HTML
USER'S
INTERACTIVE WORKBOOK

ALAYNA COHN
AND
JOHN POTTER

ISBN 0-13-017004-6

9 780130 170040

90000

PH
PTR

Prentice Hall PTR
Upper Saddle River, NJ 07458
www.phptr.com/phptrinteractive

Editorial/Production Supervision: *Wil Mara*
Acquisitions Editor: *Mark Taub*
Development Editor: *Ralph Moore*
Marketing Manager: *Kate Hargett*
Manufacturing Manager: *Alexis Heydt*
Editorial Assistant: *Michael Fredette*
Cover Design Director: *Jerry Votta*
Cover Designer: *Anthony Gemmellaro*
Art Director: *Gail Cocker-Bogusz*

Prentice Hall books are widely used by corporations and government agencies for training, marketing, and resale. The publisher offers discounts on this book when ordered in bulk quantities.
For more information, contact: Corporate Sales Department, Phone: 800-382-3419;
FAX: 201-236-7141; email: corpsales@prenhall.com
Or write: Corp. Sales Dept., Prentice Hall PTR, 1 Lake Street, Upper Saddle River, NJ   07458

Printed in the United States of America
10   9   8   7   6   5   4   3   2   1

ISBN 0-13-017004-6

Prentice-Hall International (UK) Limited, *London*
Prentice-Hall of Australia Pty. Limited, *Sydney*
Prentice-Hall Canada Inc., *Toronto*
Prentice-Hall Hispanoamericana, S.A., *Mexico*
Prentice-Hall of India Private Limited, *New Delhi*
Prentice-Hall of Japan, Inc., *Tokyo*
Pearson Education Asia P.T.E., Ltd.
Editora Prentice-Hall do Brasil, Ltda., *Rio de Janeiro*

DEDICATION

For my Mom and Dad,

Brenda and Joel Cohn. You're the best!

—Alayna Cohn

For my wife, Nisha, who allowed me to write, and my daughters, Mallika and Kanchan, who never purposely prevented me.

—John Potter

FROM THE EDITOR

Prentice Hall's Interactive Workbooks are designed to get you up and running fast, with just the information you need, when you need it.

We are certain that you will find our unique approach to learning simple and straightforward. Every chapter of every Interactive Workbook begins with a list of clearly defined Learning Objectives. A series of labs make up the heart of each chapter. Each lab is designed to teach you specific skills in the form of exercises. You perform these exercises at your computer and answer pointed questions about what you observe. Your answers will lead to further discussion and exploration. Each lab then ends with multiple-choice Self-Review Questions, to reinforce what you've learned. Finally, we have included Test Your Thinking projects at the end of each chapter. These projects challenge you to synthesize all of the skills you've acquired in the chapter.

Our goal is to make learning engaging, and to make you a more productive learner.

And you are not alone. Each book is integrated with its own "Companion Website." The website is a place where you can find more detailed information about the concepts discussed in the Workbook, additional Self-Review Questions to further refine your understanding of the material, and perhaps most importantly, where you can find a community of other Interactive Workbook users working to acquire the same set of skills that you are.

All of the Companion Websites for our Interactive Workbooks can be found at `http://www.phptr.com/phptrinteractive`.

Mark L. Taub
Editor-in-Chief
Pearson PTR Interactive

CONTENTS

ACKNOWLEDGMENTS

First and foremost, I would like to thank my coauthor, John. It truly has been enjoyable working with you. Thanks Ralph! You were my sanity on the occasion, uh, the very rare occasion, when I needed it. A very special acknowledgment goes out to our technical reviewers, Dina Thatcher and Brian Monks. Thanks for the keen eye and the never-ending questions!

—Alayna Cohn

Most of all, I would like to thank Alayna. I couldn't imagine a better person to work with. Thanks are also due to our editors, Ralph and Mark, who were the epitome of professionalism, and our technical reviewers, Dina and Brian.

—John Potter

ABOUT THE AUTHORS

Alayna Cohn has been a hostage of the computer world for a number of years. She is an experienced Web, Visual Basic, and ASP Developer. She has designed and nurtured applications from point of database design to full deployment. Many evenings, Alayna moonlights as a contracted Visual Basic instructor for the Clark University Computer Career Institute's Client/Server Program. She is proud to say she has had the pleasure of parasailing over the island of Maui.

John Potter got his first computer when he was eleven, and has been a geek ever since. He is an experienced Web developer and technical trainer, and has taught JavaScript, HTML, and Microsoft Office courses for corporate clients. He has authored articles on subjects ranging from American history to noise control in foundries.

Together, Alayna and John conceived, designed, developed, and maintained the Intranet for Community Newsdealers, Inc. Both of them have developed numerous Web-based applications utilizing such technologies as, HTML, JavaScript, DHTML, VBScript, Visual Basic, Active Server Pages, Access, and SQL Server. The authors who write together, work together as they continue to be co-workers at NewMediary, Inc. NewMediary, Inc. builds and licenses tools that efficiently connect the buyers and sellers of Internet business services. The tools allow companies to add, update and enhance their presence in a vertical directory, and then generate business by responding to "Needs" or Requests for Proposals (RFPs) posted confidentially by other firms or individuals. Feel free to visit some of their handy work at www.newmediary.com.

INTRODUCTION

Welcome to the *HTML User's Interactive Workbook*. You're about to embark on a unique learning experience, one that we hope will not only help you to learn to write HTML, but will also give you a complete understanding of how HTML is structured. Much like learning to repair an automobile, it's one thing to read about procedures in a book and answer questions about what you read. But it's another thing entirely to lift up the hood and dig right in, and you won't get to the other end of this book without doing that. By the end of this book, you will be able to design and construct web pages using only a simple text editor!

WHO THIS BOOK IS FOR

Frankly, this book is for anybody who wishes to write HTML, *no experience necessary*. Even more importantly, this book is for anybody who wishes to become a good web designer.

If you already know some HTML, you are free to pick and choose the Exercises that you need to freshen up your skills, take the Self-Review quizzes for practice, and be on your way. This book should also serve you well in the field as a basic reference.

If you are relatively new to web design, but would like to learn how to write HTML, this book will help you get there. It will also help you not just to memorize information (which is all too easily forgotten), but also to roll up your sleeves and learn by doing. And when you become active in your learning process, you retain far more than you would by simply memorizing abstract information.

Just one word of warning: HTML is not forgiving of mistakes in structure. If you have any difficulties with an exercise—for example, the page you have written does not look like the example—then the first thing to do is make sure that you have copied the example exactly. Don't be scared though; HTML is far easier to learn than any computer programming language. If you are careful to follow the directions in this workbook, you should have no major problems.

HOW THIS BOOK IS ORGANIZED

The Interactive Workbook series offers an extraordinary opportunity to explore your computer system and learn through a journey of discovery. In this book, you are presented with a series of interactive Labs that are intended to teach you the basic skills of HTML coding. Each Lab begins with Learning Objectives that show you what Exercises (or tasks) are covered in that Lab. This is followed by an overview of the concepts that will be further explored through the Exercises, which are the heart of each Lab.

Each Exercise consists of a series of steps that you will follow to perform a specific task, along with questions that are designed to help you discover the important things on your own. The answers to these questions are given at the end of the Exercises, along with more in-depth discussions of the concepts explored.

At the end of each Lab is a series of multiple-choice Self-Review Questions, which are designed to help you review what you have learned. If you feel certain that you already understand a certain Objective, you are free to skip that Exercise, but are still encouraged to take the Self-Review quiz at the end of the Lab, just to make sure. The answers to these questions appear in Appendix A. There are also additional Self-Review Questions at this book's companion Web site, found at `http://www.phptr .com/phptrinteractive/`. But we'll discuss that more in a moment.

Finally, at the end of each chapter, you will find a Test Your Thinking section, which consists of a series of projects designed to solidify all of the skills you have learned in the chapter. If you have successfully completed all of the Labs in the chapter, you should be able to tackle these projects with few problems. There are not always "answers" to these projects, but where appropriate, you will find guidance and solutions at the companion Web site.

Appendix B consists of a listing of all of the HTML tags used in this workbook, plus additional tags that you will frequently use as you write Web pages. Even when you are an experienced web designer, you will find Appendix B useful.

Appendix C consists of a basic reference to the attributes used in Cascading Style Sheets. Again, even when you are an experienced web designer, you will find Appendix C useful.

Finally, Appendix D consists of a listing of various web sites and resources related to HTML writing and design. Just remember that the web is always changing. Therefore, while Appendix D was up to date at the time this workbook was published, some of the web site addresses may have changed by the time you are reading this book.

 The final element of this book actually doesn't appear in the book at all. It is the companion Web site, and it is located at:

www.phptr.com/phptrinteractive/

This companion Web site is closely integrated with the content of this book, and we encourage you to visit often. It is designed to provide a unique, interactive, online experience that will enhance your education. As mentioned, you will find guidance and solutions that will help you complete the projects found in the Test Your Thinking section of each chapter.

You will also find additional Self-Review Questions for each chapter, which are meant to give you more experience in recognizing HTML tags, and instant results are given for each quiz. Take these quizzes after you have completed the Lab work in the book, taken the book's quizzes, and completed the Test Your Thinking sections. These online quizzes will help you gauge exactly how prepared you are to write HTML, and what areas you may need to revisit in the book.

In the Author's Corner, you will find additional information that we think will interest you, such as web design news, professional advice, and any errata that didn't make it into the book before publication.

Finally, you will find a Message Board, which you can think of as a virtual study lounge. Here, you can interact with other *HTML Interactive Workbook* readers, share and discuss your projects, and perhaps even pick up a tip or two about the HTML writing.

WHAT YOU WILL NEED

First and foremost, you will need a *PC,* on which to work. Throughout the book, we assume the PC is running some form of *Windows,* but you can use a PC running Linux or a Macintosh, if you wish. As for software, you must have—at a minimum—an Internet browser and a text editor. These requirements are discussed in more depth in Chapter 1.

You'll need a *fresh notebook* in which to jot the answers to the Exercise questions, and to take notes about what you observe as you work through the Exercises. Yes, there are answer rules provided in the book, and they will suffice for some questions, but owing to space limitations, they are primarily meant for quick notes to yourself as well as study points, not for comprehensive discussion. Of course, an electronic notebook will work just as nicely as a traditional notebook.

Finally, you'll need an *Internet connection* to gain access to the companion Web site and to visit some of the other Web sites referenced in the book. Again, we encourage you to visit the companion site frequently to share and discuss your experiences with the virtual community.

CONVENTIONS USED IN THIS BOOK

There are several conventions that we've used in this book to try to make your learning experience easier. These are explained here.

 This icon is used to flag notes or advice from the authors to our readers. For instance, if there is a particular topic or concept that you really need to understand for the exam, or if there's something that you need to keep in mind while working, you will find it set off from the main text like this.

 This icon is used to flag tips or especially helpful tricks that will save you time or trouble. For instance, if there is a shortcut for performing a particular task or a method that the authors have found useful, you will find it set off from the main text like this.

 This icon is used to flag information and precautions that will not only save you headaches in the long run, they may even save your Web site's visitors a few headaches as well.

 This icon is used to flag passages in which there is a reference to the book's companion Web site, which once again is located at:

http://www.phptr.com/phptrinteractive/

The Whole Truth

Sometimes owing to the Interactive Workbook format, some information gets watered down for efficiency's sake. Also, in some cases, certain information given will not directly apply to the Lab you are doing, but we feel that it's important to give you the bigger picture anyway. When that's the case, we have used this sidebar element to alert you that "it's not exactly as simple as that," and to offer a more detailed explanation.

A FINAL PIECE OF ADVICE

Anyone can learn to write HTML, but not everyone can design good web pages. Good web page design requires some artistic ability, color sense, and an understanding of how people use web pages. Unlike the authors of some HTML books, we have not included material on how to design attractive web pages, unless it directly relates to the HTML we are covering a particular Lab. For the most part, web design sense can only come from doing. Over time, you will learn what makes up a good web page. This book will, however, teach you to write the HTML that actually produces your design. In all cases, you will find that the discovery method employed by the *HTML Interactive Workbook* will surely enlighten and educate you unlike any other resource. However clever or comprehensive another resource might be, the discovery method is a proven training technique that is employed in classrooms and training centers around the world. This hands-on approach is the cornerstone of the International Workbook series, and we are sure that you will find it an engaging and productive way to learn. *There is no better way!*

CHAPTER 1

SETTING UP

 Genius without education is like silver in the mine.

—Benjamin Franklin

Welcome to the *HTML User's Interactive Workbook.* This is your one-stop reference and learning tool for creating and designing HTML pages for the World Wide Web. This chapter serves to get you started on the right foot by guiding you through the process of downloading, installing, and understanding all the necessary tools for HTML creation.

First, we will begin by downloading and installing two of the most popular Web browsers, Internet Explorer and Netscape Navigator (also known as Netscape Communicator). You may have one of the aforementioned browsers installed on your PC at this time. It is essential to your HTML understanding and success to download and install both browsers. We will perform a simple exercise in order to ensure that you have the most recent versions, as well.

Next, we will take the necessary steps to check your PC for the text editor you will use to design and create your HTML masterpieces.

Lastly, we will complete a few Exercises to introduce you to the Internet. This chapter includes a brief explanation of the Client/Server model that allows HTML pages to display information on anyone's computer.

L A B   1 . 1

ACQUIRING
THE NECESSARY
HTML TOOLS

LAB OBJECTIVES

After this Lab, you will be able to:

- Check the Browser Version Number
- Download and Install Browsers
- Use and Understand Both Major Browsers
- Use an HTML Editor

This Lab assumes you do not have the most recent versions of Internet Explorer and Netscape Navigator. However, it is likely that you do have one of the slightly behind-the-times versions of the browsers installed on your computer. In order to create first-rate HTML pages successfully, please be certain to download and install both of the two major browsers used throughout this book. We will discuss the reasons for doing so later in the chapter.

LAB 1.1 EXERCISES

1.1.1 CHECK THE BROWSER VERSION NUMBER

Before downloading and installing the most recent versions of Internet Explorer and Netscape Navigator, let's perform a simple check. You probably have one of the two major browsers already living on your machine.

If you have either Netscape or Internet Explorer on your PC, complete this Exercise:

Open your browser window.

From the `Help` menu, choose `About`.

a) What information do you see in the pop-up window?

_____

_____

Having both Internet Explorer and Netscape Navigator on your computer guarantees you great success in writing and understanding HTML. Both browsers are available for free download from the Internet.

Open the browser you currently have installed on your machine.

Navigate to `http://www.shareware.com`. Shareware.com is a highly reliable Web site for downloading some nifty freeware and shareware.

The Shareware.com home page contains an underlined link called `Browsers`. This link is located on the left of the page. Because Web sites change fairly often, you may have to peruse the page a bit to find the `Browser` section.

If you are unable to locate the `Browser` link, click the `CNet` logo to navigate to the `CNet` Web site to search for downloadable browsers.

Once the `Browser` page fully displays on your monitor screen, scroll down the page. Locate the `Browser Downloads` section.

b) What are the most recent versions listed for both Internet Explorer and Netscape Navigator?

_____

_____

1.1.2 DOWNLOAD AND INSTALL BROWSERS

Before grabbing the executables that will install the browsers on your PC, let's create a folder for each of them. (The executables are the programs that will run to set up the installation of the software. Executables end with a `.exe` extension.)

Right-click the `Start` button.

Choose `Explore`. The Windows Explorer window opens.

Navigate to `C drive` on the left side of the Explorer window. Click on the `C drive` icon once.

Right-click in the white area of the right side of the Explorer window. Choose `New`, then `Folder`. Name this folder `Browsers`.

Remain at the Shareware.com Web site. Compare the browser version numbers with those you have installed on your machine. If your version is behind the times, a new download is needed.

If you do not have both Internet Explorer and Netscape, you need to download and install these browsers to continue with all the Exercises and Labs in this book.

Clicking on the most recent version number of each of the browsers takes you to the download page for each.

Shareware.com provides you with a `Download Now` link to begin the process.

Shareware provides you with a summary of helpful hints and suggestions prior to the download and installation of any software. We recommend that you read the information provided. This will help to keep your PC in tip-top shape during and after installing the new software.

The download and installation process of each of the browsers is similar. In order to avoid repetition, we will discuss the download and installation steps for both browsers in one discussion.

Click the `Download Now` link.

a) What happens when you click the `Download Now` link?

_____

_____

Navigate to the `Browsers` folder you created. Save the `.exe` file(s) in this folder.

Once you have downloaded the executable(s), open Windows Explorer.

Navigate to the `Browsers` folder. If you downloaded both browsers, install one at a time.

Before installing any software on your system, we recommend closing any and all open programs. This includes exiting the Windows Shortcut Bar.

Double-click the browser executable file. You may accept the default location chosen for installation of the browsers.

b) What is the location, or path, of the browser(s) installation on your PC?

_____

_____

Follow the steps given for proper installation.

The Whole Truth

Internet Explorer and Netscape both include optional extras. For example, Netscape comes with Instant Messenger. It is a small executable for you to use as an instant chatting device while logged into your ISP (Internet Service Provider). Internet Explorer contains Microsoft Outlook. Outlook is an e-mail program. You may choose to install only the browsers sans the extra goodies. Unless you are certain you have sufficient storage space on your PC, you may wish to bypass the extras.

Each browser download requires you to answer a few questions. Be certain to read each question and message you are shown. The download process may take a bit of time, depending on your modem speed. Be sure to remain logged in to your ISP while you download the browsers.

1.1.3 USE AND UNDERSTAND BOTH MAJOR BROWSERS

In order to make the HTML creation process a bit easier, let's create a shortcut for each of the Web browsers.

Right-click on the `Start` button. Choose `Explore`. The Windows Explorer window opens.

Navigate to the folder where Netscape is installed.

a) What is the name of the Netscape file?

_____

_____

Right-click on the file and choose `Create Shortcut`.

Right-click on the shortcut and choose `Cut`.

Navigate to the `Desktop` icon on the left side of the Explorer window. Double-click on the `Desktop` icon. Right-click on the right side of the Explorer window and choose `Paste`.

Right-click on the shortcut and choose `Rename`. Name the file `Netscape`. Hit `Enter`.

Repeat this process to create a similar shortcut for Internet Explorer.

Double-click on the Internet Explorer shortcut. (From this point forward, we will refer to this as Internet Explorer.)

Allow the page to display fully.

Type the following address into the `Address` bar located at the top of the browser window:

`http://www.cnn.com`

Minimize the browser window.

Open Windows Explorer. Navigate to the folder named `Temporary Internet Files` located on your `C` drive.

Open it.

b) What do you see?

_____

_____

If you have not read the answer for the prior question, do so now.

Selecting CTRL+A selects all the files located within the Temporary Internet Files folder. Do so now.

Hit the Delete key on your keyboard.

c) Explain what happens.

_____

_____

Close Windows Explorer.

Maximize the browser window. From the Tools menu, choose Internet Options.

The General tab displays. Locate the Delete Files and Settings buttons.

d) Knowing what you learned in the last Exercise, what can you conclude are the functions of these two buttons?

_____

_____

Netscape has the same caching and refreshing capabilities as Internet Explorer.

Close Internet Explorer and open Netscape by double-clicking on the desktop shortcut.

The Refresh option is located under the same menu item as Internet Explorer.

We're going to challenge you a bit here. Locate the Preferences option from one of the menu choices and open the associated window.

Locate the Cache option within Preferences window.

e) Where is the `Cache` option located? How do the Netscape cache options compare to Internet Explorer's?

_____

_____

_____

In Netscape, navigate to `http://www.microsoft.com`.

Open Internet Explorer and open the same Web site.

Hover your mouse cursor over the main topics of the page, such as `All Products`, `Support`, `Search`, `Microsoft.com Guide`, `Downloads`, and so forth.

Perform this task in both Internet Explorer and Netscape.

f) What differences, if any, do you notice while hovering over the captions in each of the browsers?

_____

_____

1.1.4 USE AN HTML EDITOR

Open Windows Explorer.

Navigate to the `Start Menu` folder and open it.

Double-click on `Programs`.

From the right side of the window, double-click on `Accessories`.

Locate `Notepad` and `Wordpad`. Create desktop shortcuts for each of these programs as you learned previously. Place the two new shortcuts on your desktop.

Open one of your text editors. For purposes of this Exercise, you may open Notepad.

Type the following into your editor:

```
<HTML>
 <BODY>
  Hi there!
 </BODY>
</HTML>
```

From the `File` menu, choose `Save As`. The `Save As` dialog box opens. Select `All Files` from the `Save As Type` list box.

Name the file `test.html`. For now, save the new HTML file to the default location of your Windows desktop.

Close your HTML editor.

Double-click on `test.html`. If you are prompted to log in to your ISP, refuse the connection.

       a) What happens? Explain what you see.

_____

_____

Double-click the other browser to open it.

Type the following address into the address bar exactly as shown:

`C:\windows\desktop\test.html`

Hit `Enter`.

       b) What happens?

_____

_____

Close both browser windows.

Open Internet Explorer.

From the `File` menu, choose `Open`.

Using the `Browse` button, locate `test.html`. Open it.

Minimize Internet Explorer.

**LAB
1.1**

Open Netscape.

From the `File` menu, choose `Open Page`.

Using the `Choose File` button, locate and open `test.html`.

Much like many of the tasks in the Windows OS, there are numerous ways to accomplish the same goal. You may use any of the ways shown here to open and create HTML files.

As you progress through the Exercises in the book, we're certain you will become quite comfortable with the entire HTML process, from writing and designing to opening and displaying HTML pages.

LAB 1.1 EXERCISE ANSWERS

1.1.1 ANSWERS

a) What information do you see in the pop-up window?

Answer: Your answer may differ from ours depending on the browser type and version you currently have installed on your computer. When performing this check with Internet Explorer via the `About Internet Explorer` menu choice, we see product ID and copyright information. More importantly, we see the version number of the installed Internet Explorer browser on the PC. The version number is clearly printed in the pop-up window as Internet Explorer 5. When performing this check with Netscape via the `About Netscape Communicator` menu choice, we again see copyright and product information. The version number we see reads Netscape Communicator 4.7.

As of this writing, the version numbers mentioned here are the latest and the greatest of each of the two browsers. Internet Explorer and Netscape are the two most popular browsers to date. The version numbers represent the major release version from each of the browser creators. The numbers shown after the decimal point represent minor changes made to the browser since the release of the new version. It is assumed that with each new major browser release there have been significant changes and improvements to the browser. Internet Explorer is designed and developed by Microsoft. Netscape is created by Netscape Communications.

b) What are the most recent versions listed for both Internet Explorer and Netscape Navigator?

Answer: At the time of this writing, Netscape Communicator lists 4.7 as its most recent version available for free download. Internet Explorer lists version 5 as its most recent downloadable version.

The Whole Truth

Software labeled "freeware" is freely available at no cost to you. You may download, install, and use freeware as you wish. On the other hand, software labeled "shareware" comes with a price. Like freeware, shareware is most often freely available to be downloaded, installed, and used by anyone. Yet, shareware may expire after a certain number days (30, 60, or however many the maker of the software allows) and become unusable. You are usually prompted with a message stating that you must send in the appropriate amount of money to acquire a license for the software after it expires. Shareware is a nicety that allows you to test out and play with software before purchasing it.

Once again, we should *mention* that new versions of software are constantly being developed and deployed for public use. Therefore, the versions listed here are current as of this writing. Below the version numbers for each of the browsers, we see the OS compatibility listing. OS (Operating System) is the GUI (Graphical User Interface) that resides on your computer. You may have Windows 95, Windows 98 or Windows 2000 as your Operating System. Both Internet Explorer 5 and Netscape 4.7 run on either version of the Windows Operating System.

Shareware.com is usually quite helpful with browser questions. You may also contact us for tips and suggestions at the Prentice Hall Interactive Web site at http://www.phptr.com/phptrinteractive/.

1.1.2 ANSWERS

a) What happens when you click the Download Now link?

Answer: After a brief moment, you see a dialog box. The option to Save This Program to Disk *is chosen by default. Accept this choice and click* OK.

b) What is the location, or path, of the browser(s) installation on your PC?

Answer: The installation path of your browser(s) may differ from ours. When accepting the default location, each browser installs to C:\Program Files.

Internet Explorer installs at C:\Program Files\Internet Explorer\ Iexplore.exe.

Netscape Communicator installs at C:\Program Files\Netscape\ Communicator\Program\Netscape.exe.

LAB 1.1

1.1.3 ANSWERS

a) What is the name of the Netscape file?

Answer: The Netscape executable is called `netscape.exe`.

b) What do you see?

Answer: A list of files is shown inside the `Temporary Internet Files` *folder. The name of the file is listed. It is followed by the Internet address of the file origin, the size, the date of expiration, the last modified date, the last accessed date, and the last checked date.*

The files you see are contained within the pages you have just opened in your browser window. (We will discuss how these files get deposited onto your machine later in this chapter.) The important point to note here is that the files do, in fact, reside on your machine at this point. This is called the browser cache (pronounced CASH). A cached file actually remembers the HTML page you have visited by saving a copy of the HTML file on your local hard drive. The files are stored in a location on your hard drive called Memory Cache. Cached files speed up the process of HTML page retrieval should you navigate to the same page again.

Surf to the CNN Web site; there you see a file named `Cookie: anyuser@cnn.com`. By default, the browsers you have just installed accept cookies. Cookies are small text files that get deposited on your PC that "remember you." Have you ever purchased anything from Amazon.com or any other purchasing Web site from your home PC? If so, upon your next visit, a little blurb appears welcoming you back. This welcome may include your name and perhaps the date of your last visit. A cookie stores the information needed for the Web site to remember who you are. When we say "you," we mean "your computer." The cookie does not have the ability to know you personally unless you supply your name and address. Cookies are machine-specific. For instance, opening Amazon.com at work will not display a welcome to you until you log in and grab a new cookie for your work PC.

You do not create cookies with HTML, but rather you receive cookies from a Web site. Cookies are not dangerous to your PC. Webmasters use cookies to track the number of people visiting, the dates the site was visited, and so forth.

c) Explain what happens.

Answer: Assuming you have files, of any type, within the folder, you are prompted with a message box. It asks you if you are sure you want to delete the selected files. Answering `yes` *deletes the files from the folder and moves them to the Recycle Bin. Also, for every cookie you have in the folder, a message box prompts you to answer* `yes` *or* `no` *for cookie deletion.*

Cookies are safe to delete. One important note here is that if you do have an account set up with a Web site, like Amazon.com, and you delete the cookie, the Web site will no longer have the information needed in order to recognize you. In other words, the next time you open Amazon.com, you will not be greeted with your very own personal welcome. This does not mean that Amazon.com does not know you. It means it will be necessary to log in using your username and password so that the Web site may give you another cookie for recognition later. So, if you keep the cookie to a Web site to which you are registered, the site will remember you each time you log on.

d) Knowing what you learned in the last Exercise, what can you conclude are the functions of these two buttons?

Answer: Clicking the `Delete Files` *button opens a dialog box. This serves the same purpose as using* `CTRL+A` *and the* `delete` *key from the previous Exercise. This is another way to empty out the* `Temporary Internet Files` *folder. Checking the* `Delete All Subscription Content` *button will clear the cookies as well. Clicking the* `Settings` *button displays a message box. This allows you to increase or decrease the space used on your hard drive to store Internet files. Leave this at its current default setting. Internet Explorer checks for a newer version of pages you have previously visited. Leave this as is also.*

We feel it is important to use and understand browser functionality for many reasons. First, knowing the capabilities of your Web browser allows you to take control over what you see on the Internet and how you view it. Second, emptying the `Temporary Internet Files` folder frees up space on your hard drive. Lastly, should you forget to empty the cache, you may also utilize the `Refresh` option of your browser. From the `View` menu, choose `Refresh`.

The Whole Truth

The `Refresh` button works as follows: Suppose you have visited CNN.com. Afterward, you do not clear out your cache. A few days later, you return to CNN.com. The CNN home page has been changed and updated by the CNN Web developers. However, you do not see the new and improved home page. You see the page that is currently cached on your machine.

If a page has been updated or changed in any way, the `Refresh` button grabs a new copy of the page for you to see. Of course, the last Exercise showed you that Internet Explorer has a default setting that checks for a newer version of a page each time you open the browser. Yet it is possible a page you visited 20 minutes ago has been updated. The `Refresh` button allows you to stay logged onto the Internet and take control over the cached page.

Don't be concerned if some of this information we're throwing at you is a bit foreign right now. These tidbits of information will come in very handy as you progress throughout this book. You may make changes to your HTML pages and not see them upon viewing the pages in your browser. The Refresh *button will become your friend as you view your own HTML pages over and over again. Keep this information in a safe and accessible spot in your brain.*

e) Where is the Cache option located? How do the Netscape cache options compare to Internet Explorer's?

Answer: The Preferences *option is chosen from the* Edit *menu. Once the* Preferences *window opens, cache can be located by double-clicking on the* Advanced *option from within the* Category *box. Double-clicking on the* Cache *option changes the right side of the window to the associated cache choices. Netscape has a* Clear Memory Cache *button that functions in the same manner as the* Delete Files *button in Internet Explorer. Also, like Internet Explorer, Netscape includes three choices related to cache storage. These choices are located within the* Cache *dialog box below the following caption:*

Document in cache is compared to document on network.

f) What differences, if any, do you notice while hovering over the captions in each of the browsers?

Answer: While performing this task in Internet Explorer, we see a pop-up type of menu display as we hover the mouse over each one of the title captions. The same task shows no change in Netscape.

This Exercise aims to point out the differences in each of the Web browsers. Keep in mind that because a different company developed each browser, it is very likely their display properties may vary. For example, the color blue may appear as two entirely different shades of blue as it is viewed in each browser. As you move ahead through the Labs and Exercises in this book, the different HTML rendering capabilities of each browser will become quite apparent. The point to note here is the fact that HTML displays differently within each of the browsers.

1.1.4 ANSWERS

For this Exercise, you created a new HTML file called test.html and then double-clicked on it.

a) What happens? Explain what you see.

Answer: Test.html *opens in one of the recently installed browsers. The words* Hi there! *display in the browser window.*

Pretty nifty, huh? You have just created your first HTML document. Don't concern yourself with the HTML and what it means now. You will get very knowledgeable and comfortable with HTML as you progress through this book. The point to note here is that by simply changing the extension of the file from a text filename (.txt) to an HTML filename (.html), you have informed your OS you have a new HTML document.

Also, because all of the HTML files you create reside locally on your machine, there is no need to connect to the Internet. You may design all your HTML pages without ever having to log in to your ISP.

The browser set as your default browser will be the one to display test.html. *It is likely that during installation, each of the browsers asked if you would like to make that particular browser your default browser.*

There is another way to create an empty HTML file. The installation of Internet Explorer places this handy-dandy little item on your machine. Try this. Right-click on your desktop. Choose New. *Select* Microsoft HTML Document 4.0. *A new HTML file is placed on your desktop. You may name the file anything you like. However, be certain the file extension is* .html.

Your PC may or may not have this shortcut.

Next, you tried another way to open test.html.

b) What happens?

Answer: The HTML file you created, test.html, *opens and displays.*

Note here that HTML is not case-sensitive. In other words, whether you use lowercase or uppercase lettering, the meaning is the same. Both browsers understand the path of the file equally. HTML does not distinguish text case.

The Whole Truth

Both Notepad and Wordpad ship with the Windows OS. Each will work equally well as a text (HTML) editor. Use either one of these programs to write all of your HTML pages created in this book.

There are other shareware HTML editors available that you may download. A good place to find such editors is Shareware.com. But, believe us when we say you are not missing out on any functionality capabilities by using either Notepad or Wordpad. There is no new software program to learn by using one the Windows text editors. And, you never have to worry about either program expiring!

Using either of the text editors leaves plenty of room for you to concentrate on what you're here for: learning HTML.

LAB 1.1 SELF-REVIEW QUESTIONS

In order to test your progress, you should be able to answer the following questions.

1) Netscape Navigator is also known as which of the following?
   a) _____ Netscape Explorer
   b) _____ Navigator Composer
   c) _____ Internet Communicator
   d) _____ Netscape Communicator

2) Executables are programs that run to download software onto your PC.
   a) _____ True
   b) _____ False

3) An ISP is which of the following?
   a) _____ Internal Software Program
   b) _____ Internet Software Program
   c) _____ Internet Service Provider
   d) _____ Internet Software Provider

4) To select all the files in the current folder, which of the following would you press?
   a) _____ CTRL + A
   b) _____ SHIFT + A
   c) _____ CTRL + S
   d) _____ CTRL + SHIFT

5) HTML is case-sensitive.
   a) _____ True
   b) _____ False

6) The browser cache empties each time you disconnect from the Internet.
   a) _____ True
   b) _____ False

7) Cached files are located in which of the following?
   a) _____ Memory Purse
   b) _____ Temporary Cached Files
   c) _____ Memory Cache
   d) _____ Cache Memory

8) You should never delete a cookie.
   a) _____ True
   b) _____ False

9) The only way to ensure you are seeing new versions of Web pages is via your browser settings.
   a) _____ True
   b) _____ False

Quiz answers appear in Appendix A, Section 1.1.

L A B 1 . 2

UNTANGLING THE WEB

LAB OBJECTIVES

After this Lab, you will be able to:

- Understand the Client/Server Model
- View Source

The previous Lab introduced you to the two major browsers and text editors. This Lab will give you a brief explanation of the Web and how it works. Along with the first half of this chapter, the information you learn here will give you a solid understanding of how HTML pages are transferred via the Internet.

This Lab also supplies you with one of the best HTML learning tools available: learning by viewing other HTML designers' work! We will take a look at a sampling of some HTML pages currently available on the Internet.

LAB 1.2 EXERCISES

1.2.1 UNDERSTAND THE CLIENT/SERVER MODEL

Open Internet Explorer. Empty the cache. You may keep any cookies currently on your machine.

Open the Internet site for Netscape at:
`http://www.netscape.com`

Allow the page to display fully.

Close Internet Explorer.

Log off from your ISP.

Open Windows Explorer. Navigate to the `Temporary Internet Files` folder on your `C` drive. Open it.

Locate the file named `www.netscape.com`.

Right-click and drag the file to the left side of the Explorer window up to the desktop. Release the mouse button.

Choose `Copy Here`.

Close Windows Explorer.

Navigate to your desktop. Rename the file as follows: `netscape.txt`.

A message box appears as shown in Figure 1.1.

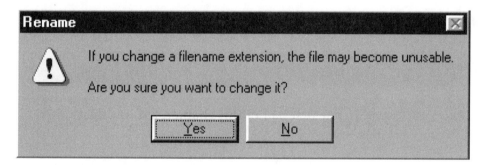

Figure 1.1 ■ *Rename* **message box.**

Answer `Yes`.

Open `netscape.txt`.

> **a)** What do you see when you open `netscape.txt`?

_____

_____

1.2.2 VIEW SOURCE

Open Internet Explorer.

Navigate to the Netscape home page once again.

Minimize the browser window.

Open Netscape.

Open the Netscape home page in this browser window also.

From the `View` **menu, choose** `Page Source`.

Maximize Internet Explorer.

From the `View` **menu, choose** `Source`.

> **a)** What information do you see as it relates to each of the browsers?

_____

_____

LAB 1.2 EXERCISE ANSWERS

1.2.1 ANSWERS

> **a)** What do you see when you open `netscape.txt`?
>
> *Answer: A text file opens. The text may be a bit jumbled and crammed together. Yet, it is indeed the file generated from surfing to the Netscape home page.*

Look through the file carefully. At this point, most likely it appears quite foreign to you (but not for long!). Upon inspection, you see words such as: `Meta`, `Table`, `Align`, `Center`, and so forth. This is the HTML of the Netscape home page.

How is it possible to have a copy of this page on your machine and not be connected to the Internet? Glad you asked. When you type a Web address into the address bar of a Web browser, you are asking a question. You are asking your browser to go out and get some information for you. In this case, your PC, the *client,* is asking Netscape, the *server,* to send you a copy of the home page. The Web works as a series of requests from a client with a corresponding response by a server. Note that there can be countless clients making requests of a single server. This exchange between browsers and servers is known as HTTP (Hypertext Transfer Protocol). Once retrieved, the response appears on your PC in the HTML format. HTML can, and does, exist independently of the Web server. Figure 1.2 illustrates a typical client/server scenario.

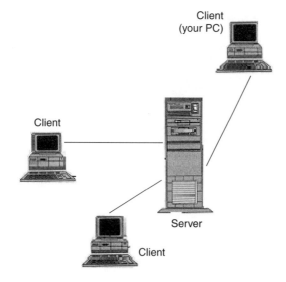

Figure 1.2 ■ Client/server model.

1.2.2 ANSWERS

a) What information do you see as it relates to each of the browsers?

Answer: The source pages generated from each browser display the same information. The files are suspiciously similar to `netscape.txt` *currently living on your desktop!*

Viewing the source HTML of a Web page will prove to be a valuable source of information as you forge ahead in the design of your own HTML pages. For example, you may see a few Web pages that capture your interest. You may want to know, "How in the world did they do that?" The `View Source` option is a great place to look to help you familiarize yourself with HTML design and creation.

The whole idea of a cached file should be very clear to you now. By having a copy of the HTML page already living on your PC, retrieving an HTML page negates impending network traffic or modem speed difficulties. In other words, it is not necessary for your Web browser to find the server (which could be on the other side of the world), get the HTML file, transport it across networks held together with electrical tape, across oceans and through hurricanes, to your PC.

LAB 1.2 SELF-REVIEW QUESTIONS

In order to test your progress, you should be able to answer the following questions.

1) A client responds to a server request.
    a) _____ True
    b) _____ False

2) Which of the following is the server for Netscape.com?
    a) _____ WWW
    b) _____ .COM
    c) _____ HTML
    d) _____ Netscape

3) There is no benefit to cached files.
    a) _____ True
    b) _____ False

4) HTML can live independently of the Web server.
    a) _____ True
    b) _____ False

5) Numerous servers are necessary for each client.
    a) _____ True
    b) _____ False

6) Generally speaking, the Internet functions as which of the following?
    a) _____ A series of responses
    b) _____ A series of requests
    c) _____ A series of requests and responses
    d) _____ A series of sources

7) HTTP stands for which of the following?
    a) _____ Hypotext To Program
    b) _____ Hypertext Transfer Protocol
    c) _____ Hypertextual Transferring Protocol

8) The exchange between browsers and servers is known as which of the following?
    a) _____ HTML
    b) _____ HPPT
    c) _____ HTTP
    d) _____ WWW

Quiz answers appear in Appendix A, Section 1.2.

C H A P T E R   1

TEST YOUR THINKING

In this chapter, we learned how to download and install the two major browsers: Internet Explorer and Netscape Communicator. We briefly covered the topic of Web servers and clients in order to get a good background understanding of how the Internet works with HTML. Knowing this information will help you move forward to the next steps of actual HTML creation.

1. Open either one of your installed browsers. Navigate to Shareware.com. Research a bit of the history on each of the browsers. What additional features are available for each browser? What is the size comparison of the browsers? Peruse around Shareware.com and get the lowdown on at least two of the lesser-known browsers. How do they compare in size and features to the major browsers?

2. Open Internet Explorer. From the `View` menu, choose `Internet Options`. Search for and locate the `'Prompt before accepting cookies'` Security setting and select it as your `Cookies` setting. Navigate to and open a few Web sites. You may try two or three of your favorites. Or, try the following: `www.boston.com`, `www.moviefone.com`, and `www.yahoo.com`. What happens upon attempting to open each of the Web sites as a result of the cookie setting? Given the information you learned in this chapter, what is the advantage of being shown a visible warning before accepting cookies? (You may set the security setting of cookies back once this project is complete.)

3. Open Netscape. From the `Edit` menu, choose `Preferences`. Search for and locate the text box from within the `Category` listing that allows you to set the `Home Page` for the Netscape browser. Set the `Home Page` as `http://www.phptr.com/phptrinteractive/`. Set the page expiration day number to seven. What is the function of the `Clear Location Bar` button?

CHAPTER 2

INTRODUCTION TO HTML

 I only ask for information.

—Charles Dickens

CHAPTER OBJECTIVES

In this Chapter, you will learn about:

In this Chapter, you'll get an overview of how HTML works and how you write it. You'll also learn to organize the basic structure that makes up an HTML document. In essence, this Chapter covers setting up the framework of the HTML document, which will be filled in with content later in the book.

L A B   2 . 1

HTML, TAGS, AND HTML DOCUMENTS

LAB OBJECTIVES

After this Lab, you will be able to:

- Understand What HTML and Tags Are, and How to Use Them
- Create an Empty HTML Document

Before you can create HTML documents, you need to understand what HTML is. HTML stands for Hypertext Markup Language. A markup language is a way of formatting text by using marks included within the text itself. In HTML, these formatting marks are called tags. Don't worry if this seems unclear; you will quickly understand it, once you get to work.

LAB 2.1 EXERCISES

2.1.1 UNDERSTAND WHAT HTML AND TAGS ARE, AND HOW TO USE THEM

As we stated earlier, a markup language is one in which the formatting information and the content are mixed together. As the browser reads the HTML document, it interprets the formatting information, so that it knows how to display the text. In HTML, the formatting information is provided by "tags." A tag is just a letter, word, or abbreviation enclosed within angle brackets (< >). A browser interprets anything enclosed within angle brackets to be a tag. For example, a browser would interpret the following code as a tag:

```
<BIG>
```

If the browser knew how to interpret the "big" tag, it would format any text following the tag as "big." If the browser didn't know how to interpret the "big" tag, the browser would ignore it. The one thing it wouldn't do is display any of the text that appeared within the tag. *Browsers never display any text that is within tags!*

Test this out for yourself. Open your text editor and type the following:

```
<Do not display this text>
```

Then, save the file as an html file and open it in your browser.

a) What do you see?

Nothing

Next, reopen the file in your text editor and edit the code so that it looks like this:

```
Do not display this text
```

Save the file as an html file and open it in your browser.

b) Now what do you see?

Do not display this text

All HTML tags come in pairs: the starting tag and the ending tag. The only difference between the starting and ending tags is a slash (/). For example, if there were a polkadot tag (there isn't, in case you are wondering), the starting tag would be as follows:

```
<POLKADOT>
```

The ending tag, however, would be like this:

```
</POLKADOT>
```

All text that was between these tags would be formatted as "polkadot" by the browser when it displayed them. In the case of our "big" tag, if you did not have an ending "big" tag, then your whole document would be formatted as "big."

c) Create your own pair of tags and write them here:

_____

_____

The most basic tag is the <HTML> tag. This tells the browser that the document it is reading is HTML. Most browsers don't actually need this information, but it is good practice to include it. Every HTML document you create should begin with an <HTML> tag and end with the ending HTML tag.

d) What do you think the ending HTML tag is?

___C/Html)_____

_____

Now that you know how to write tags, you know how to write HTML. That's all there is to it.

You may be wondering if HTML tags have to be in all capital letters. The answer to this question is that they do not. The browser doesn't care whether you use capitals or lowercase. However, it is a good habit to always use capital letters in your HTML tags because it makes reading the HTML easier. You can easily tell the tags from content (unless you write all your content in capital letters as well, which is seldom a good idea).

2.1.2 CREATE AN EMPTY HTML DOCUMENT

Now let's move on from tags to creating your first HTML document. Open your text editor and enter the following code:

```
<HTML>
</HTML>
```

Save the file as `empty.htm` and open it in your browser.

a) What do you see in the browser?

_____

_____

Next, we will create the <HEAD> section of the file.

Open the file you created previously in your text editor and edit it so that it reads as follows:

```
<HTML>
<HEAD>
Do not display this text
</HEAD>
</HTML>
```

Save the file as an HTML file, and open it in your browser.

b) What do you see in the browser?

_____

_____

c) How could you alter the text between the <HEAD> tags so that it doesn't display in the browser?

_____

_____

Next, we are going to create the body section of the document. The body section of an HTML document is where we put the content of the document that we want to be displayed by the browser. Everything that you see on a Web page is inside the body section.

To create the body section, open the file you created earlier in your text editor and edit it so that it reads as follows:

```
<HTML>
<HEAD>
</HEAD>
<BODY>
</BODY>
</HTML>
```

Then create some content for the page by entering the following line between the <BODY> and </BODY> tags:

```
This is my content!
```

Save the file as an HTML file and open it in your browser.

d) What do you see in the browser?

_____

_____

Now that we have created the basic HTML document, we will put some real content in it in the next exercise.

LAB 2.1 EXERCISE ANSWERS

2.1.1 ANSWERS

For this Exercise, refer to the following HTML document you created and opened in your browser:

```
<Do not display this text>
```

a) What do you see?

Answer: You should see a blank browser page, like the one shown in Figure 2.1.

Figure 2.1 ■ Placing text within angle brackets causes the browser to ignore it.

If you see anything other than blank space, then you must have left off one of the angular brackets (< or >), or you have text outside the brackets. Re-edit the file so that it looks exactly like the example code and try the experiment again.

Then you created a file with the following:

```
Do not display this text
```

b) Now what do you see?

Answer: You should now see a browser page, like the one shown in Figure 2.2, containing the sentence "Do not display this text."

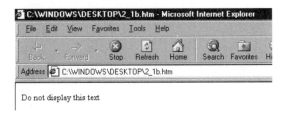

Do not display this text

Figure 2.2 ■ Removing the angle brackets from the previous example results in the text being displayed.

Any text that is not enclosed in angular brackets is considered content (i.e., the stuff you want to see in a Web page) and displayed by a browser. Any text that is enclosed in angular brackets is considered an HTML tag and is not displayed by the browser. Text and tags are the two elements that make up HTML. When writing HTML, your main task is to ensure that the browser does not mix up which is which.

Later in this Chapter, you will learn how to take advantage of the browser ignoring text within tags by adding comments within your code.

c) Create your own pair of tags and write them here:

Answer: Obviously, I don't know what tags you created, but if you had created a "fat" tag, your answer should have been:

```
<FAT> </FAT>
```

A pair of tags is characterized by two things. First, the opening and ending tags both contain the same lettering. You could not have a pair of tags where the opening tag contained the word "fat," and the ending tag contained the word "fate." That would not be a pair of tags: That would be two different tags.

Second, the ending tag must begin with a slash (/). That is how the browser knows that it is an ending tag and not the beginning of another pair of tags. The browser needs to know this because in HTML pairs of tags can be nested. That is, the ending tag in a pair of tags does not need to be the next tag after the opening tag. Instead, you will often find additional pairs of tags inserted between the opening and ending tags. The following code shows an example of nested tags:

```
<BIG>
<POLKADOT>
Some Text
</POLKADOT>
</BIG>
```

As you can see, the ending "big" tag came after both of the "polkadot" tags.

The Whole Truth

Do all tags really come in pairs? Not quite. Some tags, such as the `<IMG>` tag (it's used with images, as you will learn in Chapter 5) do not come in pairs. The `<IMG>` tag does not come in a pair because it does not format text. Other tags that do not format text (as you'll see below) also do not have to come in pairs. These tags are known as "open" tags.

With other tags, such as the `<p>` tag (you will learn about this one in Chapter 3), your browser will allow you to be lazy and only use the opening tag. Still, it's a good habit to get into to always use both the opening and closing tags when they are available. You might as well do things right from the beginning; in the future, browsers might insist on it.

---

d) What do you think the ending HTML tag is?

Answer: Given the two rules you learned previously in this Exercise, your answer should have been:

```
</HTML>
```

If that wasn't your answer, read the discussion from the previous question so that you understand why the ending HTML tag has to be `</HTML>`.

The HTML tag pair is a good example of how tags are nested in HTML. Every HTML document includes multiple pairs of tags that come between the opening HTML tag and the ending HTML tag.

2.1.2 ANSWERS

For this Exercise, you started by creating the following document and opening it in your browser:

```
<HTML>
</HTML>
```

a)   What do you see in the browser?

Answer: You should see an empty browser page, like the one shown previously in Figure 2.1.

You see a blank page, because this is a completely empty HTML document. Other than the HTML tags, which identify it to the browser as an HTML document, it contains nothing.

You then added the following text and tags and opened it again:

```
<HTML>
<HEAD>
Do not display this text
</HEAD>
</HTML>
```

b)   What do you see in the browser?

Answer: You should see a browser page, like the one shown in Figure 2.3, that contains the text, "Do not display this text."

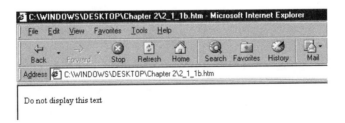

Figure 2.3 ■ By default, the browser displays any content within the `<HEAD>` section of the document that is not enclosed in angle brackets.

All information that belongs in the head section is inserted between the `<HEAD>` and `</HEAD>` tags. The head section of an HTML file is where

**LAB
2.1**

you put information that you want to include in the HTML document, but that you do not want displayed in the browser as part of the Web page. Don't worry if you can't think of what this type of information would be; you will learn what it is in the rest of this Chapter.

It is important to note, however, that even though you do not want anything in the head section displayed, your browser does not do this automatically. As you can see, the browser does not care that you have placed this text in the <HEAD> section of your document. It just displays it anyway. It is up to you to format the text so that the browser does not display it.

c) How could you alter the text between the <HEAD> tags so that it doesn't display in the browser?

Answer: You could enclose it in angular brackets. The browser assumes that the text is a tag and won't display it:

```
<DO NOT DISPLAY THIS TEXT>
```

Not only does the browser not display the text, but it ignores the information within the angular brackets, because no browser has ever heard of the "DO NOT DISPLAY THIS TEXT" tag. As you will see later in this Chapter, this is—with some minor modifications—how you put comments in your HTML documents. What comments, you ask? We'll explain that later also.

d) What do you see in the browser?

Answer: You should see a browser page, like the one shown in Figure 2.4, that contains the text, "This is my content!"

There's not much to this content, but at least it is in the right section of the HTML document: the <BODY> section. That's where we want to place all of the content that should be displayed by the browser.

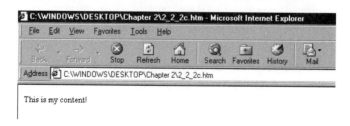

Figure 2.4 ■ A simple, but meaningless, HTML page.

LAB 2.1 REVIEW QUESTIONS

In order to test your progress, you should be able to answer the following questions.

1) HTML tags always come in pairs.
    a) _____ True
    b) _____ False

2) If you want the browser to display text, what should you do?
    a) _____ Put tags around it.
    b) _____ Don't put tags around it.
    c) _____ Put it in the <BODY> section.
    d) _____ Both b) and c).

3) Text entered into the <HEAD> section of an HTML document will be displayed when?
    a) _____ Always.
    b) _____ Only if it is within tags.
    c) _____ Never.

4) What is the ending tag for the <BODY> tag.?
    a) _____ <\BODY>
    b) _____ </BODY>
    c) _____ <\body>
    d) _____ both a) and c)

5) Do you have to begin and end an HTML document with <HTML> tags?
    a) _____ Yes.
    b) _____ No, but it is good practice.
    c) _____ Only if the document does not include a <BODY> section.
    d) _____ Only if you want Netscape Navigator to display it.

Quiz answers appear in Appendix A, Section 2.1.

L A B   2 . 2

ORGANIZING THE HEAD SECTION OF THE HTML DOCUMENT

LAB OBJECTIVES

After this Lab, you will be able to:

- Insert a Title into an HTML Document
- Insert and Use <META> Tags to Describe an HTML Document

In the previous Exercise, we created an empty HTML document with two sections. The first section we created was called the head section, and we are now going to practice organizing this section.

As you learned in the last Lab, the head section is where you place information that you do not wish the browser to display. Generally, the information in the head section is designed to provide information about your HTML document (in the future) to yourself or other HTML coders, or to Web search engines. The head section also includes the title of your HTML document, and that is what we will create first.

2.2.1 INSERT A TITLE INTO AN HTML DOCUMENT

Just above, we told you that the head section of an HTML document contains information that you did not wish the browser to display. The one exception to this is the document title. The document title is displayed by the browser in the title bar of its window (that's the colored strip at the very top). For instance, if you went to `www.microsoft.com`, you would see the following title in your browser (Figure 2.5):

Figure 2.5 ■ An example of a document title.

Now, let's put a title into the empty HTML document you created in the last Exercise. Open the document in your text editor and edit it so that it reads as follows:

```
<HTML>
<HEAD>
<TITLE>My First HTML Document</TITLE>
</HEAD>
<BODY>
</BODY>
</HTML>
```

Save the file as an HTML file and open it in your browser.

   a) What do you see in the browser?

_____

_____

On the other hand, make sure that you do not go overboard and choose an extremely long title for your page, because this can cause problems when the page is displayed. To see what can happen, open the HTML file in your text editor and edit it so that it reads as follows:

```
<HTML>
<HEAD>
<TITLE>An Extremely Long Title That Just Goes On and
On For No Particularly Good Reason, Except That I
Want It To</TITLE>
</HEAD>
```

```
<BODY>
</BODY>
</HTML>
```

Save the file as an HTML file and open it in your browser.

b) What is wrong with the way the title displays?

_____

_____

The title is just the beginning, though, of the content that goes into the head section.

2.2.2 INSERT AND USE <META> TAGS TO DESCRIBE AN HTML DOCUMENT

As we keep repeating, the head section of the HTML document is where you place information about your document that you do not want the browser to display. HTML includes a special tag, called the <META> tag, to help you do this. The tag is called <META> because meta-information denotes "information about information." Your document is information, and the <META> tag provides information about the document.

<META> tags do not come in pairs, because they do not format text. Instead, the information conveyed by the <META> tag takes the form of attributes contained within the <META> tag.

Attributes always take the following form:

Attribute Name="Attribute Value"

For example, if you had a tag attribute named SIZE, and you wanted its value to be 32, then the attribute would be expressed as follows:

```
SIZE="32"
```

Note that there are no spaces in the attribute definition.
An attribute is associated with a tag by placing it within the angular brackets of the opening tag. For example, if the attribute size were associated with the tag <BIG>, then you would use the following code:

```
<BIG SIZE="32">
```

 Attributes are extremely important because lots of tags use them, not just the <META> tag. Make sure that you understand the preceding instructions on formatting attributes. In particular, note two important things. First, there is always a space between the tag name (in this case BIG), and the attribute name. Secondly, there are no spaces between the attribute name, the equals sign, and the attribute value in quotes.

a) How would you write a <POLKADOT> tag that had the attribute COLOR with a value of pink?

_____

_____

Now that you know how to write attributes, let's look at the three attributes associated with the <META> tag as shown in Table 2.1.

Table 2.1 ■ <META> Tag Attributes

Attribute	Definition
HTTP-EQUIV	Specifies that the information is of a type that can be recognized and used by a Web browser or server.
NAME	Used in place of HTTP-EQUIV when the information in the <META> tag is of a type that cannot be used by a Web browser or server.
CONTENT	The actual information conveyed by the <META> tag.

HTTP_EQUIV and NAME attributes are always accompanied by a CONTENT attribute. This is true because HTTP-EQUIV and NAME attributes only define the type of information that is being conveyed. It is the CONTENT attribute that actually conveys the information. Therefore, a <META> tag will always take one of the two following forms:

```
<META HTTP-EQUIV="some text" CONTENT="some text">
```

or

```
<META NAME="some text" CONTENT="some text">
```

You cannot make up your own values for HTTP-EQUIV attributes, because HTTP-EQUIV attributes specify that the information is for the use of the Web browser or a Web server. Therefore, their values must be some information that the Web browser or server will recognize. The three most commonly used values for HTTP-EQUIV attributes in <META> tags are *Expires*, *Content-Type*, and *Keywords*. Expires specifies a date beyond which the content of the HTML document is not useful. *Content-Type* specifies the format in which the HTML document is presented. Most importantly, *keywords* specifies the words under which a search-engine should index the page. For *Content-Type*, you should usually specify "text/html," since you are writing HTML documents. The following example shows how this would look.

```
<META HTTP-EQUIV="Content-Type" CONTENT="text/html">
```

Now, create your own <META> tags containing HTTP-EQUIV attributes.

> **b)** How would you specify that a Web page will expire on January 1 of the year 3000?

> _____

> _____

> **c)** Suppose you wrote a Web page devoted to peanut butter. How would you specify that a search engine should index your page under "peanuts"?

> _____

> _____

Although you are restricted in which HTTP-EQUIV attribute values you can use, you are completely free to make up your own NAME attributes. Some of the more commonly used NAME attribute values are *Generator*, *Author*, and *Description*. *Generator* usually specifies the tool used to create a Web page. *Author* specifies who wrote the page, and *Description* describes the purpose or content of the page. For example, if you create a Web page using Microsoft Word 97, you should insert the following <META> tag:

```
<META NAME="Generator" CONTENT="Microsoft Word 97">
```

d) How would you specify that Joe Smith was the author of a Web page?

_____

_____

e) How would you specify that the document was created in Windows Notepad?

_____

_____

As you can see, even though the viewer of a page cannot see all the information contained in the <HEAD> section, it is very important that you take the time to create one. Without a proper title and <META> tags, you can't be sure that anyone will ever know what your Web page is about.

LAB 2.2 EXERCISE ANSWERS

2.2.1 ANSWERS

For this Exercise, you first created an HTML file with a title.

a) What do you see in the browser?

Answer: You should see a Web page that looks like the one shown in Figure 2.6.

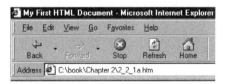

Figure 2.6 ■ **The title placed within the <TITLE> tags is displayed in the browser's title bar.**

Choosing the right title for your page is very important, not only because the title is displayed prominently at the top of the browser, but also because the title of your page will be displayed by most search engines if they return your page in answer to a search. Moreover, if a user bookmarks your page (or, in Internet Explorer, adds it to the Favorites list), it is the title of your page that is bookmarked. Therefore, choose an appropriate title that accurately conveys the content of your HTML document. A title such as "Page 1 Of My Site" conveys nothing, while a title like "Classic Cars Site" conveys just what the site is about.

Next, you created a document with an extremely long title.

b) What is wrong with the way the title displays?

Answer: When you view the page in a browser, you should see a Web page that looks like the one shown in Figure 2.7.

Figure 2.7 ■ An example of poor titling for a Web page.

As you can see, the end of the title is cut off in the browser's caption bar. Of course, the higher the resolution of the monitor on which the page is viewed, the more of the title that will be seen. You can't assume, though, that readers of your Web page have large monitors. Generally, as long as your title is sixty characters in length or less, the whole title should be visible. Remember, though, that the title of your page is also put in the browser's Favorites list, if the page is bookmarked by a user. A long title may also be cut off by this list depending upon the browser, and it is guaranteed to be annoying to the user.

2.2.2 ANSWERS

a) How would you write a `<POLKADOT>` tag that had the attribute `COLOR` with a value of pink?

Answer: The HTML code that you wrote should look like this:

```
<POLKADOT COLOR="pink">
```

Make sure that you remembered to leave a space between POLKADOT and COLOR, and that you remembered to put the quotes around the value pink, or else the browser would be unable to interpret the tag and attribute properly.

b) How would you specify that a Web page will expire on January 1 of the year 3000?

Answer: You would write a <META> tag like the following:

```
<META HTTP-EQUIV="Expires" CONTENT="1/1/3000">
```

Of course, this assumes that browsers are year 3000 compliant. Make sure when you wrote this tag that you do not misspell HTTP_EQUIV, or leave out any of the quotes. Otherwise, the browser will not interpret your Meta information correctly.

c) Suppose you wrote a Web page devoted to peanut butter. How would you specify that a search engine should index your page under "peanuts"?

Answer: The HTML code that you wrote should look like this:

```
<META HTTP-EQUIV="Keywords" CONTENT="Peanuts">
```

You can also specify more than one keyword by separating the different keywords with a comma and a space. For example, here is the *Keywords* <META> tag from www.fluffernutter.com:

```
<META HTTP-EQUIV="Keywords" CONTENT="Fluff, Marshmal-
low, Creme, Recipe, Toppings, Dips, Shakes, Dessert,
Sandwich, Peanut, Butter, Durkee, Mower, Treat, Fudge,
Baking, Cheesecake, Fluffernutter, Candy, Frosting,
Sauce, Sweet, Potatoes, Whoopie, Pie, Cookie, Salad">
```

If you put in more than one keyword, make sure that separate them properly, and enclose them all in one set of quotes.

d) How would you specify that Joe Smith was the author of a Web page?

Answer: You would write a <META> tag like the following:

```
<META NAME="Author" CONTENT="Joe Smith">
```

Again, make sure that you don't forget the spaces or quotes; HTML is very picky about those things.

e) How would you specify that the document was created in Windows Notepad?

Answer: You would write a <META> tag like the following:

```
<META NAME="Generator" CONTENT="Windows Notepad">
```

Another NAME commonly used instead of *Generator* is *Tools*, or even *Created With*. Remember, with NAME attributes, you can make up any that you want to use.

LAB 2.2 SELF-REVIEW QUESTIONS

In order to test your progress, you should be able to answer the following questions.

1) Which of the following is true of the text enclosed within the <TITLE> tags?
   a) _____ It is not displayed.
   b) _____ It is displayed in the caption bar of the browser.
   c) _____ It is used in the bookmark list when the page is bookmarked.
   d) _____ Both b) and c).

2) <META> tags can be used to convey information about the HTML document to the Web browser.
   a) _____ True
   b) _____ False

3) You can make up your own HTTP_EQUIV attributes.
   a) _____ True
   b) _____ False

4) Which of the following is incorrect?
   a) _____ <META HTTP-EQUIV="Keywords CONTENT="Peanuts">
   b) _____ <META HTTP-EQUIV="Keywords" CONTENT="Peanuts">
   c) _____ <META NAME="Subject" CONTENT="Peanuts">

Quiz answers appear in Appendix A, Section 2.2.

L A B   2 . 3

ORGANIZING THE BODY SECTION OF THE HTML DOCUMENT

LAB OBJECTIVES

After this Lab, you will be able to:

• Insert Name and Date Last Modified into an HTML Document
• Add HTML Comments to an HTML Document

The body section of the HTML document contains the actual content that you want the browser to display. However, that is not all that it contains. The body section of every document should also contain important information that is separate from the content. One of the most important parts of this information is the name of the document's author and the date that document was last modified.

LAB 2.3 EXERCISES

2.3.1 INSERT NAME AND DATE LAST MODIFIED INTO AN HTML DOCUMENT

Let's begin by creating a blank HTML document that includes the name of the author and date last modified. Open your text editor and enter the following HTML:

Make sure you substitute your name for the words "Your Name" and the current date for the words "Today's Date" in the following code.

```
<HTML>
<HEAD>
<META NAME="Author" CONTENT="Your Name">
<META HTTP-EQUIV="Content-Type" CONTENT="text/html">
<TITLE>Exercise 2.3.1 HTML Document</TITLE>
</HEAD>
<BODY>
 Created by Your Name; Last Modified On Today's Date
</BODY>
</HTML>
```

Save this file in your text editor as an HTML file and open the file in your browser.

a) What do you see displayed in your browser?

b) Why do you think it is important to include this information on your Web page?

2.3.2 ADD HTML COMMENTS TO AN HTML DOCUMENT

Although we have repeatedly stated that the body section of an HTML document is where you put the content that you want the browser to display, there is one type of content included in the body that is not displayed: HTML comments. Remember that we demonstrated, earlier in this chapter, that a browser would not display information included in angle brackets (< and >). HTML comments take advantage of this fact. However, they are not just enclosed in plain angle brackets. Instead, all comments begin with `<!--` and end with`-->`.

Open the HTML document you created in the last Exercise in your text editor and edit it so that it reads as follows:

```
<HTML>
<HEAD>
<!-- Meta Tags -->
<META NAME="Author" CONTENT="Your Name">
<META HTTP-EQUIV="Content-Type" CONTENT="text/html">
<!-- Meta Tags End -->
<TITLE>Exercise 2.3.2 HTML Document</TITLE>
</HEAD>
<BODY>
 <!-- Author And Last Modified -->
  Created by Your Name; Last Modified On Today's Date
 <!-- Author And Last Modified End -->
</BODY>
</HTML>
```

**LAB
2.3**

Save this file in your text editor as an HTML file and open the file in your browser.

a) What do you see displayed in your browser?

_____

_____

LAB 2.3 EXERCISE ANSWERS

2.3.1 ANSWERS

For this Exercise, you created a blank HTML document that includes the name of the author and date last modified.

a) What do you see displayed in your browser?

Answer: You should see a Web page much like the one shown in Figure 2.8.

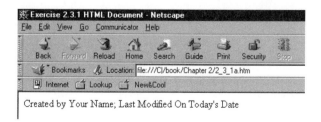

Figure 2.8 ■ A simple Web page displaying the author's name and the date that the document was last modified.

Right now, the line describing who authored the page and when it was last modified does not look very pretty. Once you have learned to format HTML, however, you can modify it so that it displays in a more attractive manner.

b)   Why do you think it is important to include this information on your Web page?

Answer: If you always include this information, everyone will know who is responsible for the HTML document and when you last worked on it.

Why is it important that everyone knows who wrote a page and when it was last modified? The reason you include the author's name (or the name of whoever is responsible for the document) is so that, if a document does not display correctly for a user, or a user has any questions about a document, they know whom to contact. The reason you include the date the document was last modified is so that the reader of the document knows how up-to-date the information on the Web page is. This information is typically included at the bottom of each Web page. For instance, if you visited the Web page of John Potter you would see the information displayed in Figure 2.9 at the bottom of the page.

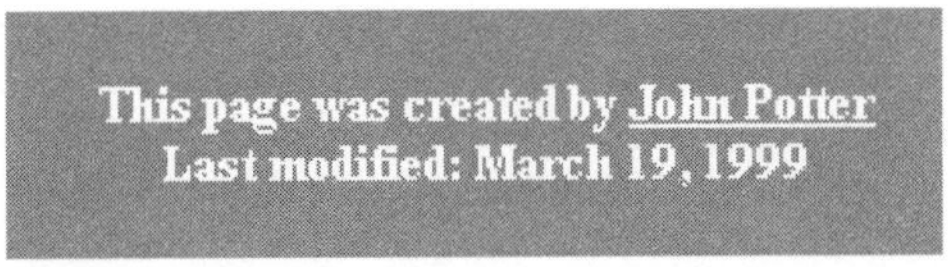

This page was created by John Potter
Last modified: March 19, 1999

Figure 2.9 ■ The author and date last modified information from John Potter's home page.

As you can see, John hasn't changed the design of his home page recently.

You may have noticed that John's name is underlined in the screen shown in Figure 2.9. This is because it is linked to an email address so you can mail him by clicking on it. You will learn all about linking in Chapter 6.

If you have looked at many Web pages, you might have noticed that not all pages include this information in the form used here. For instance, some pages contain a link to a contact page or put the last-modified information somewhere else on the page. Some badly designed pages just don't include this information at all. You might think it is excessive to have the last modified date on every page, but you can never be sure which is the first page a user will see. Just ask yourself, would you read a newspaper if you didn't know what day it was reporting on? Or, would you watch the news on television if you couldn't be sure whether they were reporting on the latest news or news that happened two years ago? Information on the World Wide Web stays around until someone removes it. So, you need to let readers of your HTML documents know how up-to-date your information is!

2.3.2 ANSWERS

For this Exercise, you created an HTML page containing comments.

a) What do you see displayed in your browser?

Answer: You should see a Web page much like the one shown in Figure 2.10.

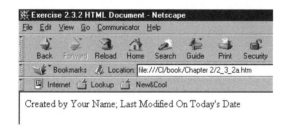

Figure 2.10 ■ Comments do not display within the browser.

Actually, the page should look exactly like the one you displayed previously in Exercise 2.3.1. If you see any of your comments displayed, go back to the file and check that you did not leave out a beginning or ending tag around the comment. This is a mistake that programmers frequently make.

Traditionally, comments are lines of text included by programmers in computer code to explain what each section of code is doing. Comments allow programmers other than the author, and sometimes the author themselves at a later time, to read the code and understand how a program works. Although HTML is far less complicated than a programming language, it is important to include comments in your HTML. This is particularly true if more than one author is working on a Web site. Typically, comments are inserted before the code or HTML they describe, but they can also be inserted afterward. Moreover, comments can also be inserted into the head section of the HTML document.

Before we leave the subject of comments, there are two important points that need to be made. First, even though the browser will not display your comments, they can still be seen by anyone who views the source of your page. So, do not put in any comments that you don't want to be seen by everyone. Secondly, while it may seem silly to include comments in such simple pages, it is still a good habit to get into. Eventually you (or a team of Web designers that you are a part of) may be writing long, complex HTML documents that include extensive formatting and scripting. When that time arrives, you will be grateful that you got into the habit of including comments early on.

In this Lab, you learned how to create an empty HTML document that can be used as a template for every HTML document you ever create in the future. If you always include the <META> information, a good title, HTML comments, and put the name and date last modified in every HTML document you create, you will have provided a good foundation for the pages you create, regardless of the content.

LAB 2.3 SELF-REVIEW QUESTIONS

In order to test your progress, you should be able to answer the following questions.

1) Where in an HTML document can comments be placed?
   a) _____ In the head section.
   b) _____ Inside <META> tags.
   c) _____ In the body section.
   d) _____ Both a) and c).

2) Everything in the body section is displayed by the browser.
   a) _____ True
   b) _____ False

3) Which of the following is true of the date a document was last modified?
   a) _____ It typically appears at the end of an HTML document.
   b) _____ It should always appear in an HTML document.
   c) _____ It could appear anywhere in an HTML document.
   d) _____ All of the above.

4) Which of the following is true regarding how to contact the author of an HTML document?

    a) _____ It typically appears at the end of an HTML document.

    b) _____ It should never appear in an HTML document.

    c) _____ It should only appear on the first page of a Web site.

    d) _____ All of the above.

5) Why is it important to include the date a document was last modified?

    a) _____ So everyone can see how hard you are working designing and updating Web pages.

    b) _____ So the reader knows how current the information on the page is.

    c) _____ So the browser knows when the page expires.

    d) _____ So your page can be listed in the correct order with other search results.

Quiz answers appear in Appendix A, Section 2.3.

LAB
2.3

C H A P T E R   2

TEST YOUR THINKING

In this Chapter, we learned how to create a properly structured HTML document. In order to gain a deeper understanding of what this means, complete the following tasks.

1) Visit several Web sites and view the page sources. Look for <META> tags in the head section of each page. Are any of the <META> tags that we discussed omitted? Are there any additional <META> tags that we did not discuss in this Chapter?

2) Visit several Web sites and look for author and contact information on each page. Look where and how this information is presented. For example, is it always at the bottom of the page? Is it even included?

3) Visit several Web sites and view the page sources. Look for comments embedded into the HTML of the page. Are there many comments? What are the site authors using them for?

CHAPTER 3

CREATING AND ORGANIZING CONTENT

 There is nothing more difficult to take in hand, more perilous to conduct, or more uncertain in its success, than to take the lead in the introduction of a new order to things.

—Niccolo Machiavelli

In Chapter 2, "Introduction to HTML," you created an empty HTML document that you could use as a template to create future HTML documents. In this Chapter, we are going to use that template to create an HTML document with content. We are going to organize that content by dividing it into headings and paragraphs. We will also break up the content into sections using horizontal rules.

Throughout this Chapter, we will work on a Web page for the imaginary Pete's Peanut Company. We will begin by organizing the main outline of the content using headings and horizontal rules.

L A B   3 . 1

USING HEADING AND HORIZONTAL RULE TAGS

LAB OBJECTIVES

After this Lab, you will be able to:

- Use Heading Tags to Organize Content
- Use the Align Attribute of the Heading Tags
- Use Horizontal Rule Tags to Divide Content

A heading in HTML is like the headline of a newspaper story or the chapter title in a book. It is a group of words that describe the content that follows. Headings can also be nested. That is, a heading can be followed by a sub-heading. If you have ever created an outline for a school paper, then you have used headings with sub-headings. For example, the outline for this chapter used three nested levels of headings:

Heading Level 1: Creating and Organizing the Content

    Heading Level 2: Using Heading and Horizontal Rule Tags

        Heading Level 3: Using Heading Tags to Organize Content

Now, let's see how this applies to creating HTML documents.

Throughout this Chapter, make sure you substitute your name for the words "Your Name" and the current date for the words "Today's Date" in the HTML code examples.

LAB 3.1 EXERCISES

3.1.1 USE HEADING TAGS TO ORGANIZE CONTENT

Let's begin by organizing our content using headings. Open the blank HTML document you created in the last Chapter in your text editor and edit it so that it reads as follows:

```
<HTML>
<HEAD>
<META NAME="Author" CONTENT="Your Name">
<META HTTP-EQUIV="Content-Type" CONTENT="text/html">
<TITLE> Pete's Peanut Company's Web Page </TITLE>
</HEAD>
<BODY>
 <H1>Pete's Peanut Company's Web Page</H1>
  Created by Your Name; Last Modified On Today's Date
</BODY>
</HTML>
```

Save it as an HTML file and open it in your browser.

a) How does the heading display in your browser?

_____

_____

Now that you have a main heading for Pete's Web page, you need to divide the content into sections. Pete's content is divided into two main sections: Peanut Products Offered and How to Purchase Pete's Peanuts. Each of these sections will be a heading level two. In HTML, the heading level two tag is written <H2>.

b) How would you edit the HTML document we created above to include these two headings?

_____

_____

You will now place level-three headings under each of the level-two headings we just created.

c) How do you think the heading level-three tag is written in HTML?

_____

_____

Open the HTML file you have created in your text editor. After the first level-two heading, insert the following level-three headings: Pete's Roasted Peanuts and Pete's Boiled Peanuts. After the second level-two heading, insert the following level-three headings: Order by Mail and Order by Phone. Save the text as an HTML file and open it in your browser.

d) How do the level-three headings display in your browser? How much space does the browser place between each heading?

_____

_____

Finally, you are going to format the Author and Date Last Modified statement that appears at the end of the document.

e) How would you format the Author and Date Last Modified statement as a level-four heading?

_____

_____

Now, you have finished creating all the heading levels we need. Before you move on, though, make sure you edit the HTML file to include all the formatted headings listed above.

3.1.2 USE THE ALIGN ATTRIBUTE OF THE HEADING TAGS

The HTML document that you have created is well-organized, but it is visually boring. In this Exercise, we will make the document more visually appealing, while emphasizing its organization, by modifying the alignment of the various headings.

In HTML, by default, all headings are aligned with the left edge of the document. You can modify this default alignment using the ALIGN attribute of the six heading tags. Like all attributes, the ALIGN attribute takes the form

`NAME="Value"` and is placed within the opening tag. The `ALIGN` attribute can have the values *Center, Right,* or *Left.*

a) How would you set the `ALIGN` attribute of an `<H1>` tag to the value *Center?*

_____

_____

You are going to organize the Pete's Peanut Company page so that all Level-one and three headings are aligned in the center of the page, all Level-two headings are aligned to the left of the page, and the Level-four heading is aligned to the right of the page.

b) Write an example of each heading with the appropriate `ALIGN` attribute.

_____

_____

Now, open the HTML file you created earlier in your text editor and edit it so that all the headings are aligned as described above. Save it as an HTML file and open it in your browser.

c) Did the file display in your browser as you expected?

_____

_____

3.1.3 USE HORIZONTAL RULE TAGS TO DIVIDE CONTENT

Although Pete's Peanuts page is well-organized, it could be made even better by dividing up the content some more. Open your HTML file in your text editor and edit it so that it reads as follows:

```
<HTML>
<HEAD>
<META NAME="Author" CONTENT="Your Name">
<META HTTP-EQUIV="Content-Type" CONTENT="text/html">
<TITLE> Pete's Peanut Company's Web Page </TITLE>
```

```
</HEAD>
<BODY>
 <H1 ALIGN="Center">Pete's Peanut Company's Web
  Page</H1>
<HR>
 <H2 ALIGN="Left"> Peanut Products Offered</H2>
 <H3 ALIGN="Center">Pete's Roasted Peanuts</H3>
 <H3 ALIGN="Center">Pete's Boiled Peanuts</H3>
<HR>
 <H2 ALIGN="Left"> How To Purchase Pete's Peanuts
 </H2>
 <H3 ALIGN="Center">Order By Mail</H3>
 <H3 ALIGN="Center">Order By Phone</H3>
<HR>
 <H4 ALIGN="Right">Created by Your Name; Last Modified
  On Today's Date</H4>
</BODY>
</HTML>
```

Save the file as an HTML file and open it in your browser.

a) What changed in the way the page displayed in your browser?

_____

_____

Now, suppose you like the way the horizontal rules divide up the page, but you do not want them to run all the way across the page or to all be the same size. You can adjust the way the horizontal rules display using attributes. Horizontal rules have four main attributes: WIDTH, SIZE, ALIGN and COLOR. You will work will all of these now, except for color, which is covered in Chapter 7, "Formatting the Page." The first attribute you will use is WIDTH.

Edit the <HR> tags in your document so that they read as follows:

```
<HR WIDTH="300">
```

Save the document as an HTML file and open it in your browser.

b) How did setting the WIDTH attribute affect the way the horizontal rules displayed?

The WIDTH attribute can be set in either number of pixels or percentage of the page width.

> **c)** What HTML would you use to set the width of a horizontal rule to 50% of the Web page's width?

_____

_____

The <HR> tag has an ALIGN attribute with the same values (*Left, Center,* and *Right*) as the various heading tags do. Even if you like the way that your browser aligns the horizontal rules by default, in Pete's Peanuts Page, it is a good idea to set the align attribute. Open your HTML file in your text editor and set the alignment of all horizontal rules to *Center*. Then save the file as HTML and open it in your browser.

> **d)** What HTML did you enter to set the ALIGN attribute to *Center?* Did inserting the ALIGN attribute change the way in which the horizontal rules were displayed by the browser?

_____

_____

The last attribute of the <HR> tag you are going to use is the SIZE attribute. Open your HTML file in your text editor and set the SIZE attribute of the last <HR> tag to *20*. Then save the file as HTML and open it in your browser.

> **e)** What HTML did you enter to set the SIZE attribute to *20?* How did setting the SIZE attribute change the way in which the horizontal rule was displayed by the browser?

_____

_____

We are now finished organizing the content of Pete's Peanuts Page. In the next Exercise, we will actually add in the content.

LAB 3.1 EXERCISE ANSWERS

3.1.1 ANSWERS

a) How does the heading display in your browser?

Answer: When you view the file in a Web browser, it should look like the screen shown in Figure 3.1.

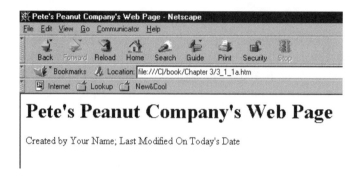

Figure 3.1 ■ Example of using the heading level-one tag.

In HTML, you use different heading tags to organize your content. When a browser reads your file, the browser displays each heading type differently so that the organization of the document is clear. HTML has six levels of headings numbered (as you might expect) one through six. <H1> is the heading level one tag.

The browser automatically makes the text enclosed in <H1> tags bold. The browser also uses a larger font (letter) size for level-one headings. It will use an increasingly smaller font size for other heading levels, but the text will always remain bold. Remember, different browsers will format heading text in different ways. Only the relative size of the heading levels will remain the same. Therefore, you can count on a level-one heading always to be larger than a level-two heading, but you cannot count on it looking the same in every browser. In Chapter 7, "Formatting the Page," you will learn how to set the size of text directly.

b) How would you edit the HTML document we created above to include these two headings?

Answer: Your HTML document should read as follows:

```
<HTML>
<HEAD>
```

```
<META NAME="Author" CONTENT="Your Name">
<META HTTP-EQUIV="Content-Type" CONTENT="text/html">
<TITLE> Pete's Peanut Company's Web Page </TITLE>
</HEAD>
<BODY>
 <H1>Pete's Peanut Company's Web Page</H1>
 <H2> Peanut Products Offered</H2>
 <H2> How To Purchase Pete's Peanuts </H2>
  Created by Your Name; Last Modified On Today's Date
</BODY>
</HTML>
```

When you display the page in your browser, you should see a page like the one shown in Figure 3.2.

Figure 3.2 ■ Example of multiple heading levels.

It is usually a good idea to make the title of the Web page and the text of the <H1> heading the same. This provides a unified organization of the HTML document, since the title and the highest level heading appear to the Web page viewer to be equivalent in importance.

c) How do you think the heading level-three tag is written in HTML?

Answer: It should look like the following HTML code:

```
<H3></H3>
```

All heading tags are written in the same way. The only difference between them is the number, which denotes the level of heading.

d) How do the level-three headings display in your browser? How much space does the browser place between each heading?

Answer: When you view the file in a Web browser, it should look like the page shown in Figure 3.3.

Figure 3.3 ■ Another example of multiple heading levels.

Your browser should display a blank line between each heading.

It is important to realize that a heading is not automatically preceded with and followed by a blank line. Instead, the way the browser actually formats the page is to place a blank line before or after the heading, *only if one does not already exist.* While this appears to be a minor point, it actually has important formatting implications. For example, it means that you cannot put any text on the line directly preceding a heading. It also means that if you place two headings adjacent to one another, there will only be one blank line between them.

e) How would you format the Author and Date Last Modified statement as a level-four heading?

Answer: Your HTML code should look like the following:

```
<H4>Created by Your Name; Last Modified On Today's
Date</H4>
```

By formatting your Author and Date Last Modified statement as the lowest heading type on a page, you clearly place it within the structure of your HTML document. It is good practice to format the Author and Date Last Modified statement as the lowest heading level on the page.

At this point in the chapter, your HTML file should look like this:

```
<HTML>
<HEAD>
<META NAME="Author" CONTENT="Your Name">
<META HTTP-EQUIV="Content-Type" CONTENT="text/html">
<TITLE> Pete's Peanut Company's Web Page </TITLE>
</HEAD>
<BODY>
  <H1>Pete's Peanut Company's Web Page</H1>
  <H2> Peanut Products Offered</H2>
  <H3>Pete's Roasted Peanuts</H3>
  <H3>Pete's Boiled Peanuts</H3>
  <H2> How To Purchase Pete's Peanuts </H2>
  <H3>Order By Mail</H3>
  <H3>Order By Phone</H3>
  <H4>Created by Your Name; Last Modified On Today's
   Date</H4>
</BODY>
</HTML>
```

3.1.2 ANSWERS

a) How would you set the ALIGN attribute of an <H1> tag to the value *Center?*

Answer: You would type the following HTML:

```
<H1 ALIGN="Center">
```

Like all attributes, the ALIGN attribute takes the value NAME="Value" . Make sure that you space the attribute correctly and do not forget the quotes.

b) Write an example of each heading with the appropriate ALIGN attribute.

Answer: You would type the following HTML:

```
<H3 ALIGN="Center">Order By Mail</H3>
<H2 ALIGN="Left">How To Purchase Pete's Peanuts</H2>
```

```
<H4 ALIGN="Right">Created by Your Name; Last Modified
On Today's Date</H4>
```

c) Did the file display in your browser as you expected?

Answer: When you view the file in a Web browser, it should look like the screen shown in Figure 3.4.

Figure 3.4 ■ Example of using the ALIGN attribute with headings.

Whether you like the way this document looks, with various headings aligned differently, is a question of taste. Some Web designers align all their headings in the same way, some mix up the alignment to add visual variety. It is decisions like this that make creating HTML as much a matter of design as it is one of coding. Increasingly, though, one designer is doing the visual design of Web pages, and another person is doing the actual coding. So, you may never get to make decisions like these.

3.1.3 ANSWERS

a) What changed in the way the page displayed in your browser?

Answer: When you view the file in a Web browser, it should look like the screen shown in Figure 3.5.

Figure 3.5 ■ **Example using horizontal rules.**

You have inserted three horizontal rules into the Web page. A horizontal rule is a line that runs (horizontally, of course) from one side of the Web page to another. You created a horizontal rule using the <HR> tag. Since a horizontal rule does not format text, the <HR> tag does not require an ending tag.

If you are using a different browser, then the horizontal rules may appear slightly different. By default, Netscape Navigator tends to give more thickness to a rule than Internet Explorer does.

b) How did setting the WIDTH attribute affect the way the horizontal rules displayed?

Answer: When you view the file in a Web browser, it should look like the page shown in Figure 3.6.

The horizontal rules now only extend part way across the Web page. The width of the horizontal rules should be about equal to a third of the page (if your display is 800 x 600 pixels), and the rules should be centered in the page (if your browser is Internet Explorer or Netscape Navigator).

The WIDTH attribute sets the length of the horizontal rule. You used the WIDTH attribute to set the length of the horizontal rule to 300 pixels. By default, the width of the horizontal rule is the same as the page width. The WIDTH attribute can be set in either pixels or percentage of page width. The default unit is pixels.

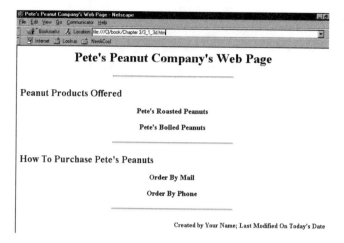

Figure 3.6 ■ Using the WIDTH attribute of horizontal rules.

Your computer screen displays a picture that is made up of thousands of individual dots of color. A pixel is a single dot of color. Typically, computer displays are 800 pixels by 600 pixels, but your computer may have a smaller (such as 640 x 480 pixels) or a larger display (such as 1024 x 768 pixels).

c) What HTML would you use to set the width of a horizontal rule to 50% of the Web page's width?

Answer: You would type the following HTML:

```
<HR WIDTH="50%">
```

Whether you set the width of your horizontal rules in pixels or percentage of page width is a question of personal preference. Some Web designers prefer to use the percentage, so that the relative width of the rule and the page never change. Others prefer to use a constant width, so that the height-to-width ratio of the horizontal rule itself is constant. There is really no "right" answer to the question of which is better.

d) What HTML did you enter to set the ALIGN attribute to *Center*? Did inserting the ALIGN attribute change the way in which the horizontal rules were displayed by the browser?

Answer: You would type the following HTML:

```
<HR ALIGN="Center">
```

Inserting the ALIGN *attribute and setting its value to* Center *should not have changed the way the horizontal rules were aligned, because both Internet Explorer and Netscape Navigator center horizontal rules by default. It's still a good idea to specify the alignment, though, because you cannot count on all browsers following this rule.*

e) What HTML did you enter to set the SIZE attribute to *20?* How did setting the SIZE attribute change the way in which the horizontal rule was displayed by the browser?

Answer: You would type the following HTML:

```
<HR SIZE="20">
```

When you view the file in a Web browser, it should look like the page shown in Figure 3.7.

Figure 3.7 ■ Using the SIZE attribute of the horizontal rule.

The last horizontal rule in the page should now look like a box instead of a line.

The SIZE attribute controls the thickness (or height) of the horizontal rule. The value of the SIZE attribute is set in pixels. Using the SIZE attribute has a lot more visual impact once you add color to a page. You may be wondering, as we have often done, why the SIZE attribute is not called the HEIGHT attribute, since this would seem to correspond better with WIDTH. Unfortunately, there is no good answer for this. It was just a decision that some employee of Netscape made a long time ago, and we are all stuck with it.

**LAB
3.1**

At this point in the Chapter, your HTML file should look like this:

```
<HTML>
<HEAD>
<META NAME="Author" CONTENT="Your Name">
<META HTTP-EQUIV="Content-Type" CONTENT="text/html">
<TITLE> Pete's Peanut Company's Web Page </TITLE>
</HEAD>
<BODY>
 <H1 ALIGN="Center">Pete's Peanut Company's Web
   Page</H1>
<HR ALIGN="Center" WIDTH="300">
 <H2 ALIGN="Left"> Peanut Products Offered</H2>
 <H3 ALIGN="Center">Pete's Roasted Peanuts</H3>
 <H3 ALIGN="Center">Pete's Boiled Peanuts</H3>
<HR ALIGN="Center" WIDTH="300">
 <H2 ALIGN="Left"> How To Purchase Pete's Peanuts
 </H2>
 <H3 ALIGN="Center">Order By Mail</H3>
 <H3 ALIGN="Center">Order By Phone</H3>
 <HR ALIGN="Center" WIDTH="300" Size="20">
 <H4 ALIGN="Right">Created by Your Name; Last Modified
 On Today's Date</H4>
</BODY>
</HTML>
```

LAB 3.1 SELF-REVIEW QUESTIONS

In order to test your progress, you should be able to answer the following questions.

1) How many levels of headings are there in HTML?
   a) _____ 4
   b) _____ 6
   c) _____ 10
   d) _____ 8

2) The heading tags have a SIZE attribute.
   a) _____ True
   b) _____ False

3) What is the default alignment for horizontal rules in Netscape Navigator and Internet Explorer?

    a) _____ Center

    b) _____ Left

    c) _____ Right

    d) _____ Justified

4) A blank line always follows headings in HTML.

    a) _____ True

    b) _____ False

5) What unit do you use to set the width of a horizontal rule?

    a) _____ Pixels

    b) _____ Percent of the page

    c) _____ Either of the above

    d) _____ Inches

Quiz answers appear in Appendix A, Section 3.1.

L A B 3 . 2

USING PARAGRAPH, BREAK, AND BLOCK QUOTE TAGS

LAB OBJECTIVES

After this Lab, you will be able to:

- Use the Paragraph and Break Tags to Organize Content
- Use the Block Quote Tag and ALIGN Attribute to Organize Content

---

In the previous Lab, you created an outline for the Web page of a mythical company called Pete's Peanuts. In this Lab, you are going to create some content and organize it into paragraphs and block quotes. You will begin by using the paragraph tag to do some basic organization of the content you create.

LAB 3.2 EXERCISES

3.2.1 USE THE PARAGRAPH AND BREAK TAGS TO ORGANIZE CONTENT

Let's begin by creating some content to go below the headings on the Pete's Peanuts Web page. Open the HTML document you created in the previous Lab in your text editor and edit it so that it reads as follows:

```
<HTML>
<HEAD>
<META NAME="Author" CONTENT="Your Name">
<META HTTP-EQUIV="Content-Type" CONTENT="text/html">
<TITLE> Pete's Peanut Company's Web Page </TITLE>
</HEAD>
<BODY>
 <H1 ALIGN="Center">Pete's Peanut Company's Web
 Page</H1>
 The Best Peanuts In The World!
<HR ALIGN="Center" WIDTH="300">
 <H2 ALIGN="Left"> Peanut Products Offered</H2>
 <H3 ALIGN="Center">Pete's Roasted Peanuts</H3>
 Pete's Roasted Peanuts are slow roasted for that
 true peanut taste.
 They won the 1999 Best Roasted Peanut award at the
 prestigious International Peanut Festival.
 Available in 1, 5, and 10 pound canisters.
 <H3 ALIGN="Center">Pete's Boiled Peanuts</H3>
 Pete's Boiled Peanuts are boiled until they are
 soft and delicious with just a hint of salt.
 Available in 1, 5, and 10 pound canisters
<HR ALIGN="Center" WIDTH="300">
 <H2 ALIGN="Left"> How To Purchase Pete's Peanuts </H2>
 <H3 ALIGN="Center">Order By Mail</H3>
 Pete's Peanuts
 555 Peanut Street
 Peanutville, GA, 55555
 <H3 ALIGN="Center">Order By Phone</H3>
 Monday Through Friday, 8:30 AM to 5:00 PM
 Call (555)-555-5555
<HR ALIGN="Center" WIDTH="300" Size="20">
 <H4 ALIGN="Right">Created by Your Name; Last Modified
 On Today's Date</H4>
</BODY>
</HTML>
```

Save it as an HTML file and open it in your browser.

a) How does the text we just inserted display in your browser?

_____

_____

Open the Pete's Peanuts page in your text editor and edit it so that it reads as follows:

```
<HTML>
<HEAD>
<META NAME="Author" CONTENT="Your Name">
<META HTTP-EQUIV="Content-Type" CONTENT="text/html">
<TITLE> Pete's Peanut Company's Web Page </TITLE>
</HEAD>
<BODY>
 <H1 ALIGN="Center">Pete's Peanut Company's Web
   Page</H1>
<P>The Best Peanuts In The World!</P>
<HR ALIGN="Center" WIDTH="300">
 <H2 ALIGN="Left"> Peanut Products Offered</H2>
 <H3 ALIGN="Center">Pete's Roasted Peanuts</H3>
<P>Pete's Roasted Peanuts are slow roasted for that
   true peanut taste.</P>
<P>They won the 1999 Best Roasted Peanut award at the
   prestigious International Peanut Festival.</P>
<P>Available in 1, 5, and 10 pound canisters.</P>
 <H3 ALIGN="Center">Pete's Boiled Peanuts</H3>
<P>Pete's Boiled Peanuts are boiled until they are
   soft and delicious with just a hint of salt.</P>
<P>Available in 1, 5, and 10 pound canisters</P>
<HR ALIGN="Center" WIDTH="300">
 <H2 ALIGN="Left"> How To Purchase Pete's Peanuts </H2>
 <H3 ALIGN="Center">Order By Mail</H3>
<P>Pete's Peanuts
 555 Peanut Street
 Peanutville, GA, 55555</P>
<H3 ALIGN="Center">Order By Phone</H3>
<P>Monday Through Friday, 8:30 AM to 5:00 PM</P>
 Call (555)-555-5555
<HR ALIGN="Center" WIDTH="300" Size="20">
 <H4 ALIGN="Right">Created by Your Name; Last Modified
   On Today's Date</H4>
</BODY>
</HTML>
```

Then save your file as an HTML file and open it in your browser.

b) Give an example of the paragraph tags you inserted. How does the browser now display the text?

_____

_____

Now that the text is divided into separate paragraphs, Pete's Peanuts page looks a lot better. However, there is still a problem with the mailing address. Ideally, you want the mailing address to display as three, single-spaced lines. If you enclose it in a single set of paragraph tags, though, the browser displays the address as a single line. On the other hand, if you put each line within <P> tags, then the browser will display the address with a blank line between each line of text. Luckily, there is a tag that can solve this formatting problem.

Open the Pete's Peanut page in your text editor and edit the mailing address to match the following:

```
<P>Pete's Peanuts<BR>
555 Peanut Street<BR>
Peanutville, GA, 55555</P>
```

Save your file as an HTML file and open it in your browser.

c) How does the mailing address display now?

_____

_____

At this point, Pete's Peanuts page is essentially complete. All that's left is making it a little more visually interesting.

3.2.2 USE THE BLOCK QUOTE TAG AND *ALIGN* ATTRIBUTE TO ORGANIZE CONTENT

As we noted above, we are going to try to make the complete Pete's Peanuts page a little more visually interesting. We will begin by using the block quote tag to format the "Best Peanuts In the World" slogan at the top of the Pete's Peanuts page. Open the HTML file you created in the previous Exercise and edit the slogan text so that it reads as follows:

```
<BLOCKQUOTE>
 "The Best Peanuts In The World!"
</BLOCKQUOTE>
```

Save the file and open it in your browser.

> **a)** How does the slogan display now that you have formatted it as a block quote?

_____

_____

Now, you are going to change the alignment of some of the paragraphs.

Open the HTML file you created in the previous Exercise and edit it so that it reads as follows:

```
<HTML>
 <HEAD>
 <META NAME="Author" CONTENT="Your Name">
 <META HTTP-EQUIV="Content-Type" CONTENT="text/html">
 <TITLE> Pete's Peanut Company's Web Page </TITLE>
 </HEAD>

<BODY>

<H1 ALIGN="Center">
 Pete's Peanut Company's Web Page
</H1>

<BLOCKQUOTE>
 "The Best Peanuts In The World!"
</BLOCKQUOTE>

<HR ALIGN="Center" WIDTH="300">

<H2 ALIGN="Left"> Peanut Products Offered</H2>
<H3 ALIGN="Center">Pete's Roasted Peanuts</H3>

<P>
 Pete's Roasted Peanuts are slow roasted for that
 true peanut taste.
</P>

<P>
 They won the 1999 Best Roasted Peanut award at the
 prestigious International Peanut Festival.
</P>

<P>Available in 1, 5, and 10 pound canisters.</P>

<H3 ALIGN="Center">Pete's Boiled Peanuts</H3>
```

```
<P>
 Pete's Boiled Peanuts are boiled until they are soft
 and delicious with just a hint of salt.
</P>

<P>Available in 1, 5, and 10 pound canisters</P>

<HR ALIGN="Center" WIDTH="300">

<H2 ALIGN="Left"> How To Purchase Pete's Peanuts </H2>
<H3>ALIGN="Center">Order By Mail</H3>

<P ALIGN="Center">
 Pete's Peanuts<BR>
 555 Peanut Street<BR>
 Peanutville, GA, 55555
</P>

<H3 ALIGN="Center">Order By Phone</H3>

<P ALIGN="Center">
 Monday Through Friday, 8:30 AM to 5:00 PM
</P>

<P ALIGN="Center">Call (555)-555-5555</P>

<HR ALIGN="Center" WIDTH="300" SIZE="20">

<H4 ALIGN="Right">
 Created by Your Name; Last Modified On Today's Date
</H4>

</BODY>

</HTML>
```

Save the file and open it in your browser.

b) How do the paragraphs display now?

_____

_____

With these final changes, the Pete's Peanuts page is complete. You have created your first Web page!

LAB 3.2 EXERCISE ANSWERS

3.2.1 ANSWERS

a) How does the text we just inserted display in your browser?

Answer: When you open the file in your browser, it will look like the screen shown in Figure 3.8.

All of the text under each heading is run together as a single line (of course, it is wrapped to fit the browser window). Regardless of how you entered the text into the editor, no formatting is preserved.

The reason the content text looks different from what you typed, when display by the browser, is that in HTML all formatting depends on tags. Therefore, the browser ignores any carriage returns or empty lines that you type, unless you tell the browser how to format the text using HTML tags. The main tag for formatting text is the paragraph tag, which is written <P>. To format text into a paragraph, you simply enclose it in opening and closing paragraph tags. Here is an example:

```
<P>This is a paragraph</P>
```

Figure 3.8 ■ Example of a page with unformatted paragraphs.

b) Give an example of the paragraph tags you inserted. How does the browser now display the text?

Answer: When you open the file in your browser, it will look like the page shown in Figure 3.9.

Order By Mail

Pete's Peanuts
555 Peanut Street
Peanutville, GA, 55555

Figure 3.9 ■ Example of a page with formatted paragraphs.

Notice how the browser places a blank line before the text formatted with paragraph tags. The browser does not, however, place a blank line after the paragraph. This is very different from the way in which the browser formats text enclosed in heading tags.

c) How does the mailing address display now?

Answer: The mailing address should now be single-spaced. When you open the file in your browser, it will look like the page shown in Figure 3.10.

Figure 3.10 ■ Example of formatting using the break tag.

The break tag, written as <BR>, tells the browser to insert a carriage return. The break tag does not require a closing tag, because it does not format text. Instead, you place a <BR> wherever you want the text to break to the next line. The major use of break tags, though, is to create blank space on a Web page. You do this by using several break tags together. Putting multiple break tags in a row causes the browser to display multiple blank lines. Break tags are also very useful for spacing horizontal rules, because horizontal rules do not put a blank line before or after themselves. Although we did not explore this use of break tags in this Lab, if you keep writing HTML, you will constantly find yourself using break tags for spacing.

At this point in the Chapter, your HTML file should read as follows:

```
<HTML>
<HEAD>
<META NAME="Author" CONTENT="Your Name">
<META HTTP-EQUIV="Content-Type" CONTENT="text/html">
<TITLE> Pete's Peanut Company's Web Page </TITLE>
</HEAD>
<BODY>
  <H1 ALIGN="Center">
    Pete's Peanut Company's Web Page
  </H1>
<P>The Best Peanuts In The World!</P>
<HR ALIGN="Center" WIDTH="300">
  <H2 ALIGN="Left"> Peanut Products Offered</H2>
  <H3 ALIGN="Center">Pete's Roasted Peanuts</H3>
<P>
  Pete's Roasted Peanuts are slow roasted for that
  true peanut taste.
</P>
<P>
  They won the 1999 Best Roasted Peanut award at the
  prestigious International Peanut Festival.
</P>
<P>Available in 1, 5, and 10 pound canisters.</P>
 <H3 ALIGN="Center">Pete's Boiled Peanuts</H3>
<P>
   Pete's Boiled Peanuts are boiled until they are
   soft and delicious with just a hint of salt.
</P>
<P>Available in 1, 5, and 10 pound canisters</P>
<HR ALIGN="Center" WIDTH="300">
 <H2 ALIGN="Left">How To Purchase Pete's Peanuts</H2>
 <H3 ALIGN="Center">Order By Mail</H3>
<P>
 Pete's Peanuts<BR>
 555 Peanut Street<BR>
 Peanutville, GA 55555
</P>
 <H3 ALIGN="Center">Order By Phone</H3>
<P>
  Monday Through Friday, 8:30 AM to 5:00 PM
</P>
Call (555)-555-5555
<HR ALIGN="Center" WIDTH="300" SIZE="20">
```

```
<H4 ALIGN="Right">
 Created by Your Name; Last Modified On Today's Date
</H4>
</BODY>
</HTML>
```

3.2.2 ANSWERS

a) How does the slogan display now that you have formatted it as a block quote?

Answer: When you open the file in your browser, it will look like the page shown in Figure 3.11.

Figure 3.11 ■ Example of formatting using the block quote tag.

The block quote tag, written <BLOCKQUOTE>, formats text as a quote. The text enclosed in the block quote tags is indented from the left margin of the page, but not centered. If you entered enough text to wrap to the next line, you would find that the text is also indented from the right margin of the page.

The block quote tag is not used by many Web designers, because the results are often visually unappealing. Generally, we would recommend that you only use block quote tags for long quotes that continue for several lines. For short quotes like the slogan, "best peanuts in the world" at the top of the Web page we would normally just center the line of text in the page. Again, though, this is a question of personal design preference.

You inserted ALIGN attributes into some of the paragraphs.

b) How do the paragraphs display now?

Answer: The mailing address, the hours to call, and the phone number should all be aligned in the center of the page, and when you open the file in your browser, it should look like the page shown in Figure 3.12.

The ALIGN attribute of the paragraph tag, just like the ALIGN attribute of the heading and horizontal rule tags, allows you to set the alignment of a paragraph's text. In addition, the paragraph tag's ALIGN attribute has exactly the same possible values (*Left, Center,* and *Right*) that the heading and horizontal rule tags' ALIGN attribute has.

Order By Mail

Pete's Peanuts
555 Peanut Street
Peanutville, GA, 55555

Order By Phone

Monday Through Friday, 8:30 AM to 5:00 PM

Call (555)-555-5555

Figure 3.12 ■ Example of formatting using the ALIGN attribute of the paragraph tag.

Using the ALIGN attributes of the heading, paragraph, and horizontal rule tags is only one way of aligning text in HTML. In Chapter 7, "Formatting the Page," and Chapter 9, "Cascading Style Sheets," you will learn two other methods. Each of the methods has different advantages and disadvantages, and only experience will tell you which method is right for a particular page.

It should be noted that the block quote tag also has an ALIGN attribute, but it does not work usefully in either Netscape Navigator or Internet Explorer. We suggest that you ignore it and don't try to use it.

If your page is not displaying in the way the Chapter text says it should be, check your HTML against the code examples given in this Chapter.

LAB 3.2 SELF-REVIEW QUESTIONS

In order to test your progress, you should be able to answer the following questions.

1) Text formatted with <BLOCKQUOTE> is indented from where?
    a) _____ The left margin of the page.
    b) _____ The right margin of the page.
    c) _____ Both side margins of the page.
    d) _____ The top margin of the page.

2) Which of the following tags does not have an ALIGN attribute?
    a) _____ <P>
    b) _____
    c) _____ <HR>
    d) _____ <BLOCKQUOTE>

3) Many Web designers find text formatted with the block quote tag visually unappealing.
    a) _____ True
    b) _____ False

4) Which of the following is correct HTML?
    a) _____ `<PALIGN="Center">`
    b) _____ `<P ALIGN="Center">`
    c) _____ `<BR ALIGN="Center">`
    d) _____ `<P ALIGN="Center">`

5) What is the default alignment for paragraph tags?
    a) _____ Right
    b) _____ Center
    c) _____ Left
    d) _____ None

Quiz answers appear in Appendix A, Section 3.2.

**LAB
3.2**

C H A P T E R   3

TEST YOUR THINKING

1) Visit several Web sites and view the sources of the pages. Do the pages use differ-
    ent level headings? How many different levels of headings are typically used? How
    are the headings aligned?

2) Visit several Web sites and view the sources of the pages. How are the paragraphs
    divided? Did the designer use break tags to create empty space? How are the para-
    graphs aligned? Are they all aligned the same?

3) Take a sales or advertising brochure from a company and pretend it is your job to
    translate the content of the brochure into a Web site. How would you organize
    the site and divide up the content? Create and write the HTML for a sample page
    of your design.

USING LISTS

 I hear and I forget. I see and I remember. I do and I understand.

—Confucious

CHAPTER OBJECTIVES

In this Chapter, you will learn about:

In Chapter 3, "Creating and Organizing Content," you learned how to organize the content of your HTML pages by breaking it up into sections. In this Chapter, you will learn how to use lists to organize the content of your HTML document. Lists are very useful. They allow you to:

- Draw the reader's eye to the points you want to make.
- Demonstrate the relationships between items in your document.
- Make an organized table of contents or menu.

Best of all, lists make your document easy to read!

There are two main types of lists in HTML: ordered and unordered. We will begin with ordered lists.

L A B   4 . 1

USING ORDERED LISTS

LAB OBJECTIVES

After this Lab, you will be able to:

- Create an Ordered List
- Change the Type of Ordered List
- Start Ordered Lists at Different Numbers or Letters

An ordered list is one that has a number or letter before each list item. In other words, the list is numbered 1, 2, 3 or ordered A, B, C. You use ordered lists when you are presenting information that is organized into steps that have to be carried out in a particular order. Common uses of ordered lists are for instructions, recipes, and outlines of documents. You can tell when to use an ordered list by asking yourself, "Does it matter which list item comes before the other?" If you answer "Yes," then you need to use an ordered list.

The Whole Truth

As usual, before we begin the Exercise, we must pause here to tell you that the way your lists look will vary depending upon on which browser and on which type of computer the page is being viewed. Overall, the differences in the ways in which lists display are minor. Just be aware that they exist.

LAB 4.1 EXERCISES

4.1.1 CREATE AN ORDERED LIST

Ordered lists are defined by using the <OL> tag. The heading of the list is de-fined using the <LH> tag. Individual items in the list are defined using the <LI> or list item tag. Now, let's create an ordered list. Make an HTML document by entering the following in your text editor:

```
<HTML>
<HEAD>
<TITLE>AN ORDERED LIST EXAMPLE</TITLE>
</HEAD>
<BODY>
 <OL>
   <LH>My Favorite Browsers
   <LI>Netscape Navigator
   <LI>Internet Explorer
   <LI>Opera
 </OL>
</BODY>
</HTML>
```

Save it as an HTML file and open it in your browser.

> **a)** How does the list display in your browser?

_____

_____

Now, reopen the file and add a </LI> tag to the end of each line in the list that begins with <LI>. Then, add a </LH> tag to the end of the line that begins with </LH>. Save it as an HTML file and open it in your browser.

> **b)** Is there any difference in the way the list displays in your browser now, compared to the previous file?

_____

_____

Many lists, particularly instructions, are more complicated than the example you have created above. Let's see how HTML deals with more complicated lists. Open the HTML file you created above in your text editor and edit it so that it reads as follows:

```
<HTML>
<HEAD>
<TITLE>A HIGH CONTENT ORDERED LIST EXAMPLE</TITLE>
</HEAD>
<BODY>
<OL>
 <LH>My Favorite Browsers
  <LI>Netscape Navigator
   <P>
    I like Netscape, because of that cool N logo in
    the corner.
   </P>
   <P>
    Also, it was the first browser I ever used.
   </P>
  <LI>Internet Explorer
  <BR>
   I like Internet Explorer, because it has a lot of
   neat features.
  <LI>Opera
  <P>
   I like Opera, because you can have multiple pages
   open at the same time.
  </P>
</OL>
</BODY>
</HTML>
```

Save the text as an HTML file and open it in your browser.

> **c)** How does the list display in your browser and what is the difference between how the text is separated by the `<BR>` tag and how the text is separated by the `</P>` tags?

_____

_____

4.1.2 CHANGE THE TYPE OF ORDERED LIST

So far, we have only created a list that is ordered numerically (1, 2, 3). This type of ordering is the default setting. In other words, if you do not specify a type of ordering, the browser will always order your list that way. We can, however, change the ordering of the list by specifying a different type of ordering. As we have seen in earlier Chapters, many HTML tags can contain attributes, and <OL> tags are among these. You can change the type of ordering by adding a type specification (or attribute) inside the <OL> tag. To do this, open the HTML file you created earlier in your text editor and edit it to match the following example:

```
<HTML>
<HEAD>
<TITLE>ANOTHER ORDERED LIST EXAMPLE</TITLE>
</HEAD>
<BODY>
 <OL Type="A">
  <LH>My Favorite Browsers
   <LI>Netscape Navigator
   <LI>Internet Explorer
   <LI>Opera
 </OL>
</BODY>
</HTML>
```

Save it as an HTML file and open it in your browser.

a) How does the list display in your browser?

_____

_____

Of course, there is more than one setting for the TYPE attribute. Let's see what happens when you would change the attribute inside the <OL> tag. Open your HTML file again and replace the line:

```
<OL Type="A">
```

with the line:

```
<OL Type="a">
```

Then, save it as an HTML file and open it in your browser.

b) How does the list display now?

_____

_____

c) How do you think you would make the list display an order of i, ii, iii?

_____

_____

4.1.3 START ORDERED LISTS AT DIFFERENT NUMBERS OR LETTERS

Strange as it may seem, there are cases where you do not want your list to begin at step one. Luckily, HTML provides a way of doing this, so let's try it out. Open your text editor and enter the following text:

```
<HTML>
<HEAD>
<TITLE>USING START IN AN ORDERED LIST EXAMPLE</TITLE>
</HEAD>
<BODY>
 <OL Start="44">
   <LH>My Favorite Browsers
     <LI>Netscape Navigator
     <LI>Internet Explorer
     <LI>Opera
 </OL>
</BODY>
</HTML>
```

Save it as an HTML file and open it in your browser.

a) How did you think the list would display in your browser? Were you right?

_____

_____

Suppose, though, that you had used the same starting point for a list that also had a type attribute other than the default? To see what happens, open the file you just created and change the line containing the <OL> tag so that it reads as follows:

```
<OL Type="A" Start="44">
```

Save it as an HTML file and open it in your browser.

> **b)** How does the list display in your browser now?

_____

_____

Of course, you don't just arbitrarily start lists at higher numbers for no reason. Instead, you will usually start a list at a higher number when you have the parts of a list separated by intervening material. To see an example of this, open your text editor and enter the following text:

```
<HTML>
<HEAD>
<TITLE>USING START IN AN ORDERED LIST EXAMPLE</TITLE>
</HEAD>
<BODY>
<OL>
 <LH>My Favorite Browsers
  <LI>Netscape Navigator
</OL>
   <P>
     Some Intervening Material That Breaks
     Up The List
   </P>
<OL Start="2">
   <LI>Internet Explorer
   <LI>Opera
</OL>
</BODY>
</HTML>
```

Save it as an HTML file and open it in your browser.

> **c)** How does this page display in your browser?

_____

_____

> **d)** Can you think of any drawbacks to using the START attribute with ordered lists?

_____

_____

The `<LI>` tag has an attribute that is much like the START attribute of the `<OL>` tag—the VALUE attribute. To see an example of how the VALUE attribute is used, open your text editor and enter the following text:

```
<HTML>
<HEAD>
<TITLE>USING VALUE IN AN ORDERED LIST EXAMPLE</TITLE>
</HEAD>
<BODY>
 <OL>
   <LH>My Favorite Browsers
    <LI>Netscape Navigator
 </OL>
<P>Some Intervening Material That Breaks Up The
List</P>
 <OL>
   <LI Value="2">Internet Explorer
   <LI>Opera
 </OL>
</BODY>
</HTML>
```

Save it as an HTML file and open it in your browser.

e) How does the list, using the VALUE attribute, display in your browser?

_____

_____

f) Can you think of any drawbacks to using the VALUE attribute with ordered lists?

_____

_____

LAB 4.1 EXERCISE ANSWERS

4.1.1 ANSWERS

a) How does the list display in your browser?

Answer: When you view the file in a Web browser, it should look similar to Figure 4.1.

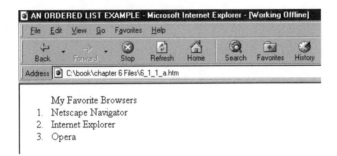

Figure 4.1 ■ Example of an ordered list.

Notice how the list heading (the text after the <LH> tag) is indented, so that it lines up with the list entries. A lot of Web authors (including both of this book's authors) do not like how this type of list heading looks. Instead of using the <LH> tag to put a heading on the list, they leave the <LH> out and put the list heading in <H1> or <H2> tags *before the <OL> tag.* If you want to put the heading inside the <OL> tag, you have to use the <LH> tag, however.

The <LH> tag does not work correctly in Internet Explorer 2 or 3. If you do not put a break tag at the end of the text following the <LH> tag, then Internet Explorer will put the text on the same line as the first <LI>. This bug has been fixed in Internet Explorer 4 and later, but you should keep it in mind when designing your lists.

b) Is there any difference in the way the list displays in your browser now, compared to the previous file?

Answer: There should be no difference in the way the files display. In each case, they should look like the screen shown in Figure 4.1.

The <LH> and <LI> tags are both "open" tags. That means that they do not require a closing tag. On the other hand, closing these tags does not do any harm and may be required in the future. Therefore, putting closing tags in is probably a good habit to get into as you learn HTML. Because closing tags are not required, though, we have not used them in all of our examples.

c) How does the list display in your browser and what is the difference between how the text is separated by the <BR> tag, and how the text is separated by the </P> tags?

Answer: As you can see, lists are not restricted to only one line of text per entry. You can include as much text as you like in your list, and even break it up into paragraphs. When you view the file in a Web browser, it should look like Figure 4.2.

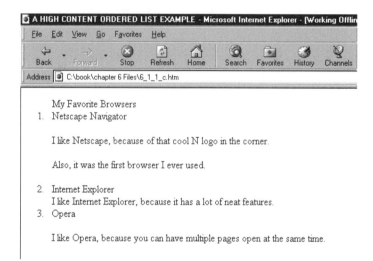

Figure 4.2 ■ Example of a badly organized multiline list.

Notice the difference in separation between the text defined within the <P> tags and the text that is merely separated with a <BR> tag. The text within the <P> tags is separated from the preceding text by a blank line. The text following the <BR> tags begins on the next line. You should also notice just how bad this list looks. If you are going to include a lot of text within your lists, you have to put a lot of thought into designing a list that looks good!

4.1.2 ANSWERS

a) How does the list display in your browser?

Answer: When you view the file in a Web browser, it should look like the screen shown in Figure 4.3.

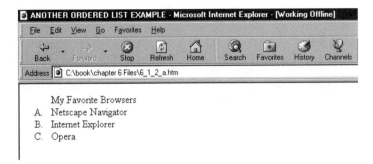

Figure 4.3 ■ Example of an ordered list using the TYPE **attribute.**

By using the TYPE="A" attribute within the <OL> tag, you directed the browser to use A, B, C for the list items, instead of using the default numbering.

b) How does the list display now?

Answer: When you view the file in a Web browser, it should look like the screen shown in Figure 4.4.

Figure 4.4 ■ Example of an ordered list using the TYPE **attribute set to** "a".

By using the TYPE="a" attribute within the <OL> tag, you directed the browser to use a, b, c for the list items, instead of using A, B, C, as you did in the previous file. If the list is not displayed with lowercase letters before the items, go back to your file and check that you used a lowercase "a" when specifying the TYPE attribute.

c) How do you think you would make the list display an order of i, ii, iii?

Answer: You would edit the <OL> *tag so that it read as follows:*

```
<OL Type="i">
```

As a result of making this change, when you view the file in a Web browser, it should look like the screen shown in Figure 4.5.

My Favorite Browsers
i.   Netscape Navigator
ii. Internet Explorer
iii. Opera

Figure 4.5 ■ Example of an ordered list using the TYPE attribute set to "i".

In all, there are five types of ordered lists you can use:

TYPE="1"   This forces use of the default 1, 2, 3 numbering.

TYPE="I"   This forces use of I, II, III numbering (Roman numerals).

TYPE="i"   This forces use of i, ii, iii numbering.

TYPE="a"   This forces use of a, b, c ordering.

TYPE="A"   This forces use of A, B, C ordering.

Which TYPE setting you use is simply a question of personal preference. For maximum cross-browser compatibility, however, you should stick to the default numbering.

4.1.3 ANSWERS

a)   How did you think the list would display in your browser? Were you right?

Answer: When you view the file in a Web browser, it should look like the screen shown in Figure 4.6.

The list begins at the number 44 because you set the START attribute of the <OL> tag to that number. The START attribute is used to tell an ordered list at which number to start. The list will always start at whatever number you set.

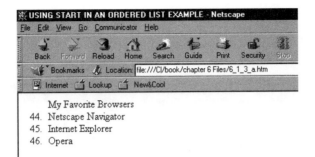

Figure 4.6 ■ Example of an ordered list with the START attribute set to 44.

b) How does the list display in your browser now?

Answer: When you view the file in a Web browser, it should look like the screen shown in Figure 4.7.

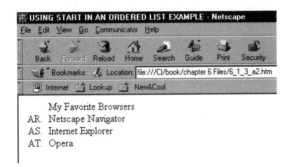

Figure 4.7 ■ Example of an ordered list using both the START and TYPE attributes.

The list starts at item AR. Each of the ordering systems has a way of going on forever (just like regular numbering), so don't worry about running out. If you had used the value 4444 for the starting point for a Type="A" list, it would have started at FHX. For all practical purposes, though, you will never use such high starting points, and from a design standpoint, it's a good thing!

The list shows FHX, because that is the number equal to 4,444 in Base 26. The X represents 24. The H represents 8 × 26 or 208. The F represents 6 × 27 × 26 or 4,212. Together, they make 4,444. In the Base 10 numbering we normally use, you start a new column every time you get to 10. In Base 26 numbering, though, you start a new column every time you get to 26. For example, the number 27 in Base 26 is AA. The left-hand A represents 26, and the right-hand A represents 1. Add them together and you get 27.

c) How does this page display in your browser?

Answer: When you view the file in a Web browser, it should look like the screen shown in Figure 4.8.

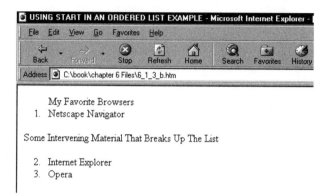

Figure 4.8 ■ Another example of an ordered list using the START attribute.

The first list starts at 1 (the default) because you used no START attribute. The second list starts at 2 (the value of the START attribute that you set). To the viewer of the page, they will look like a single list.

d) Can you think of any drawbacks to using the START attribute with ordered lists?

Answer: The biggest disadvantage is the amount of rewriting you will have to do if you decide to insert a new list item, or delete an existing one, near the start of the list. If you use a single list, without setting any START attributes, the list will automatically renumber when you insert or delete an item. If you have set START attributes, however, to make several lists look like one, then you will have to do all the renumbering yourself. This does not mean that you shouldn't use the START attribute. In many cases, it is the only way to make a complex list display in an attractive and readable manner. Just bear in mind that every design decision has both advantages and disadvantages.

Another disadvantage is that it gives you, the Web author, an additional opportunity to make mistakes. The browser never skips a list number or uses one twice when setting up a list. People, on the other hand, regularly make this type of mistake. As a general rule, remember the computer is better at counting than you, so whenever possible, let it do all the arithmetic.

e) How does the list, using the VALUE attribute, display in your browser?

Answer: When you view the file in a Web browser, it should look just like the screen shown in Figure 4.8.

The VALUE attribute of the <LI> tag directly sets the value the <LI> tag takes. The first list starts at 1 (the default) because you used no START or VALUE attributes. The second list starts at 2 (the value of the VALUE attribute that you set in the first <LI> tag). The following <LI> tags take their numbering based on the value set for the preceding <LI> tag. To the viewer of the page, they will look like a single list.

f) Can you think of any drawbacks to using the VALUE attribute with ordered lists?

Answer: All the disadvantages that apply to the use of the START attribute apply to the use of the VALUE attribute too. If you use VALUE attributes, it makes it very hard to reorganize lists, or to insert new values in the middle of the list.

At this point, you may be wondering if there is any good use for the START or VALUE attributes. Actually, there is. They are very useful when you are referring to (or quoting from) a list in a document. For example, if this book was in HTML, I would probably have frequently used the VALUE or START attributes when restating the questions in this answer section. When you have large amounts of material between list items, it is often more convenient to use multiple lists and directly set their starting points instead of using a single list.

LAB 4.1 SELF-REVIEW QUESTIONS

In order to test your progress, you should be able to answer the following questions.

1) To create an ordered list, which of the following tags would you use first?
  a) _____ <LO> tag
  b) _____ <OL> tag
  c) _____ <L> tag
  d) _____ <L1> tag

2) The NUMBER attribute sets which number an <LI> tag displays.
  a) _____ True
  b) _____ False

3) The START attribute is used with which of the following tags?
  a) _____ <OL> tag
  b) _____ <LI> tag
  c) _____ Both of the above
  d) _____ <L> tag

4) You can include more than one paragraph in a list item.
   a) _____ True
   b) _____ False

5) Which of the following is the default type setting for an ordered list?
   a) _____ i, ii, iii
   b) _____ 1, 2, 3
   c) _____ A, B, C
   d) _____ a, b, c

   Quiz answers appear in Appendix A, Section 4.1.

LAB 4.2

USING UNORDERED LISTS

LAB OBJECTIVES

After this Lab, you will be able to:

- Create Unordered Lists
- Change the Type of Bullet Used by the List

Ordered lists are not the only kind of lists you can use on your Web pages. You can also use unordered lists. Unordered lists do not have any numbering. Instead, each item in the list is preceded by a bullet point. Unordered lists are used when it doesn't really matter in which order a list is presented—when every item in a list is of equal importance.

LAB 4.2 EXERCISES

4.2.1 CREATE UNORDERED LISTS

The way you construct an unordered list is very similar to creating an ordered list. Instead of using an <OL> tag, though, you use a <UL> tag. Just as with ordered lists, the heading of the list is defined using the <LH> tag, and individual items in the list are defined using the <LI> tag. Now, let's create your first unordered list. Make an HTML document by entering the following in your text editor:

```
<HTML>
<HEAD>
<TITLE>AN UNORDERED LIST EXAMPLE</TITLE>
```

```
</HEAD>
<BODY>
 <UL>
   <LH>My Favorite Browsers
     <LI>Netscape Navigator
     <LI>Internet Explorer
     <LI>Opera
 </UL>
</BODY>
</HTML>
```

Save it as an HTML file and open it in your browser.

a) How does the unordered list display in your browser?

_____

_____

b) What do you think would happen if you added a START attribute statement (for example, START="3") to the <UL> tag?

_____

_____

4.2.2 CHANGE THE TYPE OF BULLET USED BY THE LIST

So far, the unordered list you have created is preceded by solid, black circles (also known as bullets). Just as you can force the browser to start with different numbers or letters for ordered lists, you can force the browser to use a different symbol to precede each item in an unordered list. You do this by using the TYPE attribute of the <UL> tag. Open the HTML file you created in the previous Exercise, and edit it so that it reads as follows:

```
<HTML>
<HEAD>
<TITLE>ANOTHER UNORDERED LIST EXAMPLE</TITLE>
</HEAD>
<BODY>
 <UL Type="circle">
   <LH>My Favorite Browsers
     <LI>Netscape Navigator
```

```
       <LI>Internet Explorer
       <LI>Opera
     </UL>
  </BODY>
  </HTML>
```

Save the file and open it in your browser.

> **a)** How does the unordered list display now that you have added the TYPE attribute?

_____

_____

Now, open the file in the text editor and change the TYPE attribute so that it reads as follows:

```
  <UL Type="square">
```

Save the file and open it in your browser.

> **b)** How does the unordered list display now that you have changed the TYPE attribute?

_____

_____

You can also force the browser to use a different symbol to precede each item by using a different attribute. In unordered lists, the <LI> tags also have a TYPE attribute. Open the HTML file you created in the previous Exercise and edit it so that it reads as follows:

```
     <HTML>
     <HEAD>
     <TITLE>ANOTHER UNORDERED LIST EXAMPLE</TITLE>
     </HEAD>
     <BODY>
      <UL>
        <LH>My Favorite Browsers
         <LI Type="circle">Netscape Navigator
         <LI>Internet Explorer
         <LI Type="square">Opera
      </UL>
```

```
</BODY>
</HTML>
```

Save the file and open it in your browser.

c)   How does the unordered list display now that you have added the TYPE attribute to the <LI> tags?

_____

_____

LAB 4.2 EXERCISE ANSWERS

4.2.1 ANSWERS

a)   How does the unordered list display in your browser?

Answer: When you open the file in your browser, it will look like the screen shown in Figure 4.9.

Figure 4.9 ■ Example of an unordered list.

Each item in the list is preceded by a solid black circle, called a bullet.

b)   What do you think would happen if you added a START attribute statement (for example, Start="3") to the <UL> tag?

Answer: Nothing would change about the way the file displayed because the <UL> tag does not have a START attribute, and browsers ignore any HTML tags or attributes that they do not understand.

4.2.2 ANSWERS

a) How does the unordered list display now that you have added the TYPE attribute?

Answer: When you open the file in your browser, it will look like the screen shown in Figure 4.10.

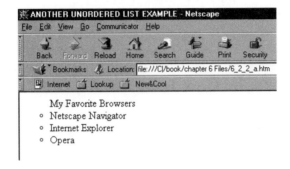

Figure 4.10 ■ Example of an unordered list using the TYPE attribute.

Each item in the list is preceded by a hollow circle.

b) How does the unordered list display now that you have changed the TYPE attribute?

Answer: When you open the file in your browser, it will look much like the screen shown in Figure 4.11.

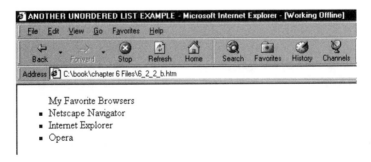

Figure 4.11 ■ Another example of an unordered list using the TYPE attribute.

Each item in the list is preceded by a black square. The square bullets do not display the same in each browser, however. In Macintosh browsers, the squares are hollow. In Internet Explorer, on the other hand, the squares are smaller than they are in Netscape Navigator.

You have now seen all three possible TYPE attributes for unordered list. They are:

TYPE="disc"—This is the black circle (it is the default).

**LAB
4.2**

TYPE="circle"—This is the hollow circle.

TYPE="square"—This is the black square.

A common mistake is to misspell the value to which you are setting the TYPE attribute. If you do this, the Web browser will just ignore your TYPE setting and use the default TYPE. If you are not getting the kind of unordered list that you expect, the first thing to check is the spelling.

c) How does the unordered list display now that you have added the TYPE attribute to the <LI> tags?

Answer: When you open the file in your browser, it will look like the screen shown in Figure 4.12.

Figure 4.12 ■ Example of an unordered list using the TYPE attribute of the <LI> tag.

The first two items in the list are preceded by black circles. The last item in the list is preceded by a black square. As you can see, succeeding list items take their TYPE from the setting of the items that preceded them in the list. Unless, of course, you set the item's TYPE explicitly. In general, though, if you need to set the TYPE of an unordered list, it is better practice to set it in the <UL> tag. It leads to less confusion for you.

LAB 4.2 SELF-REVIEW QUESTIONS

In order to test your progress, you should be able to answer the following questions.

1) To create an unordered list, you would use which of the following tags?
   a) _____ `<LU>` tag
   b) _____ `<UL>` tag
   c) _____ `<L>` tag
   d) _____ `<U>` tag

2) The `SHAPE` attribute sets which bullet shape an `<LI>` tag displays.
   a) _____ True
   b) _____ False

3) The `TYPE` attribute is used in unordered lists with which of the following tags?
   a) _____ `<UL>` tag
   b) _____ `<LI>` tag
   c) _____ Both of the above
   d) _____ `<U>` tag

4) The `TYPE="square"` attribute displays the same in every browser.
   a) _____ True
   b) _____ False

5) Which of the following is the default `TYPE` setting for an unordered list?
   a) _____ Hollow circle
   b) _____ Square
   c) _____ Black circle
   d) _____ None of the above

Quiz answers appear in Appendix A, Section 4.2

LAB
4.2

L A B   4 . 3

COMBINING LISTS

LAB OBJECTIVES

After this Lab, you will be able to:

- Combine Ordered and Unordered Lists

Very often, you will not want to use only one type of list on a Web page. For example, often when you have a Web page with an outline of a document or presentation on it, you will need to combine both ordered and unordered lists. In this Lab, we cover how to do this.

LAB 4.3 EXERCISES

4.3.1 COMBINE ORDERED AND UNORDERED LISTS

Make an HTML document by entering the following in your text editor:

```
<HTML>
<HEAD>
<TITLE>A COMBINED LIST EXAMPLE</TITLE>
</HEAD>
<BODY>
 <OL>
  <LH>My Favorite Browsers
   <LI>Netscape Navigator
   <UL>
    <LI>The first browser I used
   </UL>
   <LI>Internet Explorer
   <UL>
    <LI>Has some nifty features
```

```
   </UL>
   <LI>Opera
   <UL>
    <LI>Can open more than one page at a time
   </UL>
  </OL>
 </BODY>
 </HTML>
```

Save it as an HTML file and open it in your browser.

a) How does the combined list display in your browser?

_____

_____

As we have seen from the previous example, you can nest lists, and the browser will understand what you are trying to do. Now, suppose you wanted to add the following list below the line reading "Has some nifty features".

```
i.  DHTML
ii. XML (in IE5)
```

b) What HTML would you add to the previous file?

_____

_____

LAB 4.3 EXERCISE ANSWERS

4.3.1 ANSWERS

a)   How does the combined list display in your browser?

Answer: When you open the file in your browser, it will look like the screen shown in Figure 4.13.

Each main item in the list is preceded by a number, and each sub-item in the list is preceded by a circle. You may have expected the sub-items to be preceded by a black disc, since this is the setting for unordered lists. For some unknown reason, though, both Internet Explorer and Netscape Navigator use the hollow circle, instead.

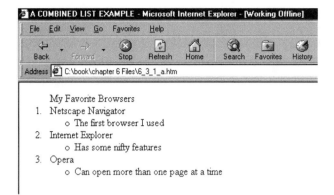

Figure 4.13 ■ Example of a nested list.

What you have been doing in this Exercise is called "nesting tags." This is when you enclose one pair of tags within another pair. This is frequently done in HTML, and it usually does not cause any problems. You can even nest a pair of tags within a pair of the same kind of tags. Just make sure that you have the same number of opening and closing tags!

b) What HTML would you add to the previous file?

Answer: You would edit the file so that it reads as follows:

```
<HTML>
<HEAD>
<TITLE>A COMBINED LIST EXAMPLE</TITLE>
</HEAD>
<BODY>
 <OL>
  <LH>My Favorite Browsers
   <LI>Netscape Navigator
 <UL>
  <LI>The first browser I used
 </UL>
   <LI>Internet Explorer
 <UL>
  <LI>Has some nifty features
  <OL>
   <LI type="i">DHTML
   <LI> XML (in IE5)
  </OL>
 </UL>
  <LI>Opera
  <UL>
```

```
    <LI>Can open more than one page at a time
  </UL>
 </OL>
</BODY>
</HTML>
```

When you open this file in a browser, it should look like the screen show in Figure 4.14.

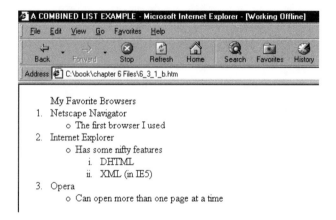

Figure 4.14 ■ Another example of nested lists.

As you can see, you can do a lot with nested lists. You have to be careful not to make any mistakes, though. Make sure you remembered the `TYPE="I"` attribute in the `<OL>` tag, or else you will get another list numbered 1, 2, 3. Also, make sure that you didn't forget to put in the ending tags for the nested lists, or you can get some unexpected effects.

LAB 4.3 SELF-REVIEW QUESTIONS

In order to test your progress, you should be able to answer the following questions.

1) Under what circumstance do you often need to combine lists?
    a) _____ When you make a page containing an outline.
    b) _____ When you make a page containing a presentation.
    c) _____ When you make a page containing a recipe.
    d) _____ both a) and b)

2) You cannot put an unordered list within an ordered list.
    a) _____ True
    b) _____ False

3) You cannot combine more than two lists at a time.

    a) _____ True

    b) _____ False

4) An unordered list enclosed within an ordered list will use a solid circle as the default bullet type.

    a) _____ True, in Internet Explorer and Netscape Navigator

    b) _____ False

    c) _____ True, but only in Internet Explorer

    d) _____ True, but only in Netscape Navigator

Quiz answers appear in Appendix A, Section 4.3.

LAB 4.3

CHAPTER 4

TEST YOUR THINKING

1) What are some of the most common uses of lists on the World Wide Web? Browse through several large sites on the Web and see if you can find any uses that you didn't think of.

2) If you were putting a menu on a Web site, would you use an ordered or un-ordered list? What are the advantages (if any) of each type of list in this situation?

C H A P T E R 5

ADDING IMAGES TO YOUR WEB PAGES

 A picture is worth a thousand words; a thousand pictures are way too many!

—Alayna Cohn

In this Chapter, we'll start off learning about the different types of images available for HTML pages. By now you should be familiar with the available browsers. And, with this knowledge, you should be aware that each browser renders HTML code differently. This rule applies to images as well. Therefore, a clear understanding of the types of images is important.

Everyone wants pictures on their HTML pages. And why not? Images, pictures, graphics—whatever you would like to call them can truly add pizzazz to your HTML. Yet, overkill is the most common mistake made by new HTML designers. Therefore, the second half of this Chapter will be devoted to learning how and when to insert images onto your HTML pages.

In order to proceed with this Chapter, you should have your browser open and minimized.

L A B   5 . 1

TYPES OF IMAGES

LAB OBJECTIVES

After this Lab, you will be able to:

- Create a Folder for All Your Images
- Create Simple Images
- Check the Size of Your Images
- Understand the Different Types of Images

Before beginning the wonderful, creative process of adding images into your HTML files, you need to be certain you have the necessary tools. If you have Windows installed on your system, then you should have the Paint program installed.

CHECKING YOUR SYSTEM FOR PAINT

You can and should be able to open Paint on your Windows PC. Paint is a drawing program shipped with the Windows OS. Let's check to make certain Paint is on your machine.

Click the `Start` button on your desktop. Navigate up to `Programs`, then to `Accessories` and over to `Paint`. Choosing `Paint` opens the application.

Also, in order to proceed with the Exercises in this Chapter, you must download and install Paint Shop Pro.

Microsoft Paint allows you to create graphics, yet only the bitmap format is available. We highly recommend downloading a free trial version of Paint Shop Pro from `http://www.shareware.com`. *As of this writing, Paint Shop Pro v5.01 is the latest version of the software available for download. Paint Shop Pro lets you get your feet wet in the process of gen-*

erating graphic files. The option to save graphics in many different file formats is available. Also, Paint Shop Pro allows much more creative freedom. Should you decide to become a graphic-making whiz, there are other graphic software programs available for retail purchase.

Now that you are prepared to create your own images, let's take a moment to understand what actually makes up a picture or image. All graphic files are stored as a series of pixels (or dots) used within a group to create an image. Pixels can actually use up to 16,777,216 different colors to make up a single image. Basically, there are three types of images you can display within an HTML file: .gif, .jpeg (or .jpg), and .bmp. The major browsers currently support all three types of images. We'll discuss all of these formats shortly. The higher the compression, the clearer and crisper the image will appear. *Compression* is a term used to describe how the image is stored. In turn, the more pixels used in the image, the more bytes the image will require. So, there is a price to pay for sharp, clear images. We have all experienced a slow download of an image from a Web site. This experience is usually associated with a large, or "byte-heavy," image. We will go into more detail on these subjects within this Chapter. This Chapter will help you create images that not only add to the overall design and attractiveness of your HTML pages, but allow for a pleasant experience for any user surfing through your Web site.

LAB 5.1 EXERCISES

5.1.1 CREATE A FOLDER FOR ALL YOUR IMAGES

 There is nothing worse than saving a file or files and then not knowing where you put them! Let's start off on the right foot and create a folder to hold all of our images.

Create a folder/directory right on the root of the C drive.

Open Windows Explorer and maximize it.

Click once on the C drive icon on the left side of the window.

Right-click anywhere within the white space on the right side of the Explorer window, which should be showing all of the folders available on the C drive.

A pop-up menu will appear. Choose `New`, then `Folder` and a new folder will be created on the C drive.

Name the folder *Images*.

Move the *Images* folder to a more logical place on your hard drive.

a) Where is the best place to keep the *Images* folder?

_____

_____

5.1.2 CREATE SIMPLE IMAGES

To make the graphic creation process a bit smoother, let's create a shortcut and place it on the desktop.

The shortcut will point to the Windows Paint program.

Open Windows Explorer.

Click once on the `Start` menu on the left of the Explorer window.

Click once on the `Programs` folder on the left of the Explorer window.

Double-click `Accessories` on the right of the window.

Right-click the `Paint` shortcut and drag and it onto your desktop. Choose `Copy Here`.

Next, open `Paint` and create your first image. Follow these steps to create an image for this Exercise.

Paint creates a new file upon opening the program. By default, the Paint Tools toolbar should be displayed within the Paint design environment. If you do not see it, navigate to the `View` menu and choose `Tool Box`. While you are there, check that the `Color Box` and the `Status Bar` are chosen, as well.

Click on the text tool, which has an uppercase **A** on it.

Move the mouse over the empty Paint development area.

a) How is the mouse cursor displayed at this point?

_____

_____

Click and drag the text tool over the blank image file. Release the mouse when you have the size you want. For this exercise, a rectangular shape of approximately 2" x 3" will be fine.

From the `View` menu, choose `Text Toolbar` in order to format the text for your image.

Choose the font and font size.

Any text typed into the text image will be black. Should you desire to change the color of the text, click one of the colors from the `Colors` toolbar. By default, this toolbar is bottom-aligned within the Paint design environment.

Type the word *Welcome* inside your text image.

Save your image as `welcome.bmp` and place it in your `Images` folder. Place all future images in this folder.

You have just created the first image you may insert into your HTML.

■ *FOR EXAMPLE:*

Figure 5.1 shows a simple example of welcome text.

Welcome

Figure 5.1 ■ Simple example of welcome text.

b) What file types are available to save your graphics in Paint?

_____

_____

c) What are some other images you could create to add value to your HTML?

_____

_____

Once again, to make the creative process a bit easier, let's create another desktop shortcut. It will be created from `psp.exe`: the Paint Shop Pro executable.

Locate `psp.exe`.

Right-click on it and choose `Create Shortcut`.

`Cut` the shortcut and `Paste` it onto your desktop.

Open Paint Shop Pro. Start thinking about a color scheme for your Web site. For this Exercise, we'll create some bullets, but first take a look at the Color Palette located on the right within the Paint Shop Pro environment. If it is hidden, navigate to the `View` menu and check off `Color Palette`.

Click on the foreground colored square on the Color Palette (see Figure 5.2).

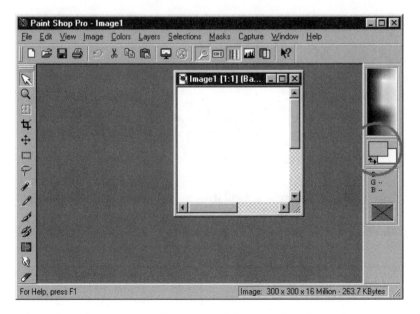

Figure 5.2 ■ The foreground and background colored squares of the Color Palette (circled).

d) What happens when you click on the black double-headed arrow between the two colored squares?

_____

_____

Sliding the small black arrow on the left of the `Color` dialog box, you are able to customize the color of your choice. Once you have the perfect color, click the `Add to Custom Colors` button.

Next, from the `File` menu, choose `New`.

For the purpose of this Exercise, let's make the image 50 pixels wide and 50 pixels high. Open the drop-down box of the `Background Color` option and choose `white`. Click `ok`.

To create bullets for this Exercise, we'll use the airbrush tool (see Figure 5.3).

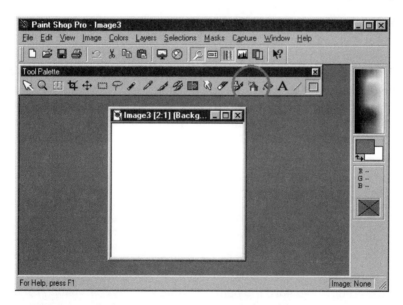

Figure 5.3 ■ The airbrush tool (circled), located on the Tool Palette, is normally used to create an airbrush effect, but we've found that it makes perfect bullets.

The Whole Truth

It is not uncommon to discover that the color you have carefully chosen for your images has "disappeared". When it came time to utilize the airbrush tool, the color had magically changed to a dull gray! Fear not. Navigate to the `Colors` menu. Note the `Decrease Color Depth` and `Increase Color Depth` choices. These options will allow you to get your original color choice back.

We are merely becoming familiar with Paint Shop Pro in this Exercise. We encourage you to become very comfortable with this software. Try out each and every image tool to find out what it does. For example, the `Image` menu contains many different options to enhance your images. Since you have Paint Shop Pro open, now may be a good time to experiment with these options.

Choose a size between `15` and `20`, a shape of `round`, leave the opacity and the paper texture at the default settings, `128` and `None`, respectively.

Next, position the airbrush tool over the image and click and hold until the bullet is to your liking.

To save your bullet image, choose `Save As` from the `File` menu. Save the image as a bitmap file (`.bmp`). Design two additional bullets using a different color for each.

e) What are the best names for your new images?

_____

_____

First impressions mean quite a lot, whether it is meeting a person for the first time or someone viewing the first page within your Web site. A professional appearance will most certainly encourage the "surfer" to look further into your HTML pages. Having the ability to create your own graphics is great. If you have the right software, such as Paint Shop Pro or Adobe Illustrator, designing your own graphics can be fun and exciting. Yet, most of us have limited time to sit and work out all the particulars of an image. There are many Web sites devoted to supplying free graphics to users.

Here are some Web sites that offer free graphics for you to use as you wish.

`http://www.altavista.com`—Navigate to the Altavista photo site by clicking on the **AV Photo and Media Finder** link. This site offers free high quality images for you to download.

`http://www.octagamm.com/boutique/mainball.htm`—Lots of bullets, letters, animations, buttons, and so forth.

`http://www.media-graphics.net/`—Every month this site offers a free download that includes different graphics and animations.

Using your favorite search engine, find some other sites that offer free graphics for download.

f) What other sites did you find?

_____

_____

To ask about other suggested Web sites for free downloadable images or to inquire about other information pertaining to this book, please go to the companion Web site at:

`http://www.phptr.com/phptrinteractive/`

SAVING GRAPHICS FROM AN EXTERNAL WEB SITE

When visiting some of these sites, you may notice a note indicating that you may copy and save images to your own directory. Here's how you can do this:

Right click on the image you wish to save.

Choose `Save Image As…` or `Save Picture As…`

Navigate to your *Images* folder.

You may rename the image at this point.

Click the `Save` button.

Your new image is now saved onto your drive. Name the image something meaningful that you will easily recognize when searching through all of your graphic files.

■ *FOR EXAMPLE:*

An image from an external Web site may be called `t672902.gif`. If the image were a picture of a Porsche, then re-naming it `porsche.gif` in your folder would make for easy searching later on.

The Whole Truth

Saving graphic files from an external source without permission is not a very good idea. Publishing your HTML pages to the Internet allows anyone and everyone to view your Web pages. If a graphic file is seen on your site, being used without explicit and/or written permission, a lawsuit is not out of the question.

Also, when saving an image file from an external site with `Save Picture As…`, be sure to save the image with the original file extension. For example, say you have found a free image from an external Web site. The file format of that image is `.jpeg`. You want to save it as a `.bmp` file. Saving it as a bitmap can corrupt the file and therefore make it impossible for you to open and edit. The safest way to keep a file from being corrupted is to save it with the original file extension. Or you can open Paint Shop Pro, edit the file if you wish, then save the file as a new graphic type. Paint Shop Pro can handle the transformation of one graphic file type to another.

5.1.3 CHECK THE SIZE OF YOUR IMAGES

Ever visited a Web site with large graphics only to get discouraged and move on to another site? Loading large images can be excruciatingly slow. Graphics should be used to enhance your HTML pages. Knowing the size of the images you will be inserting can be very useful.

Go back to the first image you created called `welcome.bmp`. Right-click on the file and choose `Properties`.

a) What information do you see related to the size of the file?

_____

_____

5.1.4 UNDERSTAND THE DIFFERENT TYPES OF IMAGES

First off, let's discuss bitmaps (.bmp). You may be familiar with the common Windows wallpaper choices supplied by Microsoft. All of these images are bitmaps. Because Microsoft created this format, it only makes sense that Internet Explorer will always recognize the bitmap format. The bitmap will display in other browsers, yet a different coding convention must be used to do so with some of the lesser-known browsers. For purposes of the following Exercises, be assured that any code used here will work with either Internet Explorer or Netscape.

Open Paint Shop Pro. Let's create a new image. No Web site is complete without a logo.

■ *FOR EXAMPLE:*

A logo can be a simple display of your initials, as seen in Figure 5.4.

Figure 5.4 ■ A simple example of a logo.

Design a logo for your Web site. For purposes of this Exercise, an image with a size of 150 x 150 is fine. Save your new image as a bitmap from the File menu by clicking on Save As. Name the image logo.bmp. Navigate to the View menu and click on Image Information.

   a) What do you see?

   _____

   _____

Stay in the Paint Shop Pro environment. The logo should still be displayed within the palette. Save the image once again. This time save the image with the .jpg extension. Name the image logo.jpg. You will find this option from the Save As Type drop-down box.

b) What message box appeared as a result of saving the image as a .jpg?

_____

_____

View `Image Information` for `logo.jpg`. From the `Colors` menu, choose `Count Colors Used`. Perform this action for both the .bmp and the .jpg files.

c) What differences are apparent between `logo.bmp` and `logo.jpg`?

_____

_____

Close all open images, leaving Paint Shop Pro open. There is another useful tool for viewing image information. Follow these steps:

From the `File` menu, choose `Open`.

Navigate to the *Images* folder. You should see both formats of the logo image.

Click once on `logo.bmp`.

Click the `Details` button from within the `Image Information/Preview` frame box.

Note the information displayed.

Do the same for `logo.jpg`.

d) How does the information differ for each image?

_____

_____

Once again, remain in the Paint Shop Pro design environment. Open `logo.jpg`. This time save the logo as a .gif file. Name the file `logo.gif`.

e) What happened this time?

_____

_____

Even though, jpg files result in smaller file sizes overall, they can still run large due to the 16 million color capacity. This is where the compression feature comes in quite handy. Let's try it out.

Open `logo.jpg`. Save the logo three times, each with a different compression value. Follow these steps:

From the `File` menu, choose `Save As`.

Click the `Options` button. Change the compression value to `25`. Save the new file as `logo2.jpg`.

Make the second compression value `50` and name and save the file as `logo3.jpg`.

Make the third compression value `55` and name and save the file as `logo4.jpg`.

Next, navigate to each of the logo images. Right-click on each and make note of the properties.

> **f)** What differences did you notice between each of the compressed images?

_____

_____

LAB 5.1 EXERCISE ANSWERS

5.1.1 ANSWERS

a) Where is the best place to keep the *Images* folder?

Answer: It's up to you if you prefer to keep the Images *folder on the root of your C drive. We like to keep everything in our projects organized.*

Working on an HTML project one day and returning to it two weeks later with everything in its place makes files easier to find and makes for a more efficient working environment. So, we suggest creating a folder called *Projects* for all of your HTML pages and placing the *Images* folder within the *Projects* folder.

5.1.2 ANSWERS

a)   How is the mouse cursor displayed at this point?

Answer: Upon choosing the text tool, the mouse cursor is displayed as a crosshair.

Each of the design tools within Paint will display as a different mouse cursor when viewed over the Paint palette.

b)   What file types are available to save your graphics in Paint?

Answer: Paint has four different bitmap formats to choose from when saving an image.

- **Monochrome bitmap**—*This file format will save images using the range from white to black, which includes the entire gray scale. The gray scale uses shades of gray to display an image. Computers, unlike photographs, are able to display 16 or 256 different shades of gray only.*

- **16-color bitmap**—*The maximum number of colors an image can have is 16. As mentioned in the introduction to this Chapter, an image is comprised of pixels. A 16-color bitmap may contain any number of pixels, yet no more than 16 colors will be included in the image.*

- **256-color bitmap**—*A bitmap saved in this format may contain up to 256 colors, but no more.*

- **24-bit bitmap**—*An image saved with this format will be very crisp and clear and have a photograph-like quality.*

The smallest unit of computerized information or data is a bit. A bit is either a one or a zero and is either black or white. For example, if a pixel is denoted as one bit-per-pixel, then it is either black or white. If a pixel is denoted as four bits-per-pixel, then the color may be set to any one of four colors. A pixel set as eight bits-per-pixel may be set to as many as 256 colors. Additional discussion on bitmaps is found later in this Chapter.

c)   What are some other images you could create to add value to your HTML?

Answer: There's no right answer here. That's the great thing about creating and adding images to your HTML. You can be as creative as you would like.

You may want to think about adding a border to either the left or right of your HTML main page. Some of the most common graphic additions to any Web site are buttons, lines, dots, and background images. One idea you may want to think about is designing a logo for your main HTML page. Key points you wish to get across to your viewers can be accented with colorful bullets. The ideas are endless, so don't be afraid to experiment. If you add an image to the HTML and decide you don't like it, you can always remove it later. If you are at a loss for ideas, go to the heart of it all: the Internet. The Web is flooded with sites that can spur some interesting ideas you may incorporate into your own Web site. Surf the Web, and we're sure you will find some great ideas out there.

d) What happens when you click on the black double-headed arrow between the two colored squares?

Answer: Each of the colored squares located on the right side of the Paint Shop Pro environment represents the foreground and background color of the current image. Clicking on the arrow changes the foreground color to the background color and vice versa.

For example, in Figure 5.2, the foreground color is shown as a light purple (although you can't see it as such in this book, trust us on this one). Any additions made to Image 1, such as text or any shapes added to the image, will display as light purple. Clicking the black arrow once forces light purple to become the background color of the given image.

e) What are the best names for your new images?

Answer: As mentioned earlier, when naming images, as well as any of your other HTML components, you should always use a name that you will easily recognize later.

I created three bullets, one blue, one light blue, and one light purple. The best names for these bullets would be `blueBullet.bmp`, `liteblue Bullet.bmp`, and `litepurpleBullet.bmp`, respectively. The point here is to name them something that makes sense to you!

f) What other sites did you find?

Answer: Please note that Web sites come and go every day. If one search fails, try another.

The resources available via the Internet are endless. We used AltaVista as our search engine and performed a search on "free graphics." Here are some of the sites we found:

```
http://conceptcorps.hypermart.net/
http://users.ccnet.com/~elsajoy/free.html
http://www.flash.net/~dsquard7/backgrounds.html
```

5.1.3 ANSWERS

a) What information do you see related to the size of the file?

Answer: The size you see will be different depending on how large you made your image.

You can view all the image details via the `View` menu, by choosing `Image Information`. Figure 5.5 shows what we saw when checking our image.

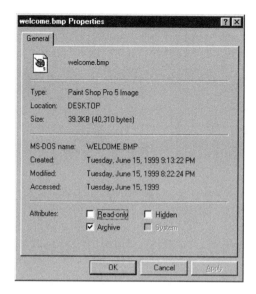

Figure 5.5 ■ The Image Properties dialog box can be opened by right-clicking on the file name.

Note the size of welcome.bmp. The size is 39.3 kilobytes, which is equivalent to 40,310 bytes. This number is not significant, but having the ability to check the size can help you design your images accordingly. Later in this Chapter, we'll learn how to reduce the image (compression) for easier and faster download to the browser.

5.1.4 ANSWERS

a) What do you see?

Answer: Choosing View, *then* Image Information *displays the* Current Image Information *dialog box.*

Once again, your image information will appear slightly different from what is shown in Figure 5.6.

Some key points you should notice here include: File Type, Image Dimensions, Pixels per Inch, Pixel Depth/Color and, lastly, Memory Used In RAM, which is located in the lower framed box. In this case, File Type informs us of the current image format. Being aware of the Image Dimensions will come into play when we discuss height and width size in Lab 5.2. The advantage of using bitmaps is that they are fairly simple images to create. Bitmaps are simply a series of colored dots or *pixels*. The more stacking of pixels you create, the more colors are added to the bitmap. In turn, the more colors used, the more byte-hungry the bitmap becomes. For example, let's say we have two images, both 2 inches wide. One image uses

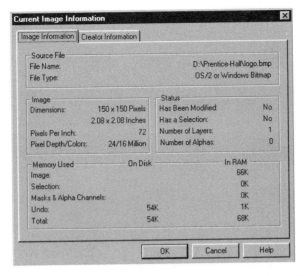

Figure 5.6 ■ You can view all of a particular file's details by selecting `Image Information` **from the** `View` **menu.**

50 pixels to cover the width. The other image uses 500 pixels to cover the same image width. The image using 500 pixels is using smaller pixels. This image will be display the most clearly and crisp of the two. And, as a result, the more pixels, the more bytes the image will require.

b) What message box appeared as a result of saving the image as a `.jpg`?

Answer: Figure 5.7 shows the message box displayed upon saving the image from a bitmap to a `.jpg` file.

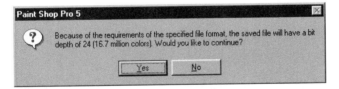

Figure 5.7 ■ Resaving a `.bmp` file in `.jpg` format results in this message box.

See the discussion following the next question for an explanation of this message.

c) What differences are apparent between `logo.bmp` and `logo.jpg`?

Answer: Isn't this interesting? Not only does the `.jpg` file format increase the color depth to 16 million colors, now we have an image using many more colors to create our image, as opposed to the `.bmp` format.

Your color count will differ from the count we viewed. Our logo.jpg file has a color count of 2143, whereas our logo.bmp file has a color count of only 46. The logo saved in the .jpg format increases the colors used quite a bit. So, if we incorporate what we learned earlier in this Chapter with this new knowledge, we can undoubtedly be certain that using a .jpg over a .bmp will display a much crisper image.

The .jpg (or .jpeg) file was created by the Joint Photographics Expert Group. Note that you may use the .jpg or the .jpeg file extension names. Either extension is recognizable by all browsers.

d) How does the information differ for each image?

Answer: What you saw here should have surprised you somewhat. Your details will vary from the information we saw. When viewing the details of our logo.bmp *file, we discovered a file size of 67,854, as opposed to the* logo.jpg *file size of 3,187. What an incredible difference.*

Perhaps you are thinking the same thing we are thinking. A bitmap takes up so much space, whereas a .jpg does not. Why use a bitmap in any Web pages? The answer is simple. The bitmap is easy to create. Period. The downside is that the bitmap, as discussed above, is quite inefficient at storing data compared to the .jpg. In turn, the .jpg file format will load into the receiving browser more quickly than the bitmap.

e) What happened this time?

Answer: A message box appears as shown in Figure 5.8.

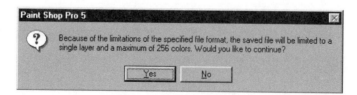

Figure 5.8 ■ Saving the same file in a .gif format results in this message box.

The .gif file format saves a maximum of 8 bits per pixel or 256 colors for any given image. If you want or need more colors, using the .bmp or .jpg is necessary. The .gif extension stands for Graphic Interchange Format. CompuServe created it in 1987. The .gif is the most common image format used on the Web today.

The Whole Truth

Animated images use the `.gif` file format. Animated images can be a fun and interesting addition to your Web site. When adding animated images to your Web site, beware of overkill. Should you decide to add some of these images to your HTML pages, follow the same steps for saving an image from an external Web site. The key point to saving an animated image is to keep the name of the original file. Changing the file name or extension runs the risk of corrupting the image.

Here are some Web sites that contain free animated `.gif` files:

`http://www.animatedgifs.simplenet.com`

`http://www.fg-a.com/gifs.html`

Creating animated `.gif` files are beyond the realm of this book. Here's a brief explanation of how they are created. Do you remember the popular flip-books from when you were a kid? You could flip through the pages quickly to see what appeared to be an image or images moving. Also, you may be familiar with how cartoons are generated. Each individual cell is strung together to create the illusion of movement. Animated images work in the same manner. Paint Shop Pro 5.01, the version you installed, contains an Animation Shop with sample animated `.gif` files.

If you would like more information on animated `.gif` files and how to create them, try out the following Web sites:

`http://members.aol.com/royalef/gifmake.htm`

`http://www.hotwired.com/webmonkey/multimedia/`
`multimedia_more.html#animation`

f) What differences did you notice between each of the compressed images?

Answer: Physically, all the compressed images are the same size. The higher the compression, the less storage space the `.jpg` file will take up on your hard drive. Your figures will differ here.

My first image compressed at the default rate of 15% has a size of 14.8KB. The same image saved with a compression rate of 55% is 9.37KB. And, my third image saved at a 100% compression rate has a size of 3.46KB. There is an interesting fact to note here. Compressing an image does minimize the storage space required on your hard drive. However, the quality of the image diminishes. You may find it necessary to experiment more with compression in order to achieve the image quality and memory storage balance for a high-quality downloadable image for your HTML.

LAB 5.1 REVIEW QUESTIONS

In order to test your progress, you should be able to answer the following questions.

1) Images are stored as a series of dots called *pixels*.
   a) _____ True
   b) _____ False

2) Compressing an image makes the physical size of the image smaller.
   a) _____ True
   b) _____ False

3) The easiest way to view the properties of an image downloaded from an external Web site is which of the following:
   a) _____ Open the image with the image editor and check `Image Information`.
   b) _____ Open the browser, navigate to the Web site of origin, right-click the image and view its properties.
   c) _____ Open your `Images` folder, right-click the image, and choose `Properties`.

4) Which of the following is the correct maximum number of colors that pixels may use to make up a single image?
   a) _____ 16
   b) _____ 256
   c) _____ 16,777,216
   d) _____ 24

5) The correct file extension name for the image created by the Joint Photographics Experts Group is which of the following:
   a) _____ `.jpg`
   b) _____ `.jpeg`
   c) _____ `.JPG`
   d) _____ `.JPEG`
   e) _____ All of the above

6) Two hundred fifty six is the maximum number of colors allowed in which of the following image formats:
   a) _____ `.bmp`
   b) _____ `.gif`
   c) _____ `.jpg`

7) Animated images use which of the following file format:
   a) _____ `.bmp`
   b) _____ `.gif`
   c) _____ `.jpg`

Quiz answers appear in Appendix A, Section 5.1.

L A B   5 . 2

HOW TO INSERT
IMAGES

LAB OBJECTIVES

After this Lab, you will be able to:

- Use the `HEIGHT` and `WIDTH` Attributes
- Use the `BORDER` Attribute
- Use the `ALT` Attribute
- Align Images

Being able to insert and display images within your HTML pages in a professional manner is very important. It can surely augment and even define the look and feel of your HTML pages. Inserting images in specific locations or making images clickable links adds value to any Web site.

In this Lab, you will learn how to use all the associated tags necessary to get the most out of your images. The first tag you must know about is the `<IMG>` tag. The `<IMG>` tag tells HTML that the following syntax will represent an image, as opposed to text or any formatting code for the page. The *SRC* attribute of the `<IMG>` tag indicates the location of the image to be displayed. The `<IMG>` tag must be used hand-in-hand with the *SRC* attribute.

■ *FOR EXAMPLE:*

The following code might be used to display the `welcome.bmp` image:

```
<IMG SRC = "C:/Projects/FirstProj/Images/welcome.bmp">
```

This example tells the HTML the entire path location of the image. Note how the path is enclosed in quotes. Also, much like some of the previously mentioned tags, the IMG tag does not require an end tag. Using this syntax would insert the welcome.bmp image into the HTML, yet it would lack any positioning or other attributes. Let's continue on to add other attributes to HTML embedded images.

LAB 5.2 EXERCISES

5.2.1 USE THE **HEIGHT** AND **WIDTH** ATTRIBUTES

Start a new HTML page. Using the <IMG> tag and the SRC attribute, add the logo.gif image, placing the code within the body of your HTML page. Save the file and view it in your browser.

a) What do you see?

_____

_____

Using the ordered list syntax from the previous Chapter, place your image into a list as a list item.

b) What is the syntax used to do this?

_____

_____

Using Paint Shop Pro, view the Image Information of logo.gif. Note the height and width properties of the image. The HEIGHT and WIDTH attributes of the <IMG> tag can be used to display images differently from their original size. Both the HEIGHT and WIDTH attributes are specified in pixels. Change both attributes to 50 pixels. Add the HEIGHT and WIDTH attributes to the list you created.

■ *FOR EXAMPLE:*

```
<IMG SRC="C:/Projects/FirstProj/Images/logo.gif"
HEIGHT="50" WIDTH="50">
```

c) What is the output in your browser?

_____

_____

You may also use the HEIGHT and WIDTH attributes with a percentage specification. Using the same number that you used above, change the pixel sizing measurements to a percentage value. Use the % sign. Resize the browser a few different sizes.

d) What is different about the display of your image now?

_____

_____

5.2.2 USE THE BORDER ATTRIBUTE

The BORDER attribute can be used to specify a border to be displayed around an image. The border is specified in pixels.

Start a new HTML page. Code the necessary shell values required for an HTML page. Using the <IMG SRC=> tag, specify logo.gif in the path. Specify a border size of 20.

■ FOR EXAMPLE:

```
<IMG SRC="C:/Projects/FirstProj/Images/logo.gif"
BORDER="20">
```

Save the file. Open your browser.

a) What do you see?

_____

_____

Open your editor and change the BORDER attribute to 2. Save the file. View it in your browser.

b) What do you see?

_____

_____

5.2.3 USE THE ALT ATTRIBUTE

The ALT attribute of the <IMG> tag stands for Alternative Text. In other words, a tool tip is displayed for each image when you utilize the ALT attribute. Hovering the mouse cursor over an image using the ALT attribute will display text. The ALT text should be enclosed in double quotes. Add the ALT attribute to the <IMG> tag and specify some text.

■ FOR EXAMPLE:

```
<IMG SRC = "C:/Projects/FirstProj/Images/logo.gif" ALT =
"This is my fantastic logo.">
```

Save the file. View the HTML page in your browser.

a) What do you see when the HTML is opened in your browser?

_____

_____

Purposely change the path of your image to an incorrect SRC path. Save the file once again.

b) What do you see in your browser now?

_____

_____

5.2.4 ALIGN IMAGES

In order to display images in various locations within an HTML page, it is necessary to have the ability to use the ALIGN attribute. The ALIGN attribute has the following associated properties: *left, right, top,* and *bottom.* Once again, the properties are text values and should be enclosed in double quotes.

Add the ALIGN attribute to your existing HTML. Set the ALIGN property to a value of *right.* Here's how you can do this:

```
<IMG SRC = "C:/Projects/FirstProj/Images/logo.gif" ALT =
"This is my fantastic logo." ALIGN = "right">
```

a) What do you see when viewing the saved HTML in your browser?

_____

_____

The best use of the ALIGN attribute comes into play when displaying an image in relation to some surrounding text. Four other properties can be used here: *top, left, bottom,* and *middle.*

Open and edit your HTML page. Add a line of text immediately prior to the <IMG> tag. At this point, simply add the text with no other attributes associated with the text. Change the ALIGN attribute property to *top.* View the file in your browser.

b) What is the output?

_____

_____

Change the ALIGN attribute property to *bottom.*

c) What is the difference between the *bottom* property and the *top* property when viewing the HTML in your browser?

_____

_____

 The best thing about HTML and its tags and attributes is having the ability to create numerous scenarios within your Web pages. Don't be afraid to experiment with different properties when it comes to formatting and displaying images, as well as experimenting with all the other tags for HTML coding.

Add a `<P>` tag at the end of the text line you just created. Once again, save the file and open your browser.

d) What difference did the `<P>` tag make in the display of your image?

_____

_____

Previously, we learned how to insert horizontal rules into HTML pages.

Place a horizontal rule immediately before and immediately after the `<IMG>` tag.

e) What is the syntax to do this?

_____

_____

f) How does the page display in your browser?

_____

_____

LAB 5.2 EXERCISE ANSWERS

5.2.1 ANSWERS

a) What do you see?

Answer: What you should see is `logo.gif` *in the upper left-hand corner of your browser window.*

b) What is the syntax used to do this?

Answer: Your source path will be different for the `<IMG>` *tag. This is what our HTML code looked like:*

```
<OL>
 <LI>
  <IMG SRC = "C:/Projects/FirstProj/Images/logo.gif">
 </LI>
</OL>
```

c) What is the output in your browser?

Answer: Coding the HEIGHT *and* WIDTH *attributes of an image will drastically affect the way it is displayed within the browser. The* logo.gif *file, with the* HEIGHT *and* WIDTH *set to 50, will display the image quite small. The* HEIGHT *and* WIDTH *attributes can resize an image for you rather than going back to the drawing board and redesigning the image. Recall the introductory Chapters and note here that the* HEIGHT *and* WIDTH *properties will set aside the specified space for an image as the HTML loads to a client machine.*

d) What is different about the display of your image now?

Answer: Ah, this is interesting. What you should have noticed is quite different from specifying the HEIGHT *and* WIDTH *in pixels. First, this is what my HTML code looked like with the percent values:*

```
<IMG SRC = "C:/Projects/FirstProj/Images/logo.gif"
HEIGHT = "50%" WIDTH = "50%">
```

Note how the carriage return within my HTML code did not affect the ability for the browser to understand the code.

The percentage additions to the HEIGHT and WIDTH attributes actually re-size the image in accordance with the size of the browser.

5.2.2 ANSWERS

a) What do you see?

Answer: The output of the image in the browser displays a solid border around logo.gif. *Figure 5.9 shows what we viewed in our browser.*

LAB 5.2

Figure 5.9 ■ The result of adding a border of size 20 around a logo when opened in a browser.

b) What do you see?

Answer: The border is much smaller now.

The BORDER attribute is a handy little property. You can easily add a border of any size without changing the original image.

5.2.3 ANSWERS

a) What do you see when the HTML is opened in your browser?

Answer: Figure 5.10 shows what displayed in my browser when hovering the mouse over the image.

b) What do you see in your browser now?

Answer: Well, what you should see is no display of your image. Yet, the ALT attribute is displayed on the HTML page.

If the user's browser does not support the <IMG> tag or if the user has stopped the loading of the page, the alternative text will still be displayed.

This is my fantastic logo.

Figure 5.10 ■ As you can see, the ability to add alternative text to your images can be valuable. If the browser were unable to find your image, the ALT text would still display.

5.2.4 ANSWERS

a) What do you see when viewing the saved HTML in your browser?

Answer: By specifying the right property of the ALIGN *attribute, the image should be right-justified within the HTML page.*

The properties of the ALIGN attribute may or may not be surrounded by double quotes. Choose which you prefer and be consistent in your HTML coding. In other words, if you use the quotes in one line and not another, it's just plain sloppy.

b) What is the output?

Answer: Here you should see how the image is positioned in relation to the text you have added. The text is positioned in the upper-left corner of the browser.

Figure 5.11 is similar to what you should see in your browser.

c) What is the difference between the *bottom* property and the *top* property when viewing the HTML in your browser?

Answer: The bottom property actually aligns the bottom of the image with the base-line of the text. Note how the middle, top, and bottom properties differ. The relation of the image should vary slightly with each of the aforementioned ALIGN *properties.*

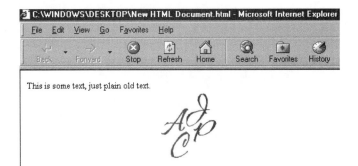

Figure 5.11 ■ As you can see, setting the ALIGN attribute to top will align the text along the top edge of the image file.

d) What difference did the <P> tag make in the display of your image?

Answer: The <P> tag inserts a paragraph break and moves the image below the line of text.

e) What is the syntax to do this?

Answer: The following code shows the <HR> tags as well as the <P> tag from the prior Exercise. Note how the code is lined up—neatness counts!

```
This is some text, just plain old text.<P>
<HR>
<IMG SRC = "C:/Projects/FirstProj/Images/logo.gif"
 ALIGN = "top">
<HR>
```

f) How does the page display in your browser?

Answer: The HTML page displayed in your browser should have the text line first. Then, there should be one horizontal rule, followed by the image and then the other horizontal rule. This is a good example of how you can utilize different HTML tags and embed them within each other to achieve the look you want.

LAB 5.2 REVIEW QUESTIONS

To test your progress, you should be able to answer the following questions.

1) Which of the following is the only way to specify the path of an image within an <IMG> tag?

a) _____ With an end </IMG> tag

b) _____ With the *SRC* attribute

c) _____ With the exact location of the image

d) _____ With the name of the image in double quotes

2) You must enclose the path to the image in double quotes.
   a) _____ True
   b) _____ False

3) The `<IMG>` tag must have an end tag to function properly.
   a) _____ True
   b) _____ False

**LAB
5.2**

4) The `HEIGHT` and `WIDTH` attributes are used to make the browser understand the exact original size of the image.
   a) _____ True
   b) _____ False

5) The percentage value of the `HEIGHT` and `WIDTH` properties achieves which of the following results?
   a) _____ Displays the image in a percentage of the original size.
   b) _____ Does nothing.
   c) _____ Resizes the image in relation to the size of the browser window.

6) What is the default color displayed around an image when using the `BORDER` attribute?
   a) _____ Blue
   b) _____ Black
   c) _____ Red
   d) _____ White

7) Which of the following is true of the `ALT` attribute?
   a) _____ It displays a line of text immediately to the right of the image in the browser window.
   b) _____ It displays an alternative image if the original image cannot be located.
   c) _____ It displays a tool tip when the mouse hovers over the image.

Quiz answers appear in Appendix A, Section 5.2.

C H A P T E R   5

TEST YOUR THINKING

In this Chapter, we learned how to create and insert images into our HTML pages. The Windows OS comes with the Paint program to get us started. Also, a free trial version Paint Shop Pro is available for download at `http://www.shareware.com`. Once we created our masterpieces, we then moved on to inserting the images into the HTML. Once again, we encourage you to practice using the different properties associated with `<IMG>` tag.

1) Using all of the skills learned in this and prior Chapters, create a new HTML page. Use an unordered list to display three images accompanied by textual descriptions of each. Also, incorporate the `ALIGN` properties to display the images and text in a visually pleasing fashion.

2) Using the HTML from the preceding project, add some <HR>, <BR>, and <P> tags. There is no right answer here. The purpose of this project is to get you comfortable with all the tags you have learned to this point. This is where you can begin to put the pieces together to display your dream home page.

3) Recall the introductory Chapters that explain the client/server concept. Why is it so important to save images from an external Web site to your local drive rather than using the `<IMG SRC=>` tag to grab the image?

4) This Chapter has allowed you to dip into the world of inserting images and image creation. Yet, there is a world of knowledge out there in cyberland! There are two image formats we did not have the time or the allotted space to cover within this Chapter. To extend your image knowledge, we encourage you to define and understand both the Raster image format and the Meta/Vector image format. One format stores the image as data, whereas the other stores the image as pixels. Which is which?

CHAPTER 6

CREATING HYPERLINKS

 Keep away from people who try to belittle your ambitions. Small people always do that, but the really great make you feel that you, too, can become great.

—Mark Twain

CHAPTER OBJECTIVES

In this Chapter, you will learn about:

This Chapter is devoted to the soul of HTML: hyperlinks. Hyperlinks, hypertext links or, simply, links, are what make your HTML pages a whole Web site. Links allow you to weave together all your HTML pages seamlessly for navigation from one page to the next. Without links, Web sites would be virtually worthless and very boring.

The second portion of this Chapter concentrates on teaching you how to receive feedback from users who have visited your HTML pages. If you have an email address, you are halfway there. If you do not have an email address, we'll make sure you have one before moving ahead.

L A B   6 . 1

ADDING LINKS

LAB OBJECTIVES

After this Lab, you will be able to:

*   Understand and Use External Hyperlinks
*   Create an Internal Text Link
*   Create an Internal Image Link

Links hold the key to navigation throughout the Internet. Most often, an underlined word or words on an HTML document designate a link. Clicking on a link tells the browser to look for the address attached to that link. The Exercises in this Lab introduce you to links, the "glue" that helps you organize your HTML pages into a complete Web site.

 If you have not done so, download and install both of the major browsers, Internet Explorer and Netscape Communicator (Navigator) now. Refer to Chapter 1 for complete details.

PREPARE YOUR BROWSER

As you have seen in previous Chapters, browsers differ slightly. In order for you to get the most out of the Exercises, perform the following check:

If you are using Internet Explorer, you may skip this check. If you are using Netscape, take a moment to be certain your browser options are set correctly.

1.   Open Netscape. Whether you are online or offline at this time does not matter. This check may be performed either way.
2.   Navigate to the `Edit` menu.

3. Choose `Preferences`.
4. Click the `Appearance` option from within the `Category` frame.
5. Choose `Colors`.
6. The `Underline Links` check box should be checked.

LAB 6.1 EXERCISES

6.1.1 UNDERSTAND AND USE EXTERNAL HYPERLINKS

In order to create links, you must have the Uniform Resource Locator (URL) of the place you wish to link. The URL is just a fancy name for the address to where the link points.

Open your browser.

Type the following URL into your browser's address bar:

`http://www.cnn.com`

Once the Web site has loaded, hover your mouse over a couple different links. They are usually a few words of text in blue and underlined. Another way to distinguish a link from other static text is by keeping an eye on your mouse cursor. Much of the time, the mouse cursor will display itself as a hand icon when it is hovering over a link.

Take a look at the status bar of your browser window as you hover over links. The status bar is at the bottom of the window. It is the place where you usually see the words, `Document Done` once a page has finished loading.

Locate the link to the weather, books, and travel.

     a) What appears in the status bar as you hover over each of the links?

_____

_____

To create a link, you must use an anchor tag. An anchor tag begins with a starting `<A>` and must end with a closing `</A>`.

The anchor tag must be used with the *HREF* attribute. *HREF* stands for Hyper-Text Reference. Simply, this tells the browser where it will go when you click on the link. To prepare the browser for the address, use <A HREF = as your beginning link tag.

Once you have the opening anchor tag, you must supply the full address to the page you want linked enclosed in double quotes. End the URL with a closing angle bracket (>).

Using this information, write out the link syntax for the CNN URL.

b) How did you create this link?

_____

_____

External links are any links that do not belong to your Web site. If you have not designed the pages, then it is an external Web site. To link to an external Web site or to individual external pages, you must use the full URL.

Create a new HTML file. Add the external link you created for the previous question.

Save the file as FirstLink.html.

View the HTML file in your browser.

c) What do you see?

_____

_____

Return to your editor window.

Add a meaningful word or words between the anchor tags that best describes the URL.

Save the file and view it your browser window.

d) How does the display differ from the preceding question?

_____

_____

6.1.2 CREATE AN INTERNAL TEXT LINK

An internal link is one that links *your* HTML together. That is, any HTML page designed by you may be linked together using an internal link. When referencing an internal link, the full URL is not necessary. The file name alone informs the browser that the link is part of the same site.

Open your HTML editor.

Create a second HTML page. You may name it `second.html`.

Using the experience you gained from Chapter 5, "Adding Images to Your Web Pages," add two `.gif` images to `second.html`. Be certain to use all the proper conventions for this file.

Save the file.

Open `FirstLink.html` in your editor. Using only the file name, add an internal link pointing to `second.html`.

Save the file.

Open `FirstLink.html` in your browser. Click the link to `second.html`.

> **a)** How did you write the code to accomplish this task?

_____

_____

Edit `second.html` to include a link back to the first page.

Save the file.

Check to be sure your links work and you are able to navigate back and forth between the two pages.

> **b)** How did you add the link in `second.html`?

_____

_____

There are other additions available for your links that can make them a bit more interesting.

Open `FirstLink.html` in your editor.

Edit the link for CNN as follows:

```
<A HREF = "http://www.cnn.com"
 onMouseOver='status="Click here for the latest news
 from CNN."'
 onMouseOut='status=""'> CNN </A>
```

Save the file. View the file in Internet Explorer. Place your mouse cursor over the edited CNN link.

> **c)** What difference does the newly added code make when viewing the file in Internet Explorer?
>
> _____
>
> _____

Now, open `FirstLink.html` in Netscape. Once again, hover over the edited link.

> **d)** What difference do you notice in Netscape?
>
> _____
>
> _____

Edit `FirstLink.html` again.

> Add the following to the link pointing to `second.html` just as shown here:
>
> ```
> <A TITLE = "If you click here you will be
>  transported to the second page. Don't worry,
>  you can come back to this page anytime you
>  want. I would never leave you stranded in
>  cyberland with no place to go."
>  HREF="second.html">Please, browse on! </A>
> ```

Save the file.

View it in both Internet Explorer and Netscape.

> **e)** What happens when hovering over the link to `second.html` in each of the browsers?

_____

_____

6.1.3 CREATE AN INTERNAL IMAGE LINK

Now that the creation of text links is under your belt, let's add more flexibility to your links.

Open `second.html` in your HTML editor.

`Comment out` the text link pointing to `FirstLink.html`. Remember to use comments, and use them often.

Add the necessary anchor tags around the `<IMG>` tag for `welcome.gif`. If you did not use the `ALT` attribute upon designing `second.html`, do so now.

Also, include the `TITLE` attribute from the previous Exercise for the anchor tag.

Save the file.

> **a)** What syntax did you use to do this?

_____

_____

View your file in both of the browsers.

You should observe a couple of key changes to the image as it is displayed here.

> **b)** What differences do you notice between the two browsers?

_____

_____

LAB 6.1 EXERCISE ANSWERS

6.1.1 ANSWERS

For this Exercise, you visited the CNN Web site.

a) What appears in the status bar as you hover over each of the links?

Answer: The weather link shows the URL `http://www.cnn.com/WEATHER`. *The books link shows* `http://www.cnn.com/books`. *Lastly, the travel link shows the address* `http://www.cnn.com/travel`. *The status bar is the place to look for the address of where the link is pointing.*

b) How did you create this link?

Answer: **<A HREF = "http://www/cnn.com "></A>**

All links you create will use this format. Note how the URL does not contain any spaces between the words. It is important to use the URL as it exists here.

c) What do you see?

Answer: Nothing. A link is useless unless you tell the browser what the link represents.

Links should be designed and created with the Web surfer in mind. You should always be descriptive when it comes to assigning text to links. This does not mean that a link requires a lengthy textual description; however, a link's text should convey to the user exactly what the link represents.

In addition to the valuable information we supply you with in this book, the Web can most certainly give you oodles of ideas for creating links. Remember that you are designing your HTML pages to be visually pleasing, as well as useful and interesting. As you will discover as you forge ahead, employing good design practices associated with links includes using both textual and graphical representations.

d) How does the display differ from the preceding question?

Answer: Now you see the textual description for the link underlined in blue. You could use any word or words to inform the user of the address of the link. Sometimes the best solution is the simplest. The idea here is to think of the convenience of the folks who will be viewing your HTML pages. Use the text to inform your users where they will be taken upon clicking the link. The following examples demonstrate what you may use.

```
<A HREF = "http://www.cnn.com"> CNN </A>
```

or

```
<A HREF = "http://www.cnn.com"> Click here for the
latest news from CNN. </A>
```

While viewing the HTML file in your browser, note how the textual description of the links does not have any effect on the functionality of the link nor does it affect the status bar text. Both of the previous examples show how the link should be named for easy recognition by the user. Most people who surf the Web know a link when they see one. Therefore, using the "Click here" methodology may not always make sense. We recommend relying on your common sense for this one. Remember, keep it simple and useful.

Figure 6.1 illustrates both of the links in the browser.

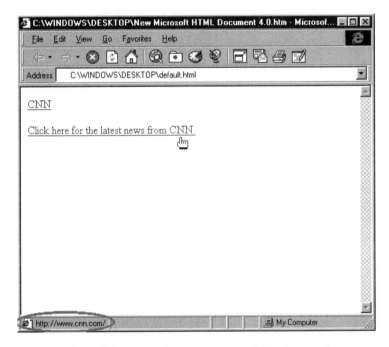

Figure 6.1 ■ The hand icon as it appears while hovering over a link. The status bar text shows the URL for CNN.

6.1.2 ANSWERS

For this Exercise, you created an internal link between two HTML files.

a) How did you write the code to accomplish this task?

Answer: FirstLink.html should have a link very similar to the following in the source code:

```
<A HREF = "second.html"> Please, browse on! </A>
```

The full URL is not needed here. The browser understands it is not necessary to look externally for this file. You may use the full URL for an internal link, but I do not recommend it. Using the full URL could, in fact, slow down the server a bit.

b) How did you add the link in `second.html`?

Answer: This is what we used to create the link from `second.html` *to* `FirstLink.html`:

```
<A HREF = "FirstLink.html">
 Return to the Main Page.
</A>
```

You may be asking yourself, "Why do I need to do that? Isn't that what the `Back` button on the browser is used for?" You are correct. But, we believe in taking care of all the needed tasks. You should not rely on the fact that people will use or know how to use the `Back` button. You should allow the user to navigate throughout your pages with ease. You may accomplish this by adding a hyperlink to each page within your Web site that links back to the main page.

c) What difference does the newly added code make when viewing the file in Internet Explorer?

Answer: As you hover over the CNN link, the sentence "Click here for the latest news from CNN" appears in the status bar of the browser window. The `onMouseOver` *keyword tells the browser to display the words following the word status in the status bar. The* `onMouseOut` *keyword tells the browser to switch back to displaying nothing. Note that both of the status keywords, like other HTML code, are not case-sensitive. You may use any form of capitalization you wish.*

Using this coding addition eliminates the need for the "Click here" link. This not only adds to the design of your HTML pages, but allows links to be as small as one word. This can save space on your HTML pages. The `onMouseOver`/`onMouseOut` combination gives you the ability to describe each link as you see fit.

d) What difference do you notice in Netscape?

Answer: There is no difference. The full URL remains displayed in the status bar.

This is a good example of why you should test your HTML in both of the major browsers. It is not a great tragedy that the newly added code does not show in Netscape. The point to note here is that you may use the `onMouseOver`/`onMouseOut` combination and it will not cause an error in Netscape. The code should degrade gracefully. It is a nifty little addition for anyone viewing your pages via Internet Explorer. It is important to use code that is cross-browser friendly.

e) What happens when hovering over the link to `second.html` in each of the browsers?

Answer: The `TITLE` *attribute of the anchor tag displays the words enclosed within the double quotes when viewed in Internet Explorer. Netscape does not recognize the* `TITLE` *attribute. Therefore, you should see no change.*

In Internet Explorer, the `TITLE` attribute acts very much like the `ALT` attribute of the image tag. You may write as much text for the `TITLE` attribute as you wish. You should note here that the text you place in the HTML source for the `TITLE` displays exactly as you wrote it, including the carriage returns of the text. If we write the text as one long line, it will display in that fashion.

Also, although Netscape does understand the `TITLE` attribute, using it does not cause any viewing problems or errors.

6.1.3 ANSWERS

For this Exercise, you created an internal link from an image.

a) What syntax did you use to do this?

Answer: Your syntax should appear as follows:

```
<A HREF ="FirstLink.html"><IMG SRC = "welcome.gif"
ALT = "So glad you could join me here today."></A>
```

b) What differences do you notice between the two browsers?

Answer: First, adding the anchor tags around `welcome.gif` *adds a border to the image. It is very much like a text link, where an underline is added, by default, to show you it is a link. Also, you should notice the border added to the image is the same default blue as seen with the text link. Figure 6.2 shows this obvious change to the image as it is displayed in either Internet Explorer or Netscape. The top image illustrates the usage of the new* <A> *tag addition. The bottom* `welcome.gif` *was designed using the* <IMG> *tag only.*

Next, the `ALT` attribute has precedence over the `TITLE` attribute no matter in which browser you view the file. So, when hovering over the image, you will see the text property you used for the `ALT` attribute.

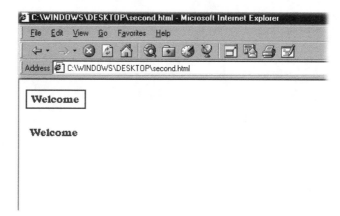

Figure 6.2 ■ `Welcome.gif` **used as a link. The** `<A>` **tag adds a border to the image.**

LAB 6.1 SELF-REVIEW QUESTIONS

In order to test your progress, you should be able to answer the following questions.

1) Links are also known as which of the following?
   a) _____ clicks
   b) _____ hypolinks
   c) _____ hyperlinks
   d) _____ activetext

2) URL is an acronym for which of the following?
   a) _____ United Real Locator
   b) _____ Universal Reel Linker
   c) _____ Universal Resource Location
   d) _____ Uniform Resource Locator

3) URL is another name for which of the following?
   a) _____ glue
   b) _____ address
   c) _____ browser

4) What icon is most often displayed when hovering over a link?
   a) _____ hand
   b) _____ arrow
   c) _____ hourglass

5) Which of the following best describes the status bar?

    a) _____ The field in which you type the Web address in a browser.

    b) _____ It displays the words "Document Done" when a page has finished loading.

    c) _____ It is located at the bottom of the Web browser.

    d) _____ All of the above

    e) _____ Both b and c

    f) _____ Both a and b

6) You can never have an internal link and an external link on the same page.

    a) _____ True

    b) _____ False

7) An anchor tag must have which of the following attributes?

    a) _____ *REF*

    b) _____ *SRC*

    c) _____ *HREF*

    d) _____ An anchor tag does not require any attributes.

8) The anchor tag does not require an ending tag.

    a) _____ True

    b) _____ False

9) You must use the full address for all links included in your HTML.

    a) _____ True

    b) _____ False

10) The `TITLE` attribute is valid in which of the following?

    a) _____ Internet Explorer

    b) _____ Netscape

    c) _____ Both

Quiz answers appear in Appendix A, Section 6.1.

LAB 6.2

USING HTML TO RECEIVE FEEDBACK

LAB OBJECTIVES

After this Lab, you will be able to:

* Use `Mailtos`
* Create a Simple Guestbook

Undoubtedly, you have been slaving over all of the previous Chapters, ensuring that you thoroughly understand all of the concepts. Hopefully, the preceding Lab supplied you with the necessary information to allow you to pull together some of the HTML pages you have already designed. Once you have completed all of the Exercises in this book, you will be armed to tackle the World Wide Web with your HTML creations. This will be a proud moment for you. Perhaps you would like to hear positive feedback from the folks who view your HTML pages.

Now, we can't guarantee all your feedback will be positive, but hopefully any criticism you receive will be constructive. This Lab is devoted to the two ways you can receive feedback from any Web surfer who wants to drop you a line.

LAB 6.2 EXERCISES

6.2.1 USE MAILTOS

Giving people the ability to write to you from any one or all of your HTML pages is a nice addition to your Web site. Using a `MAILTO:` command is how you may accomplish this goal. Note that the `MAILTO:` command is used as shown with the colon after the word `mailto`.

If you already have an email address, you are more than halfway there.

The Whole Truth

The assumption here is that because you are able to connect to the Internet and use the Web as you have been doing throughout this book, you already have an email address. But, it is never safe to assume. If you do possess an email address, you may skip this sidebar. However, if you do not have an email address, the following steps will enable you to utilize and test the functionality of the `MAILTO:` command.

As of this writing, YAHOO (`http://www.yahoo.com`) offers free email accounts. There are other free email providers out there. Yet, YAHOO offers the most user-friendly steps to obtain it.

Via your browser, navigate to the Yahoo URL.

Click on the link titled `Yahoo!Mail`. If you are unable to locate this link, you may also type the following into your browser's address textbox:

`http://www.yahoo.com/homet/?http://mail.yahoo.com`

This page displays the following message: `I'm a new user`.

Click on the link `Sign Me Up`!

This takes you to the page of legal mumbo-jumbo. Read it if you must. Click the `I Accept` button.

The sign up form appears. Fill in all the required information. You will need to think of a username and a password for yourself.

Once you have completed the necessary information, you will receive confirmation on your email name.

After completion, your email address will appear in the following format:

`[your username]@yahoo.com`

A `MAILTO:` is used in the same manner as a hyperlink. As opposed to using a URL as the address for the anchor, you use an email address.

Knowing this, open `second.html` in your editor.

Add a `MAILTO:` to the page.

Save the file.

a) What is the syntax used to do this?

View the HTML page in your browser.

Hover your mouse cursor over the new link.

b) What is displayed in the status bar?

Click the MAILTO link.

c) What happens?

6.2.2 CREATE A SIMPLE GUESTBOOK

A guestbook truly can be an impressive addition to your HTML pages. A guestbook is another way for anyone viewing your Web site to give you feedback. In order to create a guestbook, you must learn how to design forms.

A guestbook is an exception to the static HTML you have learned about up to this point. As mentioned in an earlier Chapter, HTML is most often used as display only. A guestbook permits you to have some interaction with your users.

The first step to creating a guestbook is to create the guestbook shell; using the <FORM> tag accomplishes this task. The <FORM> tag requires an ending tag.

Open second.html in your HTML editor.

Type the following HTML into second.html, placing it below the links from the previous Exercises. Replace our fictitious address with your email address.

```
<P>Write to me!
 <FORM METHOD="POST"
  ACTION="mailto:alayna@Teach.com">
 </FORM>
```

 Having come this far into the book, the assumption is that you have downloaded and installed the most current of the two major browsers: Internet Explorer and Netscape. Earlier browsers, those with version number 3 or lower, do not recognize the guestbook form.

Save the file and view it in your browser.

a) What do you observe?

_____

_____

Open second.html in your editor once again.

Immediately following the starting <FORM> tag, add a paragraph tag.

Next, add the following:

```
Let me know who you are: <INPUT TYPE = "text"
   NAME = "surfername" SIZE = "25">
```

Save your file.

View second.html in your browser.

b) What does the new HTML create?

_____

_____

This is the beginning of your guestbook! Test the newly added HTML and type a few letters into the textbox.

Return to your text editor. Edit the above textbox input field. Assign a word or words to the VALUE attribute of the textbox. For example, add the VALUE attribute and assign it the words "Your name."

Save the file.

View it in both Internet Explorer and Netscape.

       c) What do you observe?

_____

_____

Another entry addition available for your guestbook allows the surfer to choose one option within a given group for you to receive feedback from.

Open `second.html` in your editor.

Add the following below the textbox:

```
<P>
 What do you think of my new Web site?
<P>
<INPUT TYPE = "radio" NAME = first VALUE = "loveIt ">
  I love It!
<INPUT TYPE = "radio" NAME = second VALUE = "reallyLoveIt ">
  It's outstanding!
<INPUT TYPE = "radio" NAME = third VALUE = "youAreAlmighty ">
  WOW! I'm in awe.
```

Save the file.

View it in your browser.

       d) What did the new HTML create?

_____

_____

Click each one of the radio buttons.

       e) How many of the radio buttons are you able to choose at once?

_____

_____

Close your browser window.

Open `second.html` in your editor.

Modify the radio button HTML and assign the same NAME to each of the buttons.

Save the file once again.

Open second.html in your browser.

> **f)** How many are you able to choose at once now?

LAB
6.2

_____

_____

There is one more nifty input type we will cover here. It allows any surfer passing by your HTML pages to tell you just how great you are in her own words. It is called the TEXTAREA box.

Open second.html in your editor.

Add the following code immediately before the closing <FORM> tag.

```
<TEXTAREA NAME = "moreGoodNews" ROWS = 6 COLS = 50>
</TEXTAREA>
```

Save the file and view it in both Internet Explorer and Netscape.

Enter text into the new TEXTAREA boxes within both browsers.

> **g)** What differences are apparent in each of the browsers?

_____

_____

Edit second.html once again.

Add the following to the TEXTAREA tag:

```
WRAP = "VIRTUAL"
```

Save the file and view it in your browsers.

> **h)** What change did this bit of HTML invoke?

_____

_____

Now, all that is needed is the finale of your guestbook. Once a Web surfer has showered you with comments and compliments, you must provide a way for her to send you the information. This is handled with a SUBMIT button.

Open `second.html` in your editor.

Add the following HTML within the `<FORM>` tags:

```
<INPUT TYPE = Submit VALUE = "Send it!">
<INPUT TYPE = Reset VALUE = "Start over">
```

Save the file and view it in your browser.

i) What is the output?

_____

_____

Now that you have a guestbook, submit it to yourself.

Once you receive the form in your email, check out the appearance of the file.

j) What do the results of the guestbook submission look like in your email?

_____

_____

_____

LAB 6.2 EXERCISE ANSWERS

6.2.1 ANSWERS

For this Exercise, you added a `MAILTO:` to `second.html`.

a) What is the syntax used to do this?

Answer: Although your email address will differ from the one used here, the following format should be used. Note there is no space between the colon and the beginning of the email address.

```
<A HREF = " MAILTO:alayna@Teach.com ">We would love
to hear from you. </A>
```

b) What is displayed in the status bar?

Answer: What you see should be very similar to what is shown in Figure 6.3. Keep in mind you should always use a descriptive textual display to inform the net surfer this is a MAILTO *as opposed to a regular hyperlink.*

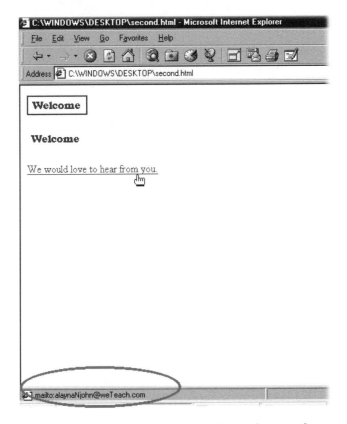

Figure 6.3 ■ The MAILTO link. The status bar shows the email address.

c) What happens?

Answer: What you see here will vary depending on where you obtained your email address.

No matter what type of email you subscribe to, a dialog box should appear. It will automatically fill in your email address in the TO: text box. Figure 6.4 shows the mailing dialog box that may appear when using Netscape.

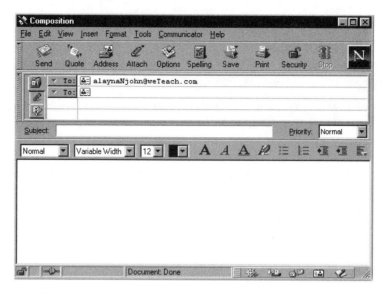

Figure 6.4 ■ The Netscape mailing dialog box.

It is here that anyone can compose and send you an email message by clicking on the SEND button as shown on the Message Toolbar.

6.2.2 ANSWERS

For this Exercise, you added the <FORM> tags to second.html.

a) What do you observe?

Answer: The words "Write to me!" are displayed.

The <FORM> tags inform the browser to prepare itself for some input, which in this case will be feedback from a user who is viewing your HTML pages. The METHOD attribute of the <FORM> tag has a value of *POST*. By declaring the *POST* value, you are telling the browser that any content within the <FORM> tags will be posted to you (at your email address). The ACTION attribute works hand-in-hand with the *POST* value to complete the task, informing the browser to complete the MAILTO: ACTION.

b) What does the new HTML create?

Answer: This is very interesting. The output shown here is quite different from anything you have seen so far. At first glance, you may mistake this new rectangular shape as an image. Upon further inspection, you will realize this is a textbox. It is a box that allows any surfer to enter text that you will later receive as a result of a completed guestbook entry.

■ *FOR EXAMPLE:*

This Exercise asked you to type this into your editor:

```
Let me know who you are: <INPUT TYPE = "text"
   NAME = "surfername" SIZE = "25" VALUE = " ">
```

In your browser, it appears as shown in Figure 6.5.

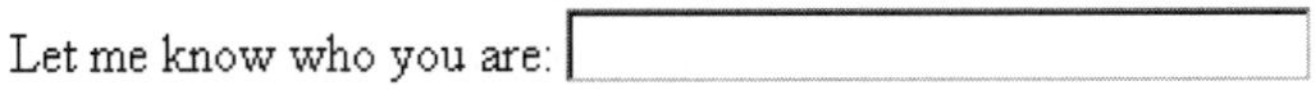

Let me know who you are: [   ]

Figure 6.5 ■ Sample textbox.

> *Since you have informed the user you are requesting a name, let's assume he has entered the name "Joel." When you receive the end result of the textbox input in your email, it may appear similar to the following:*

```
Surfername = Joel
```

Therefore, the NAME attribute helps you identify what text the surfer entered into the given field.

A form can contain different entry fields. Many of the fields follow the same format as the text box. HTML needs to know the field is an INPUT field that has a NAME, a SIZE, and a VALUE.

The INPUT TYPE informs HTML this is a textbox. There are other INPUT fields available. We will cover those shortly.

The NAME attribute assignment to the INPUT field is for your use. When you receive the feedback from the Internet user, it will not appear as shown on your HTML page. The NAME tells you what was the field of origin.

The SIZE attribute of the INPUT field informs the browser how many characters long the text box should be.

c) What do you observe?

> *Answer: Internet Explorer does recognize the text assignment to the VALUE attribute. The text used within the double quotes for the VALUE attribute displays within the textbox in the browser window. However, Netscape does not recognize the text assignment.*

The VALUE attribute allows you to assign an initial value to the field. For instance, the preceding example tells the browser you want the textbox to be displayed with no text, as indicated by the empty double quotes.

It is important to keep this in mind when designing your guestbook. Because both browsers do not understand this equally, it is best to use a few words of description placed immediately before the input field as shown in Figure 6.5.

**LAB
6.2**

d) What did the new HTML create?

Answer: Figure 6.6 shows the output of the newly added HTML.

This group is known as *option buttons*. They are often referred to as *radio* or *input buttons* also. Radio buttons are always within a group.

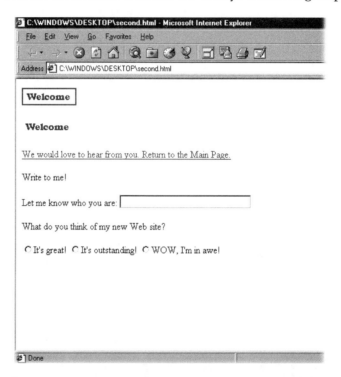

Figure 6.6 ■ Newly added options buttons to the guestbook.

A group of option buttons can be as large as you wish to design. The key to adding and using option buttons is to allow the user only one choice within the group.

e) How many of the radio buttons are you able to choose at once?

Answer: The current radio button group allows you to choose all three.

This simply won't do. Remember the whole basis for using option buttons is to give the user the ability to choose only one within a given group. The radio button HTML must be modified in order for the group to work properly.

f)   How many are you able to choose at once now?

Answer: Now, this makes more sense! By changing the NAME *attribute to the same name for all three buttons, you are able to choose only one at a time. This is perfect.*

This is the HTML I used to make the group work as intended:

```
<INPUT TYPE="radio" NAME=Opinion VALUE="loveIt">
 It's great!

<INPUT TYPE="radio" NAME=Opinion
 VALUE= "reallyLoveIt">It's outstanding!

<INPUT TYPE="radio" NAME=Opinion
 VALUE="youAreAlmighty">WOW, I'm in awe!
```

You may use any text you want for the VALUE attribute. As long as the NAME attributes are the same, only one of the buttons may be chosen at a time. The TYPE attribute tells the browser INPUT type is a radio button. The option button group works in the same manner as the textbox when you receive the feedback. For example, by choosing the first button, you will receive something similar to the following in your email:

```
Opinion = loveIt
```

So, you can see here that assigning a VALUE is key here. This will be what you see as a result from the user's choice when you receive your emailed feedback.

g)   What differences are apparent in each of the browsers?

Answer: In Internet Explorer, the TEXTAREA *box is created with a vertical scroll bar only. When entering text into the* TEXTAREA *text box in Internet Explorer, the text wraps around to the next line. It acts very much like an automatic carriage return; whereas, the* TEXTAREA *textbox in Netscape is created with both a vertical and horizontal scroll bar. When entering text into this* TEXTAREA *box, the text does invoke an automatic carriage return. Any text entered will continue to scroll horizontally as long as text is typed into the box.*

The TEXTAREA textbox does require a closing tag. Be sure to note here that TEXTAREA requires the named tags, whereas TEXT boxes do not. You may adjust the rows and the columns, customizing them to any size you need.

h)   What change did this bit of HTML invoke?

Answer: The TEXTAREA *textbox behaves the same in both browsers. Netscape's* TEXTAREA *box now is able to handle the automatic carriage return.*

i) What is the output?

Answer: Two buttons are created. The SUBMIT *button follows through on the* ACTION=POST *as written in the opening* <FORM> *tag. All the values of the form are posted to you by use of the* MAILTO: *command. The* RESET *button is understood by HTML to clear all of the input from within the form when you click on it.*

If you have not placed in the appropriate breaks and paragraphs to make the guestbook more visibly attractive, do so now. And, that's it! You have created a guestbook. Congratulations!

Figure 6.7 shows the completed guestbook output.

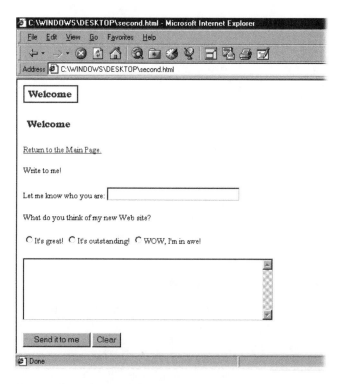

Figure 6.7 ■ Completed guestbook.

j) What do the results of the guestbook submission look like in your email?

Answer: You notice a couple of strange things here. First, it is very possible that the file has a .dat *extension. Next, the mail attachment from the guestbook appears as one long line. Lastly, you should notice that you receive no confirmation of sent mail.*

If the guestbook results arrive as .dat file, you can usually open it up in your text editor. It depends on your email service. Many email providers allow you to open attachments right in the email window. This will eliminate the need for file conversion. If you do need to convert the .dat file, try this:

Save the `.dat` file attachment onto your desktop.

Rename and save the file with a `.txt` extension.

Open the file in your text editor.

The Whole Truth

Some feedback you receive from guestbook entries appears a bit odd. Unwanted characters such as `%` `#` `/` or `+` may appear within the text when you receive it in your email. This can make for difficult reading. To correct this problem, add the following to your opening `<FORM>` tag:

`ENCTYPE="text/plain"`

ENCTYPE is an acronym for "encryption type." This small addition to your guestbook form will tell the mail server to send the feedback to you as plain text. Using `ENCTYPE` may not work all of the time. Unfortunately, HTML guestbooks are in desperate need of a hefty upgrade. Until the powers that be come up with new and fantastic HTML guestbooks, we must work with what we have!

LAB 6.2 SELF-REVIEW QUESTIONS

To test your progress, you should be able to answer the following questions.

1) Which of the following is the correct syntax for using a `MAILTO:`?
   a) _____ `< "MAILTO:`you@emailhost.com` ">`
   b) _____ `< MAILTO =` you@emailhost.com `>`
   c) _____ `<A HREF = "MAILTO =` you@emailhost.com`">`
   d) _____ `<A HREF = "MAILTO:`you@emailhost.com` ">`
   e) _____ `<A HREF = " MAILTO :` you@emailhost.com `">`

2) You must add the necessary HTML in your `MAILTO:` in order to view your email address in the status bar.
   a) _____ True
   b) _____ False

3) A guestbook must be created within the `<FORM>` tags.
   a) _____ True
   b) _____ False

4) Browsers with version number 3 or higher are able to recognize the guestbook form.
   a) _____ True
   b) _____ False

5) The NAME attribute tells the browser what type of field to create within the form.

a) _____ True

b) _____ False

6) You have received feedback from your guestbook as follows: User =Brenda. This feedback originated from the use of which of the following?

a) _____ INPUT

b) _____ NAME

c) _____ VALUE

d) _____ SIZE

7) Option buttons allow net surfers to make multiple choices within a given group of buttons.

a) _____ True

b) _____ False

8) Which of the following is the correct syntax to implement a TEXTAREA textbox?

a) _____ `<TEXT>This is a textarea box.</TEXT>`

b) _____ `<TEXT AREA TYPE  ROWS = 3 COLUMNS = 5> This is a textarea box. </TEXTAREA>`

c) _____ `<TEXTAREA NAME = "Comments" ROWS = 4 COLUMNS = 5> This is a textarea box. </TEXTAREA>`

d) _____ `<TEXTAREA NAME = "Comments" ROWS = 4 COLS = 45> This is a textarea box.</TEXTAREA>`

9) The MAILTO ACTION is which of the following?

a) _____ TYPE

b) _____ POST

c) _____ MAIL

d) _____ FORM

Quiz answers appear in Appendix A, Section 6.2.

C H A P T E R   6

TEST YOUR THINKING

In this Chapter, we learned how to create and use links, MAILTOS, and forms for guestbooks. The concepts presented in this Chapter give HTML the ability to interact with the user. Links provide the connection to produce a whole Web site from your otherwise standalone HTML pages. The following projects will help you to become much more comfortable with the subject matter presented here.

1) Using all of the skills learned in this Chapter and prior Chapters, create a new HTML page. Design a guestbook with five options buttons. Create two textbox inputs, one for entry of a name and one for entry of an email address. Add a TEXTAREA textbox with four rows and four columns. The CHECKBOX is another input type available for use within a form. It works very much like an OPTION button group, with one major difference. A group of checkboxes allows the user to choose as many boxes as she/he wishes. Add a CHECKBOX group of four to your guestbook form using the following syntax:

```
<INPUT TYPE = "CHECKBOX" NAME = "userGender" VALUE =
"MaleOrFemale">
```

2) This project asks you to do a bit of research. Another style available for use within a guestbook form is the pop-up or option selection list box. Using your favorite search engine, determine the proper usage and syntax for proper implementation in a form.

3) Chapter 5 introduced you to creating and using images within your HTML. A slick little addition is available for you to use which includes an image in place of the SUBMIT and/or RESET buttons within your guestbook form. Create two images of equal size, each representing one of the INPUT form buttons. Ensure the buttons are clearly presented for easy recognition for the user. Replace the SUBMIT and RESET buttons within your guestbook with the two images. The syntax used to make the images function as buttons should match the following format:

```
<INPUT TYPE = "image" SRC = "submit.gif" HEIGHT="30"
WIDTH="135" BORDER="0" ALT = "This is the Submit
button.">
```

CHAPTER 7

FORMATTING
THE PAGE

 Imagination is more important than knowledge. Knowledge is limited. Imagination encircles the world.

—Albert Einstein

Previous Chapters have prepared you with the necessary knowledge to create HTML pages. By now, you may be asking yourself, "How do I add a bit more character and style to my Web pages? Can I use anything else besides black for all my text?" This Chapter will answer those questions. We are certain you have experienced the misinterpretation of someone's tone of voice when it is written in an email message or a letter. It can be difficult to decipher a joke from a serious statement, or a high-priority request submitted by a boss from a miniscule one if the author is not clear with his or her intentions. Having the ability to represent your ideas clearly in your Web pages is not only fun but also necessary.

175

First, you will begin with understanding color representation and how to use it on the Web. Of course, until now, your entire HTML has been in black and white excluding, perhaps, any colored images added in Chapter 5, "Adding Images to Your Web Pages." Next, you will learn how to format the HTML using all the available tags and properties associated with text.

This Chapter will enhance your existing HTML and truly allow your personality to shine through on your Web pages. Think of this Chapter as a way to give your HTML its very own "tone of voice."

LAB 7.1

HOW THE HEX TO GET COLOR INTO HTML

LAB OBJECTIVES

After this Lab, you will be able to:

*   Use Color Codes to Change Body Text and Backgrounds
*   Add Color to Hyperlinks
*   Add Color to Text

Okay, ready for a flashback? Recall learning about primary colors in school. In a sense, you will be learning it once again. Here we go: There are three basic (or primary) colors—red, blue, and yellow. Each of these colors is a primary because there are no other colors in existence that are combined to create these colors. In other words, the primary colors cannot be broken down any further to another basic color. These three colors are used to create the others. Mixing equal parts blue and yellow creates green, mixing equal parts red and yellow creates orange, and so forth.

Unfortunately, or fortunately depending on your point of view, computers are not like the rest of the world when it comes to color. The three basic colors used by computers, and televisions, are red, green, and blue. These colors are known as additive colors.

In this Lab, you will learn and understand how color is represented within HTML. More importantly, you will learn how to implement this knowledge to enhance body backgrounds, hyperlinks, and text (which is often referred to as font).

LAB 7.1 EXERCISES

7.1.1 USE COLOR CODES TO CHANGE BODY TEXT AND BACKGROUNDS

Before adding color to absolutely everything in your Web site, first pause. You should be asking yourself questions like, "What mood do I wish to convey within my pages? Will using a little color or a lot of color benefit my HTML pages?" Other questions may come to your mind as we work our way through this Chapter.

Perhaps lime green is your favorite color. Yes, it is indeed a lovely color. Yet, is lime green the way to display all the text on your Web site? Probably not.

It's a colorful world out there in cyberland. Before beginning, taking a look at some of the Web sites out there may help spark ideas of the dos and don'ts of color usage.

Open your browser and visit some of your favorite Web sites. Also, try surfing to a couple of the following Web sites. Note the use of color in each.

```
http://www.sony.com
http://www.cliffassociates.com/
http://www.cdw.com/-default.asp
http://www.gateway.com/home/
http://www.denteco.com/
```

> **a)** If you surfed to some of your favorite sites, which ones did you choose?
>
> _____
>
> _____
>
> _____

If you chose the sites listed, you may skip this question. Yet, be sure to read the answer section for some interesting information.

Start a new HTML page. Code the necessary shell tags for the HTML document. Save the file as `color.html`. Remember that you can never save files too often. There are two color attributes associated with the <BODY> tag. The first is BGCOLOR. Add the following attribute to the <BODY> tag:

```
<BODY bgColor = "skyblue">
```

Save the file. Open `color.html` in your browser.

b) What do you see?

_____

_____

Return to your editor. Edit the BGCOLOR color code as follows:

```
<BODY bgColor = "#87CEEB">
```

Save the file once again. View it in your browser.

c) What is the output?

_____

_____

Another interesting way to get familiar with color is by using Paint Shop Pro. A prior Chapter asked you to download and install this software. The `Color Dialog Box` *allows you to manipulate colors using a color wheel. It supplies the user with the HTML Color Code associated with the chosen color from within the dialog box.*

The second way to use the `<BODY>` tag to define color is with the use of the TEXT attribute. Add the following line of text shown within the body of your HTML. Be sure to add the following TEXT attribute to your existing `color.html` also:

```
<BODY bgColor = "#87CEEB "text = "#FFD700">
 Toto, I don't think we're in Kansas anymore.
```

Save the file. Open it in your browser.

d) What is the output?

_____

_____

7.1.2 ADD COLOR TO HYPERLINKS

A previous Chapter introduced you to hyperlinks and how to add them to your HTML. There are three `<BODY>` attributes you may use to change the color of hyperlinks: `link`, `vlink`, and `alink`. Adding color to HTML links is a fun and attractive addition to your Web site.

The Whole Truth

If you are using Internet Explorer 4.0 or higher as your browser of choice, you need to check the following option before continuing with these Exercises:

From the `View` menu, choose `Internet Options`.

Choose the `Default` tab.

At the bottom of this panel, click on the `Colors` button. The `Colors Dialog Box` is displayed.

If the `Use Hover Color` box is checked, uncheck it.

Click `OK`.

The `Use Hover Color` box forces links to display a default color of red when hovering the mouse over any link. Unchecking the box allows you to have control over what color the hyperlinks will adopt.

This portion of Exercise 7.1.2 will work with Internet Explorer 4.0 and higher. Netscape 4.5 and higher does have a link option you may need to change as well.

From the `Edit` menu, choose `Preferences`.

From the `Appearance` category, click on `Colors`.

Make certain that the `Always use my colors, overriding docu-ment` is unchecked.

If you have not done so already and you have the drive space, download and install both of the major browsers: Internet Explorer and Netscape. If you do have both browsers installed on your machine, you are in luck. It truly is most beneficial for you to design and test with as many browsers as possible. This will enable you to see how most of the Web surfers will view your HTML pages. Be aware that users' browser preferences will always take precedence over any HTML you incorporate into your pages.

Open the `color.html` file in your editor. First, change the background color back to its default color of white. Next, add the necessary code for a link of your choice. For example, you may use `www.cnet.com`. Save the file and open it in your browser.

      a) What color is the hyperlink?

_____

_____

Open `color.html` in your editor. Add the link attribute within the `<BODY>` tag as follows:

```
<BODY link = "#FF0000">
```

Save the file and view it in your browser.

      b) What is the color of the link?

_____

_____

Once again, open `color.html` in your editor. Next, we'll try out the VLINK attribute. VLINK stands for "visited link". Add the VLINK attribute to the `<BODY>` tag. For example:

```
<BODY link = "#FF0000" vLink = "#00FA7A">
```

Save the file and open it in your browser. Click the link. Let the page open and display. Hit the `Back` button on your browser to return to `color.html`.

      c) What color is the hyperlink now?

_____

_____

Return to your editor. Add the color `#FF67B4` to the attribute ALINK of the `<BODY>` tag. ALINK stands for "active link". Save the file. View it in your browser.

d) What is the color of the link as you click on it?

_____

_____

7.1.3 ADD COLOR TO TEXT

Up to this point, we have experimented with changing the text color of the entire HTML document. No matter what color we specify using the TEXT attribute of the <BODY> tag, any and all text within the tags will be the same color. Lucky for us there is a way to specify colors for the exact text we want to change. The <FONT> tag allows us the freedom to do so. The font tag does require an end tag.

Open color.html in your editor.

Using CTRL+X to cut, remove the TEXT attribute from within the <BODY> tag added in the previous Exercise.

Add the starting and ending <FONT> tags to the one line of text in color.html.

Add the color and its value as follows:

```
<FONT COLOR = "7FF000"> Toto, I don't think we're in
Kansas anymore. </FONT>
```

Save the file. Open it in your browser.

a) What is the color of the line of text?

_____

_____

Return to your editor. Using CTRL+V, paste the text attribute back into the <BODY> tag. Save the file. View it in your browser.

b) What happened to the line of text?

_____

_____

LAB 7.1 EXERCISE ANSWERS

7.1.1 ANSWERS

a) If you surfed to some of your favorite sites, which ones did you choose?

Answer: Your favorite sites will differ from the ones listed in this Exercise. The Web sites listed are good examples of pages that use color in a positive and attractive way. Of course, there is one glaring exception here. We're sure you can decide which one it is.

If you did not surf to the pages listed, do so now. Among them is one glaring example of poor Web design. The background color mixed with the bright use of text color is offensive to the eyes. Upon opening the site, it is difficult for the eye to focus on one particular item on the page. Its layout is bland and lacks a nice, smooth design flow. If you would like to see other Web sites designed with a similar lack of finesse, try `http://www.webpagesthatsuck.com`. Its sole purpose is to show you good Web design by pointing out bad Web design.

b) What do you see?

Answer: The browser displays the entire page with the color sky blue as its background.

The `BGCOLOR` attribute represents the background color for the body of the HTML page. Color codes are used as easily recognizable "English words" to achieve the color you want to use within your HTML. Specifying the colors red, blue, green, yellow, and so forth in HTML is known as using *named colors*.

The Whole Truth

Contrary to the colors in a rainbow where the absence of color is black, a computer's absence of color is white. What is the default background color of an HTML page? You guessed it. The background color of any HTML document is white, the absence of color. Mixing the additive colors together is known as *subtractive coloring*. No, really, we're serious!

---

c) What is the output?

Answer: The browser displays the same sky blue background color as seen in the previous Question.

The six-digit representation of color is called the *hexadecimal color* or the *hex code*. Coding using the # sign helps the browser render the color code appropriately. Hex colors can use thousands upon thousands of six-digit combinations to display different colors. Older browsers were able to understand hex code colors only. Newer browsers are able to understand and display both hex codes and named colors.

■ FOR EXAMPLE:

There are 16 digits used for hexadecimal color codes: 0, 1, 2, 3, 4, 5, 6, 7, 8, 9, A, B, C, D, E, and F.

Any six-digit combination of these digits will result in a color that your HTML and your computer can understand. As with all other HTML code, the hex codes are not case-sensitive. Whether you decide to use lowercase or uppercase does not matter; whichever you choose, be consistent!

Some browsers may display the correct color without the use of the # sign. Internet Explorer understands hex code without the # sign. Netscape Navigator does not. I do not recommend using hex code without the # sign because you have no way of knowing what browser your users will have on their machines. Get yourself into the good habit of writing your color codes with the # sign, and you will never need to worry if the users browser will understand what color you wish to display.

Table 7.1 is a color chart for you to use as you wish. All of the colors are recognizable colors for use within HTML. This is a partial list of all the available Web-recognized colors. You may use either the color name or the hexadecimal code representation.

Table 7.1 ■ Named colors and hex colors.

AliceBlue F0F8FF	AntiqueWhite FAEBD7	Aqua 00FFFF	AquaMarine 7FFFD4
BlanchedAlmond FFEBCD	Black 000000	Bisque FFE4C4	Crimson DC143C
Coral FF7F50	Chocolate D2691E	Cyan 00FFFF	CornFlowerBlue 6495ED
DarkBlue 00008B	DodgerBlue 1E90FF	DarkKhaki BDB76B	DarkGreen 006400
DimGray 696969	FireBrick B22222	Gold FFD700	Green 008000
Gray 808080	HoneyDew F0FFF0	HotPink FF69B4	Indigo 4B0082
Khaki F0E68C	Linen FAF0E6	LightBlue Add8E6	LavenderBlush FFF0F5
LemonChiffon FFFACD	LightCoral F08080	LightGreen 90EE90	LightSeaGreen 20B2AA

Magenta FF00FF	MediumBlue 0000CD	Maroon 800000	MediumAquaMarine 66CDAA
MediumOrchid BA55D3	MintCream F5FFFA	Navy 000080	NavajoWhite FFDEAD
Orange FFA500	Olive 808000	OliveDrab 688E23	Peru CD853F
PaleGreen 98FB98	Purple 800080	PowderBlue B0E0E6	Red FF0000
RosyBrown BC8F8F	RoyalBlue 4169E1	SaddleBrown 8B4513	Sienna A0522D
SeaGreen 2E8B57	SeaShell FFF5EE	SkyBlue 87CEEB	Silver C0C0C0
SlateGray 708090	SlateBlue 6A5ACD	Salmon FA8072	White FFFFFF

This is a partial list of all the available Web recognized colors. For a larger selection of available HTML colors, use any search engine. For example, try out Yahoo, Altavista, Snap, or Webcrawler and specify 'color chart' in the search text box to point you in the right direction. Here are a few sites I found:

```
http://www.myfreeoffice.com/donnajean/chart.html
http://www.brobstsystems.com/colors.htm
http://www.leapday.demon.nl/colorchart.htm
```

d) What is the output?

Answer: The hex code used in the Exercise represents the named color gold. The line of text typed into the body of the HTML document is displayed as gold. Using the TEXT *attribute of the* <BODY> *tag will display any text within the body of the page as gold. The following Exercises will teach you how to use different font colors for different lines of text.*

7.1.2 ANSWERS

a) What color is the hyperlink?

Answer: First, this is the line of code used to add the link:

```
<A HREF = "http://www.cnet.com"> Click here to catch
up on computer news and goodies. </A>
```

What you use as the prompt can differ from what I used. The default color of a link is usually a shade of blue. For instance, Internet Explorer displays a link as a bright blue, while Netscape's default link color is a dark blue.

b) What is the color of the link?

Answer: You should see the link displayed as the color red.

c) What color is the hyperlink now?

Answer: The link displays as the named color MediumSpringGreen once you return to `color.html`. *By utilizing the* `VLINK` *attribute, the user can see where he or she has been.*

d) What is the color of the link as you click on it?

Answer: The link is now the named color HotPink.

7.1.3 ANSWERS

a) What is the color of the line of text?

Answer: The font color displays as Chartreuse.

b) What happened to the line of text?

Answer: Nothing. The point to note here is that any specification to text using the `<FONT>` *tags will override any font color attribute specified within the body of the HTML document. In other words, the* `<FONT>` *tag has higher priority over the* `TEXT` *attribute.*

LAB 7.1 SELF-REVIEW QUESTIONS

In order to test your progress, you should be able to answer the following questions.

1) The three primary computer colors are which of the following?
    a) _____ red, green, and blue
    b) _____ black, white, and red
    c) _____ red, blue, and yellow

2) The two color attributes associated with the `<BODY>` tag are which of the following?
    a) _____ `LINK` and `VLINK`
    b) _____ blue and green
    c) _____ `BGCOLOR` and `FONT`
    d) _____ `BGCOLOR` and `TEXT`

3) Which of the following is true of BGCOLOR?
  a) _____ It stands for big color.
  b) _____ It is used to specify the body color of an HTML document.
  c) _____ It is used to specify the background color of an HTML document.

4) Which of the following is the correct color usage of the body TEXT attribute?
  a) _____ `<BODY COLOR = "76BB00">`
  b) _____ `<BODY TEXT COLOR = "76BB00">`
  c) _____ `<BODY TEXT = "#76BB00">`
  d) _____ `<BODY TEXT = "76BB00#">`

5) To add color to links, use which of the following attributes?
  a) _____ LINKCOLOR
  b) _____ LINK
  c) _____ LINK, ALINK
  d) _____ VLINK
  e) _____ All of the above
  f) _____ a, b, and d
  g) _____ b, c, and d

6) Older browsers understand named colors over hex code.
  a) _____True
  b) _____False

7) Hex color codes can use any five-digit combination of 14 possible hexadecimal digit choices.
  a) _____True
  b) _____False

8) In the world of computers, which of the following is the absence of color?
  a) _____White
  b) _____Black
  c) _____Gray

Quiz answers appear in Appendix A, Section 7.1.

8

8   *Lab 7.2: Sizing Up the Text*

L A B   7 . 2

**LAB
7.2**

SIZING UP THE TEXT

LAB OBJECTIVES

After this Lab, you will be able to:

- Use FONT FACE
- Specify Font Size in HTML
- Use Heading Tags

The previous Lab introduced you to adding color to your existing HTML text. This Lab will concentrate on giving you more flexibility for the text in your files. Color is great, but HTML would be quite a boring sight without some other visual text variety. You'll start out by learning how to change the font of HTML text. Next, you will learn and experiment with the different recognizable font sizes. The last Exercise of this Lab will introduce you to formatting font using the heading tags.

LAB 7.2 EXERCISES

7.2.1 USE FONT FACE

Much like the COLOR attribute allows you to indicate what color you would like to associate with the <FONT> tag, the FACE attribute allows you to specify the style, or face, of the <FONT> tag. The FACE attribute allows you to assign different styles to individual lines or blocks of text.

Create a new HTML file and add in the necessary shell information. Name it `sizing.html`.

Add the following into the body section:

```
<FONT FACE = "Arial" COLOR = "#7AB777">Toto, I don't
 think we're in Kansas anymore.</FONT>
<P>
<FONT FACE = "Courier New" COLOR = "#800000">There's
 no place like home.</FONT>
<P>
<FONT FACE = "Verdana" COLOR = "#8B008B">Why does the
 muskrat guard his musk? Courage.</FONT>
<P>
<FONT FACE = "Times New Roman" COLOR = "#20B2AA">I'll
 get you, my pretty. And your little dog too.</FONT>
```

Save the file. Open `sizing.html` in your browser.

a) What do you see?

_____

_____

You may also use multiple FACE attributes within one `<FONT>` tag. For instance, modify and add the font face Helvetica to the first line of text in `sizing.html` as follows:

```
<FONT FACE = "Arial,Helvetica" COLOR = "#7AB777">
 Toto, I don't think we're in Kansas anymore.
 </FONT>
```

Save the file once again. Open it in your browser.

b) What do you see?

_____

_____

7.2.2 SPECIFY FONT SIZE IN HTML

Having the ability to specify color and font face for your HTML text leaves the door wide open for an endless number of design possibilities. This Exercise allows for even more creative freedom. Here you will learn how to assign font size to the text within your HTML.

There are 12 font sizes available. The different degrees of font sizes vary from +6 to +1 and −1 to −6.

Open `sizing.html` in your editor.

Add the `SIZE` attribute to each of the four lines of text you added from the previous Exercise (hint: It can be added very much like you added the `COLOR` attribute).

Add the size of +5 to the first line.
Add the size of +3 to the second line.
Add the size of −1 to the third line.
Add the size of −4 to the fourth line.
Save the file. View it in your browser.

a) What code is used to do this?

_____

_____

b) Which of the font sizes used is the largest? Which is the smallest?

_____

_____

7.2.3 USE HEADING TAGS

Another way to size up your text is by using heading tags. The heading tag requires a beginning tag and an ending tag. Where `<FONT>` tags are used for individual or multiple lines of text, heading tags are used to specify headings in HTML. There are six available heading tag sizes.

The syntax used for Heading 1 is as follows:

```
<H1>This is a heading one example.</H1>
```

Each of the six heading sizes uses similar syntax. The syntax used for Heading 2 is as follows:

```
<H2>This is a heading two example.</H2>
```

Open `sizing.html` in your editor.

Remove all the `<P>` tags from the file and replace them with break tags.

Type the following lines into your file right after the starting `<BODY>` tag.

```
<H1>The Wizard of Oz in a nutshell.</H1>
<H5>A Y2K film.</H5>
```

Save the file. Open it in your browser.

a) What is noticeably different about the heading tags?

_____

_____

Adding color to heading tags is easy. You should follow this rule: Font tags should be placed within heading tags.

Open `sizing.html` in your editor.

Add the font color `4B0082` (indigo) to heading five.

Save the file. View it your browser.

b) What is the syntax used to do this?

_____

_____

Edit `sizing.html` in your text editor.

Add a new line of text to `sizing.html`. Assign the line of HTML as follows:

`Heading 2`

`Font size of -1`

Save the file. View it in your browser window.

c) Which HTML attribute takes precedence?

_____

_____

LAB 7.2 EXERCISE ANSWERS

7.2.1 ANSWERS

a) What do you see?

Answer: Your page could look slightly different from ours. If you have Arial, Times New Roman, Courier New, and Verdana fonts installed on your system, your sizing.html *should look the same as mine. Figure 7.1 shows the output in our browser.*

Figure 7.1 ■ Output using the different font faces.

b) What do you see?

Answer: You should see no change at all in the font face of the text "Toto, I don't think we're in Kansas anymore."

Internet surfers must have at least one of the specified fonts installed on their system in order to view your HTML as you designed it. Using two fonts instead of one gives you a better chance of having your HTML appear as you intended. If the user has neither of the fonts, the browser will choose one. The fonts used in this Exercise are fairly common. Almost all PCs are equipped with these fonts. Yet, not all PCs will have all the same fonts as your PC. For example, you want a line of text displayed using the font Garamond. During the testing phase of design, you see that Garamond is so fantastic that you decide to use it often. A Web surfer comes upon your HTML. This user does not have the font Garamond installed on his machine. The user will still see the text but it will not show as Garamond.

 Most likely, the machine will display whatever it thinks should be displayed, which you have no control over. Therefore, your HTML will not be seen as you originally intended. This is not a major problem and is an easy fix. Follow this rule and you should have no problems: Use the easy stuff. In other words, stick with using common font styles such as Arial, Helvetica, or Times. Using multiple fonts (usually two or three is plenty) as shown in this example is a good habit to practice, always. If the user's machine does not understand the first font, it will pick up on the second font, and so on.

The Whole Truth

Most likely, your PC is chock full of fonts. It is a good idea to know where the fonts live on your machine. Take a moment to perform this check.

Right-click on the `Start` button.

A pop-up menu appears. Choose `Explorer`.

The Windows Explorer opens. From the left side of the `Explorer` window, navigate to your master hard drive (usually called the C drive).

Scroll down to the folder called `Windows`. Click it once to open it.

Navigate to the `Fonts` folder. Click it once to open it.

Once the `Fonts` folder is open, a list of all the available fonts on your system will appear. Your list could be quite large if you have installed any software program that included extra fonts. If not, the standard Windows fonts are shown.

7.2.2 ANSWERS

a) What code is used to do this?

Answer: Your code should look like the following:

```
<FONT FACE = "Arial,Helvetica" COLOR = "#7AB777" SIZE = "+5">
   Toto, I don't think we're in Kansas anymore .
</FONT>
<P>
```

```
<FONT FACE = "Courier New" COLOR = "#800000" SIZE = "+3">
  There's no place like home.
</FONT>
<P>
<FONT FACE = "Verdana" COLOR = "#8B008B" SIZE = "-1">
  Why does the muskrat guard his musk? Courage.
</FONT>
<P>
<FONT FACE = "Times New Roman" COLOR = "#20B2AA" SIZE = "-4">
  I'll get you, my pretty. And your little dog too.
</FONT>
<P>
```

You should note here that the attributes of the <FONT> tag work no matter in which order they are placed.

b) Which of the font sizes is the largest? Which is the smallest?

Answer: Font size +5 is the largest. Font size −4 is the smallest.

Font size +6 is the largest available font size. In contrast, -6 is the smallest font size available for use in HTML. Font size increases from +1 to +6. Font size decreases from –1 to –6. Honestly, -6 is so teenie-weenie that the chance of ever using it is slim to none. The difference between +4, +5, and +6 is barely noticeable to the human eye. Likewise, there appears to be no visual difference between –2, -3, -4, -5, and –6. Why the powers that be decided on these font sizes is not important. Don't worry about it too much. Generally speaking, if you stick to using +1, +2, +3, +4 and –1, you will have all the options you need.

7.2.3 ANSWERS

a) What is noticeably different about the heading tags?

Answer: Heading tags do not need <BR> or <P> tags to set them apart from other text. Their sole purpose is to stand out as headings. In other words, headings know enough to leave plenty of "elbow room" surrounding them.

Keep in mind that by using heading tags, you will declare you do not want anything butting right up to them. As seen in this Exercise, although we typed the <H1> and <H5> lines together, the text is physically separated within the browser. We can conclude that using heading tags is much like forcing an automatic <P> tag.

b) What is the syntax used to do this?

Answer: The syntax is as follows:

```
<H5><FONT COLOR="#4B0082">A Y2K film.</FONT></H5>
```

c) Which HTML attribute takes precedence?

Answer: The heading tag overrides the `SIZE` *attribute.*

Heading tags are quite powerful. Their sole purpose is to make text stand out. Therefore, any font size assigned to a heading tag is nonexistent and unnecessary.

This is the syntax used to complete this Exercise:

```
<H2 FONT SIZE = "-1">
   This is a test of size precedence.
</H2>
```

You may comment out this line of HTML to keep `sizing.html` as originally designed.

LAB 7.2 SELF-REVIEW QUESTIONS

In order to test your progress, you should be able to answer the following questions.

1) The available attributes for the `<FONT>` tag are which of the following?
   a) _____ `STYLE`, `COLOR`, and `SIZE`
   b) _____ `COLOR`, `TEXT`, and `SIZE`
   c) _____ `HEADING`, `COLOR`, and `TEXT`
   d) _____ `FACE`, `SIZE`, and `COLOR`

2) Using multiple fonts for a single line of text is discouraged.
   a) _____True
   b) _____False

3) The range of available font sizes is which of the following?
   a) _____ –1 to –5 and +1 to +6
   b) _____ +2 to +7
   c) _____ –1 to –6 and +6 to +1

4) The font size –6 is the largest available size.
   a) _____True
   b) _____False

5) Heading tags must be separated using <P> tags.

    a) _____True

    b) _____False

6) The order of the <FONT> attributes is not important.

    a) _____True

    b) _____False

7) The syntax used for a complete Heading 4 tag is which of the following?

    a) _____ `<H FOUR> </H FOUR>`

    b) _____ `<H4> </H4>`

    c) _____ `<H4> <H4/>`

    d) _____ `<HEADING4> </HEADING4>`

8) How many heading tag sizes are available in HTML?

    a) _____ 4

    b) _____ 10

    c) _____ As many as you want

    d) _____ 6

9) You have used the font Bookman Old Style in your HTML. The user must have the font installed on her system to view it as intended in their browser.

    a) _____ True

    b) _____ False

10) Font tags should be placed inside heading tags.

    a) _____ True

    b) _____ False

Quiz answers appear in Appendix A, Section 7.2.

LAB   7.3

USING OTHER FORMATTING TAGS

LAB OBJECTIVES

After this Lab, you will be able to:

- Use the Bold Tag
- Use the Italic Tag
- Use the Center Tag
- Use the Pre Tag
- Use Other "Funky" Tags

The previous Exercises in this Chapter have taught you how to manipulate text by adding different kinds of tags, attributes, and properties. In this section, you will learn how to add even more functionality to your HTML pages. Besides color, size, and font, HTML offers you many other options to add to the appearance of your HTML pages.

The Whole Truth

Note that there are other formatting tags, yet none as common as the ones you will learn about in the following exercises. The four tags discussed here—bold, italic, center, and preformat—are the most widely used and practical of all the HTML formatting tags. For a complete list of all HTML tags, we recommend visiting the Web site of the World Wide Web consortium at http://www.w3c.org. On a regular basis, the W3C posts updates, recommendations, and new technology for anything having to do with Web design. The World Wide Web consortium is basically a group of people who get together and decide what should be the "norm" for designing HTML. The W3C reports on recommended HTML tags and specifications to achieve the most from your HTML designs. The W3C serves as a good reference to find out about new tags and which tags may be defunct. There are other tags in existence that achieve the same results as the ones you will learn here. However, many of them are being phased out and are not worth your time and effort to learn. As newer browsers are released, these older tags will no longer be recognized. In order to give you the most bang for your buck, you will learn the formatting tags that are the most useful and widely recognized by all browsers.

LAB 7.3 EXERCISES

7.3.1 USE THE BOLD TAG

Certainly, there are times when stressing a word or words is necessary. This is where a tag such as the bold tag comes into play. The bold tag is explicitly stated with a starting `<B>` and an ending `</B>`.

The important thing to remember when using multiple formatting tags is the way you embed them. For example, take a look at the following line of HTML code:

```
<FONT FACE = "Arial" SIZE = "+3"><B>This line of text
is bold.</B></FONT>
```

The outer tags are the `<FONT>` tags. The inner tags are `<B>` tags. Embedding tags properly ensures that the intended output will be correct. You may embed as many tags as you need or want. Yet, if three tags do the job of one tag, use the one tag.

Open `sizing.html` in your editor.

Add the `<B>` tags to the first line of text in the file (excluding the headings).

Save the file. View the output in your browser.

a) What is the syntax used to do this?

_____

_____

7.3.2 USE THE ITALIC TAG

Another useful tag is the italic tag. Much like the `<B>` tag, it can be used to add emphasis to text. The `<I>` tag requires a beginning and an ending tag.

Open `sizing.html` in your editor.

Edit Heading five to make it italic.

Add a link to the Web site of your choice. Format the link to be displayed as italic.

LAB
7.3

Save the file and view it in your browser.

a) What syntax did you use to complete this exercise?

_____

_____

7.3.3 USE THE CENTER TAG

You may have noticed that all the text you have added to `sizing.html` is left-justified. This is the default location of any text placed into an HTML file. The `<CENTER>` tag adds even more flexibility to the placement of your text. The `<CENTER>` tag does require both starting and ending tags.

Open `sizing.html` in your editor. Add code to center both headings and the hyperlink.

Save the file. View it in your browser.

a) How did you edit `sizing.html` to do this?

_____

_____

7.3.4 USE THE PRE TAG

The `<PRE>` tag is a handy tag to use in your HTML.

Open `sizing.html` in your editor.

Add the following lines exactly as shown below the link.

```
<CENTER>
Starring Judy Garland as Dorothy. Ray Bolger as the
Scarecrow. Jack Haley as the TinMan. And, Bert Lahr
as the Cowardly Lion.
 </CENTER>
<PRE>
Our story begins in K   a   n   s   a   s, where gray is
the color of choice.
</PRE>
```

Save the file and open it your browser.

a) Describe the output.

_____

_____

7.3.5 USE OTHER "FUNKY" TAGS

This section is devoted to what we affectionately call the "funky" HTML tags. There are times when you would like to add certain characters to your HTML but the keyboard does not have a coinciding key for it. For example, you may want to add a registered trademark symbol to an item in your HTML. Or, perhaps you may want to add an accent to a name. This Exercise will teach you to use the most common "funky" tags.

Each funky tag has a name code, number code, or both associated with it. They all begin with an ampersand (&) and end with a semicolon (;). You already have been introduced to one of the funky tags early on in the book. It is the non-breaking space .

Open `sizing.html` in your editor.

Add the following line immediately before the closing `<BODY>` tag. Add additional formatting to the line as desired, such as color or font.

```
<CENTER>&copy; Built with blood, sweat, and tears by
[insert your name here].<CENTER>
```

Save the file. Open `sizing.html` in your browser.

a) What contribution did this line add to your existing file?

_____

_____

LAB 7.3 EXERCISE ANSWERS

7.3.1 ANSWERS

a) What is the syntax used to do this?

Answer: There are two different ways to accomplish this task. Both are equally as effective.

```
<FONT FACE = "Arial,Helvetica" COLOR = "#7AB777"
  SIZE = "+5">
    <B>Toto, I don't think we're in Kansas anymore.</B>
</FONT>
```

or

```
<B><FONT FACE = "Arial,Helvetica" COLOR = "#7AB777"
  SIZE = "+5">
    Toto, I don't think we're in Kansas anymore.
</FONT></B>
```

The <STRONG> tag is very similar to the <B> tag. As mentioned in "The Whole Truth" section of this Exercise, it is one of the tags being phased out and its usage is very low. If you want bold text, use the <B> tag and you can't go wrong.

7.3.2 ANSWERS

a) What syntax did you use to complete this Exercise?

Answer: The order of your embedded tags may differ from ours. This is how we edited `sizing.html` *for this Exercise:*

```
<HTML>
<BODY link = "#FF0000" vLink = "#00FA7A"
 alink="#FF67B4">

<H1>The Wizard of Oz in a nutshell.</H1>
<H5>
 <FONT COLOR="#4B0082"><I>
  A Y2K film.
 </I></FONT>
</H5>

<FONT FACE = "Arial,Helvetica" COLOR = "#7AB777"
 SIZE = "+5"><B>
   Toto, I don't think we're in Kansas anymore.
</B></FONT>

<BR>

<FONT FACE = "Courier New" COLOR = "#800000"
 SIZE = "+3">
  There's no place like home.
</FONT>

<BR>

<FONT FACE = "Verdana" COLOR = "#8B008B"
 SIZE = "-1">
  Why does the muskrat guard his musk? Courage.
</FONT>

<BR>

<FONT FACE = "Times New Roman" COLOR = "#20B2AA"
 SIZE = "-4">
  I'll get you, my pretty. And your little dog
  too.
</FONT>

<P>

<A HREF = "http://www.amazon.com"><I>
 Click here to buy your favorite HTML book today.
</I></A>

</BODY>
</HTML>
```

Figure 7.2 shows the output in my browser:

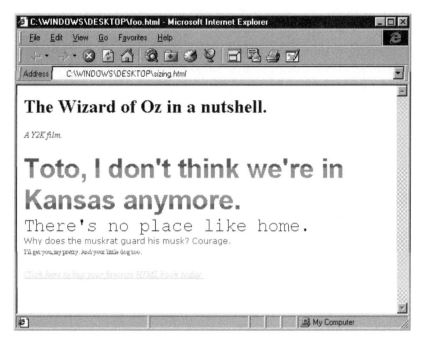

Figure 7.2 ■ Output of the revised `sizing.html` document.

7.3.3 ANSWERS

a) How did you edit `sizing.html` to do this?

Answer: This is how we coded the file to accomplish this task:

```
<HTML>
<BODY link = "#FF0000" vLink = "#00FA7A"
 alink="#FF67B4">

<H1><CENTER>
 The Wizard of Oz in a nutshell.
</ CENTER></H1>

<H5> <CENTER> <FONT COLOR="#4B0082"><I>
 A Y2K film.
</I></FONT> </CENTER></H5>

<FONT FACE = "Arial,Helvetica" COLOR = "#7AB777"
 SIZE = "+5"><B>
```

```
     Toto, I don't think we're in Kansas anymore.
</B></FONT>

<BR>

<FONT FACE = "Courier New" COLOR = "#800000"
 SIZE = "+3">
  There's no place like home.
</FONT>

<BR>

<FONT FACE = "Verdana" COLOR = "#8B008B"
 SIZE = "-1">
 Why does the muskrat guard his musk?
 Courage.
</FONT>

<BR>

<FONT FACE = "Times New Roman" COLOR = "#20B2AA"
 SIZE = "-4">
  I'll get you, my pretty. And your little
  dog too.
</FONT>

<P>

<A HREF = "http://www.amazon.com"><CENTER><I>
 Click here to buy your favorite HTML
 book today.
</I></ CENTER></A>

</BODY>
</HTML>
```

We prefer to use the identifying tag as the outer tag and the formatting tags as inner tags. For instance, Heading 5 is easily recognizable due to the fact that <H5> is the outer tag. Should you have the need to make any changes to <H5>, it is easily recognized when scanning the page. Any formatting done to Heading 5 is embedded within the line of text. For instance, once we have assigned "Y2K" as Heading 5, every other formatting addition is just gravy, so to speak.

7.3.4 ANSWERS

a) Describe the output.

Answer: The <CENTER> tag centers each individual line of text horizontally on the page. The line of text within the <PRE> tags appears exactly as typed into the HTML file.

The <PRE> tag actually preformats the text enclosed within the tag. Recall the non-breaking spaces you learned earlier. They are not needed to force spaces between the letters of the word "Kansas." Also, note the carriage return after the word "color" is literally interpreted by the browser. Much like heading tags, note here that a line break is not needed to separate the two.

7.3.5 ANSWERS

a) What contribution did this line add to your existing file?

Answer: The new line of centered text is shown with a copyright symbol placed at the beginning. This is similar to what you should see in your browser:

© Built with blood, sweat, and tears by AC.

Table 7.2 shows a list of some of the most common funky characters for you to use in your HTML.

Table 7.2 ■ Generating Alternative Funky Characters in HTML

Name Code	Number Code	Glyph	Description
	`	`	acute accent
	®	®	registered trademark
ä	ä	ä	lowercase a, umlaut
ñ	ñ	ñ	lowercase n, tilde
	°	°	degree sign

LAB 7.3 SELF-REVIEW QUESTIONS

In order to test your progress, you should be able to answer the following questions.

1) The <B> tag does not require an end tag.
   a) _____ True
   b) _____ False

2) Which of the following uses the correct syntax?

a) _____ `<CENTER>This is correct.</B><CENTER>`

b) _____ `<I><B>This is correct.<I></B>`

c) _____ `<CENTER><B>This is correct.<CENTER></B>`

d) _____ `<B><I>This is correct</I></B>`

3) You may not use more than two formatting tags for any line of text.

a) _____ True

b) _____ False

4) In order to separate a heading from text using the `<PRE>` tag, you must use either the `<BR>` or the `<P>` tag.

a) _____ True

b) _____ False

5) The symbol used to signify a registered trademark is which of the following?

a) _____ `&#reg;`

b) _____ `&reg;`

c) _____ `&#174;`

d) _____ `&174;`

e) _____ `&174#;`

6) The tag used to create text exactly as typed is which of the following?

a) _____ `<BLOCKQUOTE>`

b) _____ `<CENTER>`

c) _____ `<PRE>`

7) Links cannot embed any of the formatting tags.

a) _____ True

b) _____ False

8) All funky tags begin and end with which of the following?

a) _____ semicolon and colon

b) _____ semicolon and ampersand

c) _____ ampersand and semicolon

d) _____ ampersand and pound sign

Quiz answers appear in Appendix A, Section 7.3.

C H A P T E R   7

TEST YOUR THINKING

In this Chapter, you learned how to add many different formatting tags to your HTML pages. You also learned to add more flexibility to the `<FONT>` tag, as well as indicate size for text. An occasional visit to the World Wide Web consortium at `http://www.w3c.org` is recommended in order for you to keep abreast of any new or outdated tags.

1) Start a new HTML file. Code in all the necessary shell requirements. Design this page as a description of yourself. Using at least one list, be sure to include some of your favorite pasttimes. Center an image on the page. For example, the image could be a picture of one of your favorite hobbies. Be sure to add appropriately sized headings to include your name, or nickname, and your email address. Make your email address an italicized link.

2) Start another new HTML page. Change the background of the page to a light color that will not hinder the visibility of all other text and images. Create a link to the first page from project one. Add a centered paragraph of text to the page. The paragraph may be brief, but be sure it is relevant to you. For example, it should describe your typical day. Add the hex code for SlateBlue and the font size of +2. Each time you mention yourself (*me, I, myself*), it should display as bold.

3) Add a preformatted paragraph of text to the previous page. Use this paragraph to describe how the weather was today in your area. Be certain to mention the temperature and use the symbol for degrees. With each mention of the words "hot," "warm," "cool," or "cold," be sure to set the words apart by formatting accordingly. For example, the word "hot" should be displayed in red, perhaps slightly larger than the other text, and use a different font.

C H A P T E R   8

DESIGNING AND FORMATTING TABLES

Success is dependent on effort.

—Sophocles

In this Chapter, we'll start off learning how to create simple tables. Tables are the crux of HTML design and creation. Tables allow you to place content exactly where you want it to be within the page. Without tables, your HTML pages would lack the flexibility of design that HTML is so very capable of handling. All prior Chapters have led you to this point.

In the first half of this Chapter, we will discuss the basics of table structure and design. As the Chapter progresses, you will discover the amazing design capabilities that table structure can offer to your HTML pages. The second half of the Chapter is devoted to learning some pretty spiffy HTML to spruce up the design of your tables.

L A B   8 . 1

CREATING TABLES

LAB OBJECTIVES

After this Lab, you will be able to:

- Create Simple Tables
- Use Cellpadding and Cellspacing
- Align and Size Table Data

HTML tables are made up of rows and columns. If you have ever used Microsoft Excel or any other spreadsheet software program, then you probably have a pretty good idea of the composition of tables. If you have not had any experience with spreadsheets, fear not. You will be a pro in no time at all.

As with all of the previous Chapters, it is recommended that you test any and all of your HTML in both Internet Explorer and Netscape. There are other browsers out in the world. Yet, Internet Explorer and Netscape are by far the most commonly used. We may be repeating ourselves here, but be certain to have both browsers open, minimized, and ready to test your newly written HTML. Remember, the HTML you write today could be viewed by Internet surfers using any browser of any version number!

LAB 8.1 EXERCISES

8.1.1 CREATE SIMPLE TABLES

Open your HTML text editor.

Start a new file. Name it `tables.html`.

LAB
8.1

Add the necessary shell HTML for a new page.

Add the following within the BODY section of the page:

```
<TABLE>
 <TR>
  <TD>This is the first cell of the first row.</TD>
 </TR>
</TABLE>
```

Save the file.

View it in your browsers.

a) What is the output?

_____

_____

Open your editor.

Add the new tags and the included text to your existing file as shown:

```
<TABLE>
<TR>
 <TD>This is the first cell of the first row.</TD>
 <TD>This is the second cell of the first row.</TD>
</TR>
<TR>
 <TD>This is the first cell of the second row.</TD>
 <TD>This is the second cell of the second row.</TD>
</TR>
<TR>
 <TD>This is the first cell of the third row.</TD>
 <TD>This is the second cell of the third row.</TD>
</TR>
<TR>
 <TD>This is the first cell of the fourth row.</TD>
 <TD>This is the second cell of the fourth row.</TD>
</TR>
</TABLE>
```

Save the file once again.

View it in your browser.

b) What is the output?

_____

_____

_____

You may be wondering how in the world this could be a table. It appears as a few lines of text. There seems to be nothing special about them. However, there is definitely something going on here. Let's examine it a little closer.

A table is defined by an opening <TABLE> tag and a closing </TABLE> tag. A table row is signified in HTML by the <TR> tag. The <TD> tag represents the table data or cells. A cell is an intersection of a row and a column. A row is any data seen horizontally on the page. Conversely, a column is any data seen vertically on the page. Both the <TR> and the <TD> tags require ending tags.

Knowing this, take another look at the table you created. Place the following HTML within the opening <TABLE> tag:

```
BORDER = "1"
```

Save the file.

View it in your browser window.

c) How many cells exist within this table?

_____

_____

The table design is much clearer now. You can see each intersection of row and column. As you can see, a table is still a table with or without the BORDER attribute. A table *border* is defined as the outer line of the table.

This is the whole premise of table design. It may seem a bit confusing, but look closely. Each <TR> tag creates a new row. There are three complete row tags inside this table. For each row, there are two complete <TD> tags. Each <TD> tag creates an additional column within the table. All the <TD> tags are embedded within the accompanying <TR> tags. Any text between the <TD> tags becomes data within a cell.

Knowing how many rows and columns you need for your table will keep you far ahead of the game. Let's give it a try in the text editor.

Start another new file and name it `tables2.html`.

Suppose you want a table with three columns and two rows, and a BORDER attribute with the value of two.

The first step is to grab a piece of paper and sketch out the table. Write the row and column tags you need outside the border of your table drawing. Until you become comfortable with designing tables, this method is sure to work.

Following along with your sketch, add the two <TABLE> tags within the editor.

Add the necessary row tags.

Then, add the column tags. Place a few words of text within each cell. Stating the position of the cell as shown in the previous example is fine.

Lastly, add the BORDER attribute to the table.

Save the file.

View it in your browser.

    d) What is the syntax used to design this table?

_____

_____

_____

_____

8.1.2 USE CELLPADDING AND CELLSPACING

Edit `tables2.html` in your editor.

Add the following HTML commands within the starting <TABLE> tag:

```
cellPadding = "10" cellSpacing = "10"
```

Save the file.

View the output in your browser.

a) Explain how the new commands change the appearance of the table.

_____

_____

8.1.3 ALIGN AND SIZE TABLE DATA

Before starting on the particulars of this Exercise, let's try a little experiment.

Maximize the view of `tables2.html` in your browser.

Note the physical size of the table.

Resize the browser window to approximately half your monitor screen size.

Note the physical size of the table.

Resize the browser to half that size.

a) How does the table size change as it relates to the resizing of the browser window?

_____

_____

More often than not, you will have a need for a table that is less than the full width of the browser window.

Edit `tables2.html` in your text editor by adding the following to the opening `<TABLE>` tag:

```
WIDTH = "50%" HEIGHT = "80%"
```

Save the file.

View the output in the maximized browser window.

b) How did the new command affect the output of the table?

_____

_____

Edit the height and width of the table as follows:

```
WIDTH = "50" HEIGHT = "80"
```

Save the file and view it in your browser window.

   c) How did this change the output?

   _____

   _____

Edit the file once again and add the following to the opening <TABLE> tag:

```
ALIGN = "RIGHT"
```

Save the file.

View it in your browser.

   d) What is the output?

   _____

   _____

There are other alignment settings for use within the individual table cells.

Edit `tables2.html` in your editor. For clearer visibility, change the table WIDTH and HEIGHT settings back to percentage values.

Assign one of the following attributes to one of the opening <TD> tags. (Do not use any attribute more than once for this Exercise.)

```
ALIGN = "RIGHT"
ALIGN = "LEFT"
ALIGN = "CENTER"
VAlign = "TOP"
VAlign = "BOTTOM"
VAlign = "CENTER"
```

Save your file and view the output in your browser.

e) Explain how each of the alignment attributes affected each cell within the table.

_____

_____

_____

_____

Another attribute available for table cells utilizes the WIDTH attribute. You may set the WIDTH of table cells in the same manner as setting the WIDTH for tables.

Edit tables2.html in your editor as follows:

```
<TABLE BORDER = "2" CELLPADDING = "10" CELLSPACING =
  "10" WIDTH = "50%" HEIGHT = "80%" ALIGN = "CENTER">
<TR>
 <TD ALIGN = "CENTER" WIDTH = "10%">
  This is the first cell of the first row.
 </TD>
 <TD ALIGN = "RIGHT" WIDTH = "10%">
  This is the second cell of the first row.
 </TD>
 <TD ALIGN = "LEFT" WIDTH = "80%">
  This is the third cell of the first row.
 </TD>
</TR>
<TR>
 <TD vAlign = "TOP" WIDTH = "10%">
  This is the first cell of the second row.
 </TD>
 <TD vAlign = "BOTTOM" WIDTH = "10%">
  This is the second cell of the second row.
 </TD>
 <TD vAlign = "CENTER" WIDTH = "80%">
  This is the third cell of the second row.
 </TD>
</TR>
</TABLE>
```

Save the file and open it in your browser.

Examine the new HTML and the output very carefully (*hint:* Observe the cells as a whole as they relate to the row to which they belong).

f) Explain in detail how the new WIDTH attributes affect the size of the cells. Include and describe the significance of using 10%, 10%, and 80%.

_____

_____

_____

_____

Edit `tables2.html` once again.

In the third cell of the first row, delete the line of text. Replace it with a non-breaking space.

In the third cell of the second row, delete the line of text. Leave the data for this cell empty.

Save the file and view it in your browser.

g) What is the output of the edited table cells?

_____

_____

LAB 8.1 EXERCISE ANSWERS

8.1.1 ANSWERS

You created a new HTML file, added some table HTML, named it `tables.html` and viewed it in the browser window.

a) What is the output?

Answer: One line of text is seen in the browser. It is placed in the upper left-hand corner by default.

Next, you added additional tags and some new text to `tables.html`.

b) What is the output?

Answer: The output is the same for both browsers. Figure 8.1 illustrates the output.

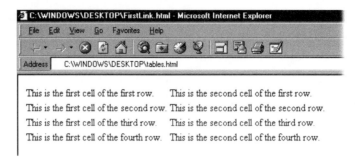

Figure 8.1 ▪ Output of `tables.html`.

c) How many cells exist within this table?

Answer: There are a total of eight cells in this table.

d) What is the syntax used to design this table?

Answer: The syntax is as follows:

```
<TABLE BORDER="2">
<TR>
 <TD>This is the first cell of the first row.</TD>
 <TD>This is the second cell of the first row.</TD>
 <TD>This is the third cell of the first row.</TD>
</TR>
<TR>
 <TD>This is the first cell of the second row.</TD>
 <TD>This is the second cell of the second row.</TD>
 <TD>This is the third cell of the second row.</TD>
</TR>
</TABLE>
```

A table may be created with as many rows and columns as you need. Note that the border size may be decreased or increased as needed, as well. Border size is represented in pixels. A border with a size of 0 eliminates any physical outline representation. Similarly, omitting the BORDER attribute from the <TABLE> tag eliminates a table border.

Figure 8.2 illustrates a sketch of the table. Your sketch should be similar.

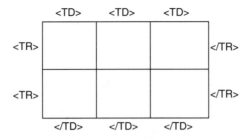

Figure 8.2 ■ **Sketch drawing of an HTML table.**

8.1.2 ANSWERS

a) Explain how the new commands change the appearance of the table.

Answer: The table appears spread out. There is more space between each cell and the border of the table. Also, the space within each of the table cells is increased. In this Exercise, both cellpadding and cellspacing are assigned a pixel size value of 10.

Specifically, cellpadding allows you to assign the amount of space in pixels between each cell within the table. Cellspacing allows you to assign the amount of space in pixels between the cell text and the cell borders. Note here that each of these commands is a single word.

Figure 8.3 illustrates two tables. Both tables use the same syntax with one small difference. The table on top includes the commands of cellspacing and cellpadding as used in this Exercise; the bottom table does not.

Figure 8.3 ■ **The top table utilizes both cellpadding and cellspacing. The bottom table does not utilize these commands.**

8.1.3 ANSWERS

a) How does the table size change as it relates to the resizing of the browser window?

Answer: The table actually resizes itself to fit the width of the browser window. This is the default reaction of any HTML table. This is known as filling 100% of the size of the browser window. The table cells react to the resizing, as well. As the window is made smaller, any text embedded in the cells react by autowrapping to fit within each cell.

This experiment proves that a table truly acts as a container for anything placed within it. No matter how we resize the browser window, no information (cells, or text) leaves the boundaries of the container. Cells are containers within the larger table container. Therefore, anything placed within a cell will never overflow the cell to which it is assigned.

b) How did the new command affect the output of the table?

Answer: The table is exactly half the width and 80% of the height of the browser window.

We encourage you to take a moment and experiment with resizing the table width and height. Use different percentage values until you become comfortable with how each attribute affects the outcome of the table in your browser window. Note that the percentage sign is required.

c) How did this change the output?

Answer: This small adjustment changes the output quite a bit. The table displays itself very differently in each of the browsers. The table is now much smaller.

By removing the percentage signs, you have designated the table width and height in pixels. Hopefully, you can see the potential danger of using pixel values. The likelihood that a table designed using pixel values will not display as you intended is high. Chapter 1, "Setting Up," taught you the different ways to set browser settings. Using percentage values allows you to keep some control over the size of your tables. It will be more cross-browser friendly. Knowing this, using percentage values allows you to have a bit more control of your original, intended table size. Using percentage values will size the table in accordance with the window and browser settings. As always, the users' settings always have priority over any HTML you write.

d) What is the output?

Answer: The table is now aligned to the right of the browser window.

Finally, we have found a command that allows you to specify the location of an HTML object. The default left location grows tired after a while, doesn't it? There are three properties available to assign to the ALIGN attribute of a table: *Right, Left,* and *Center.*

The Whole Truth

As mentioned throughout this workbook, different HTML can react differently in each of the browsers you are working with. Table HTML is no exception. The *Middle* property of the ALIGN attribute works in one of the two browsers. It functions in the same manner as the *Center* property.

Since *Middle* is recognized by only one of the browsers, it is not recommended that you use this property value for the ALIGN attribute. However, we wanted you to be aware of its existence. Knowing that it does exist can only add to your understanding of HTML cross-browser functionality. If nothing else, feel free to impress your friends and family with this knowledge.

We're not going to give away the answer to this one! Try it out in both Internet Explorer and Netscape. We just may ask you about it later.

---

e) Explain how each of the alignment attributes affected each cell within the table.

Answer: The first three ALIGN attributes set the text within each cell as stated: Right, Left, or Center, respectively. The three VALIGN attributes set the text vertically within each cell as stated: Top, Bottom, or Center, respectively.

The power of these table attributes allows for great flexibility in designing table data just as you want it to appear. The ALIGN and VALIGN attributes may be combined within an individual cell for even more design options.

■ FOR EXAMPLE:

```
<TABLE BORDER = "1" WIDTH = "40%" HEIGHT = "40%"
ALIGN = "RIGHT">
```

```
<TR>
 <TD ALIGN = "CENTER" VALIGN = "TOP">
  Put me in my place, I dare ya.
 </TD>
</TR>
</TABLE>
```

This is a one-celled table that utilizes both ALIGN and VALIGN. Using both attributes forces the text to be centered horizontally within the cell, as well as placed at the top of the cell.

Figure 8.4 illustrates the browser view of this HTML table.

Figure 8.4 ■ HTML utilizing *ALIGN* and *VALIGN*.

f) Explain in detail how the new WIDTH attributes affect the size of the cells. Include and describe the significance of using 10%, 10%, and 80%.

Answer: The newly added WIDTH attributes resize each individual cell according to the percentage setting. The three percentages—10%, 10%, and 80%—equal 100% of the width needed to complete the row.

This may have been a tough one to figure out. We didn't do it on purpose to fluster you, honest. It is truly important to have a clear understanding of setting cell width. Let's take a little closer look at it. The HTML in this file consists of one table with two rows. Each row occupies 100% of the width of the table. Each row contains three cells. The combined width of the three cells must equal 100% in order to fill the entire row. Therefore, by adding 10%, 10%, and 80%, you complete the necessary requirements to fill 100% of the row. Breaking the table into rows first, then comprehending the number of cells within each row, and lastly understanding the attributes of the cells should help you become quite proficient at designing tables.

Cells do not utilize the HEIGHT *attribute. As this Chapter progresses, you will discover other more efficient ways to manipulate and design tables. Table structure is very flexible in HTML.*

g)   What is the output of the edited table cells?

Answer: The cell containing the nonbreaking space appears as an empty cell. The second edited cell is empty as well. Yet, the cell lacks a border.

This is pretty interesting. There seems to be nothing particularly unusual about the first cell with the nonbreaking space. Of course, it becomes fairly obvious that the nonbreaking space allows the cell to maintain its border when observing the second cell. This is a handy bit of information to keep in mind as you design tables. It is very likely you will have a need for both types of cell display. Figure 8.5 illustrates the table created in this Exercise.

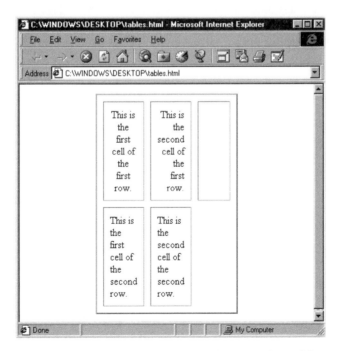

Figure 8.5 ■ **Table both using and not using nonbreaking spaces.**

LAB 8.1 SELF-REVIEW QUESTIONS

In order to test your progress, you should be able to answer the following questions.

1) Which of the following are the main tags used in table design?
   a) _____ <TR> and <TD>
   b) _____ <RT> and <DT>
   c) _____ <ROW> and <CELL>
   d) _____ <CELLPADDING> and <CELLSPACING>

2) A cell is defined as the intersection of a row and a column.
   a) _____ True
   b) _____ False

3) Which of the following is the tag used to represent table data?
   a) _____ <TABLE>
   b) _____ <TR>
   c) _____ <TD>

4) To design a table with an outline, you must use which of the following attributes?
   a) _____ OUTLINE
   b) _____ LINE
   c) _____ BORDER
   d) _____ TBORDER

5) What is cellpadding?
   a) _____ It is the space between the cell border and the table border.
   b) _____ It is the space between the cell data and the cell border.
   c) _____ It is the space between the table border and the cell data.

6) Using the WIDTH attribute in pixels will size the table as it relates to the users' screen and window settings.
   a) _____ True
   b) _____ False

7) The ALIGN attribute with the associated *Middle* property is understood by which of the following?
   a) _____ Netscape
   b) _____ Internet Explorer
   c) _____ Neither Netscape nor Internet Explorer
   d) _____ Both Netscape and Internet Explorer

8) A table must include a border to qualify as a true HTML table.
   a) _____True
   b) _____False

Quiz answers appear in Appendix A, Section 8.1.

L A B   8 . 2

USING ADVANCED TABLE HTML

LAB OBJECTIVES

After this Lab, you will be able to:

- Use COLSPAN
- Use ROWSPAN
- Add Color to Cells
- Add Images to Cells
- Add Links to Cells
- Embed Tables

The advanced table HTML you will learn in this Lab will give you the design flexibility we've been promising throughout this Chapter. We think you will enjoy this Lab. It involves incorporating many of the HTML commands you have learned in previous Chapters. So, let's get started.

LAB 8.2 EXERCISES

8.2.1 USE COLSPAN

Start a new HTML page. Code the necessary HTML shell tags.

Add one table to this new file. Design the table to half the height and width of your monitor screen.

Design the table with two rows. Give the first row one cell. Give the second row four cells. Add a word or two to each of the data cells. (Use names of family and friends or pets.)

Use the alignment attributes you learned in the last Lab to enhance the appearance of the table.

Save and name the file `advancedTable.html`.

View it in your browser.

> **a)** What do you see?

_____

_____

Edit the file and add the following attribute to the first cell of the first row:

```
COLSPAN = "4"
```

Save the file once again and view it in your browser.

> **b)** What change occurred as a result of adding this new attribute?

_____

_____

8.2.2 USE ROWSPAN

Using the information you learned in the last Exercise, it should be fairly easy to determine the output of the ROWSPAN attribute.

Let's give it a try.

Edit `advancedTable.html` and add a new table to the file. Place a break between the two tables.

Use the following HTML to create the second table.

```
<TABLE BORDER = "2" WIDTH = "50%" HEIGHT = "50%"
ALIGN = "CENTER">
  <TD ALIGN = "CENTER" ROWSPAN = "2">I need my space.
  <TD ALIGN = "CENTER">Pushy, ain't he?
```

```
<TR>
 <TD ALIGN = "CENTER">Such a bully.</TD>
</TR>
</TABLE>
```

Take a moment to examine what is happening here.

Save the file and view it in your browser.

a) What do you see?

_____

_____

8.2.3 ADD COLOR TO CELLS

Create a new HTML file and add one table with a border. Design the table with three rows and four columns.

Design the fourth cell of the first row with a nonbreaking space. The fourth cell of the second row should contain no text at all. Fill the remaining cells with some text, such as types of cars, animals, vacation favorites, and so forth.

Do not add any other table data attributes at this time.

Name and save the file as `colorTable.html`.

View and check the file for row and column accuracy.

Edit the file in your editor.

Refer to the hexadecimal color chart from Chapter 7, "Formatting the Page." Add a different hex color (preferably something light) to the last cell of each row (*hint*: Color is added to table cells in the same manner it is added to the `<BODY>` tag).

Save and view the file in both Internet Explorer and Netscape.

a) Describe the output as it relates to the cell color attributes.

_____

_____

_____

8.2.4 ADD IMAGES TO CELLS

Adding images to cells is a piece of cake.

Edit `colorTable.html` in your text editor.

Choose any small image you created from Chapter 5, "Adding Images to Your Web Pages."

Using the proper syntax to add any image to an HTML file, embed your chosen image into the table. Place the image into the last cell of the second row. (This is the cell not utilizing the nonbreaking space.)

Use the proper alignment attributes to center the image in the designated cell.

Save the file. View the output.

a) What is the syntax used to complete this Exercise?

_____

_____

_____

8.2.5 ADD LINKS TO CELLS

Adding links to table cells should come very easy to you as well. Once again, you use the same embedding format as practiced in the previous Exercise. Recalling Chapter 6, "Creating Hyperlinks," use the correct syntax and add the following link to the last cell of the first row of `colorTable.html`, replacing the nonbreaking space.

`http://www.hamsterdance.com`

Save the file and view the output in your browser.

a) What HTML did you add to create this link?

_____

_____

8.2.6 EMBED TABLES

Create a new HTML file. Code the necessary shell tags.

Add the following HTML to the BODY of the file:

```
<TABLE BORDER="1" WIDTH="50%" HEIGHT="50%"
ALIGN="CENTER">
 <TR>
 <TD>
  One big table.
<TABLE BORDER="1" WIDTH="25%" HEIGHT="25%"
ALIGN="RIGHT">
 <TR>
 <TD>
  One itty, bitty table.
 </TD>
 </TR>
</TABLE>
 </TD>
 </TR>
</TABLE>
```

Save and name the file `embedTable.html`. Study the HTML to check your understanding of the embedded table.

View the file in your browser.

a) Describe the output.

_____

_____

Edit `embedTable.html`.

Add and embed a single-celled table inside the smaller table of this page. Be sure to add a word of text inside the new table.

Save the file.

b) What HTML did you add to complete this Exercise?

_____

_____

_____

LAB 8.2 EXERCISE ANSWERS

8.2.1 ANSWERS

**LAB
8.2**

a)   What do you see?

Answer: The table has one cell on the top row that is left-justified. The bottom row contains three cells that fill the width of the table.

b)   What change occurred as a result of adding this new attribute?

Answer: The cell of the first row now fills the entire width of the table.

COLSPAN allows you to span cells across as many columns as you need. Nifty, huh? This is the way we designed the table for this Exercise. Your alignment attribute properties will most likely differ from ours. Figure 8.6 shows the table aligned in the center of the page. Refer to the table HTML as you view Figure 8.6.

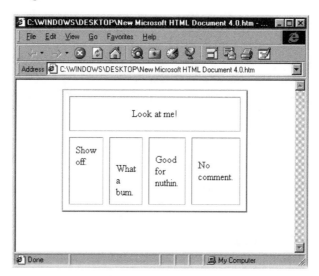

Figure 8.6 ■ Top row utilizing the COLSPAN attribute.

```
<TABLE BORDER = "2" CELLPADDING = "5" CELLSPACING =
"5" WIDTH = "50%" HEIGHT = "50%" ALIGN = "CENTER">
<TR>
 <TD ALIGN = "CENTER" COLSPAN = "4">Look at me!</TD>
</TR>
<TR>
 <TD vAlign = "TOP">Show off.</TD>
 <TD vAlign = "BOTTOM">What a bum.</TD>
 <TD vAlign = "CENTER">Good for nuthin.</TD>
```

```
<TD ALIGN = "LEFT">No comment.</TD>
  </TR>
</TABLE>
```

 We gave you the syntax here in order to mention a useful tip. Note how the two <TABLE> tags are set against the left margin of the page. Then, note the alignment of the <TR> tags. We have tabbed the row tags over slightly for better visibility. And lastly, the <TD> tags are indented slightly within the rows to which they belong. Lining up your HTML not only makes for good coding practice, but makes it much easier for you to see exactly how many cells you have embedded in the rows of your table.

8.2.2 ANSWERS

a) What do you see?

Answer: The output of `advancedTable.html` *displays a table with one cell occupying two rows in the first column and two cells occupying one row each in the second column.*

This HTML can be a bit confusing, so let's take a closer look at it. For clarity purposes, Figure 8.7 shows the display of the newly added table only. It may help to examine Figure 8.7 while looking at the HTML in your editor.

Figure 8.7 ■ **Examine the code that generated** `advancedTable.html` **and compare it to this output.**

Just as COLSPAN is used within table rows to span columns, ROWSPAN is used within table columns to span rows. Okay, digest that for a moment. The HTML used to create advancedTable.html follows this pattern. We want the first column to occupy all of the rows (in this case it is two rows). Therefore, we use a ROWSPAN of 2 within the first column, or <TD> tag.

Designing fancy tables can be confusing, but practicing table HTML is sure to help you become quite proficient. We mentioned this earlier but it is important enough to say again: Sketch out the table on a piece of paper before writing the HTML.

8.2.3 ANSWERS

a) Describe the output as it relates to the cell color attributes.

Answer: The last cell of each of the three rows contains the newly added color in Internet Explorer. The last cell in the second row viewed in Netscape shows no change in color.

First of all, this is the HTML we used to create the table for this Exercise. Your HTML should contain the same number of rows and columns. Your other table attributes may differ.

```
<TABLE BORDER="2" CELLPADDING="2" CELLSPACING="2"
WIDTH="70%" HEIGHT="60%" ALIGN="CENTER">
<TR>
 <TD>Bugs Bunny</TD>
 <TD>Daffy Duck</TD>
 <TD>Marvin the Martian</TD>
 <TD BGCOLOR="#C0FFC0"> </TD>
</TR>
<TR>
 <TD>Yosemite Sam</TD>
 <TD>Foghorn Leghorn</TD>
 <TD>Wile E. Coyote, Genius</TD>
 <TD BGCOLOR="#C0C0FF"></TD>
</TR>
<TR>
 <TD>Pepe Le Pew</TD>
 <TD>Gossimer</TD>
 <TD>Speedy Gonzales</TD>
 <TD BGCOLOR="#FFC0C0">Tweety Bird</TD>
</TR>
</TABLE>
```

As shown here, the BGCOLOR attribute is used to display color within table cells. We added a small twist to this Exercise to point out the difference in cell color display between the two browsers. Internet Explorer has the ability to display HTML cell color with or without the use of   or cell text. However, cell color will not display as you intend in Netscape without the use of either the nonbreaking space or the inclusion of cell text.

L<small>AB</small>
8.2

 If you would like to see any of the color-enhanced HTML that accompanies this Chapter or other portions of this Workbook, please navigate to the companion Web site at:

```
http://www.phptr.com/phptrinteractive/
```

We would be more than happy to upload any requested HTML.

8.2.4 ANSWERS

a) What is the syntax used to complete this Exercise?

Answer: Your original table cell will differ from the one shown here. The line formerly written as:

```
<TD BGCOLOR="#C0C0FF"></TD>
```

is changed to:

```
<TD ALIGN="CENTER" VALIGN="CENTER">
  <IMG SRC="cake.gif">
</TD>
```

The HTML cell now includes the proper image syntax as well as the ALIGN and VALIGN attributes. These attributes center the image vertically and horizontally within the cell.

Figure 8.8 illustrates the output of this image addition. For display purposes, we have deleted the color attribute.

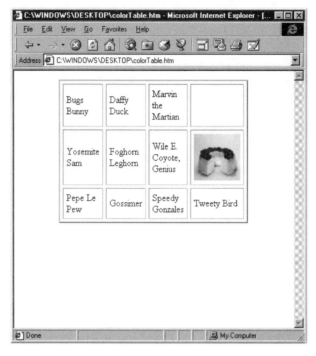

Figure 8.8 ■ Adding an image within a cell is as easy as adding it normally.

8.2.5 ANSWERS

a) What HTML did you add to create this link?

Answer: You should have added the following line:

```
<TD><A HREF="http://www.hamsterdance.com">The
Silliest Site We Know.</A></TD>
```

Hopefully, you see a pattern evolving here. Adding just about anything inside a table is simple if you follow the most basic rule. Whether it is images, links, or text, always embed the additions within the <TD> tags. Adding FONT attributes to any text within table cells follow the same rule.

■ *FOR EXAMPLE:*

```
<TD><FONT FACE="Arial" COLOR="BLUE"><I><B>Text
embedded within a cell.</I></B></FONT></TD>
```

This line of text is embedded within a table cell. It follows the HTML rules of properly ordered tags to achieve the desired output. This line of text displays in the browser as bold, italic, blue, and with the font Arial.

8.2.6 ANSWERS

a) Describe the output.

Answer: You see a table centered in the browser window. This table contains a smaller table that is right-justified within it.

A table within a table follows the same cell embedding rule you learned in the previous Exercise. In order for a table to embed itself within another table, it must follow these rules:

- It must be smaller than the parent or larger table.
- It must use the same embedding rule you learned from the previous Exercise. In other words, the embedded table should be written inside of the table data tag (the <TD> tag).

As you design more and more HTML pages, you will most certainly find a need for embedding tables. Embedded tables are perfect for arranging all your text, images, links, and other HTML goodies exactly the way you wish them to be.

b) What HTML did you add to complete this Exercise?

Answer: This is the HTML we used to complete this Exercise:

```
<TABLE BORDER="1" WIDTH="50%" HEIGHT="50%"
ALIGN="CENTER">
 <TR>
 <TD>
  One big table.
<TABLE BORDER="1" WIDTH="25%" HEIGHT="25%"
ALIGN="RIGHT">
 <TR>
 <TD>
  One itty, bitty table.
<TABLE BORDER="2" WIDTH="10%" HEIGHT="20%"
ALIGN="LEFT">
 <TR>
  <TD>
  Hi
  </TD>
 </TR>
```

```
    </TABLE>
     </TD>
     </TR>
    </TABLE>
     </TD>
     </TR>
    </TABLE>
```

Your table attributes and their properties will differ slightly. No matter what properties you used here, the new table must have a smaller height and width than the second table. Note where the new table is embedded within the HTML. It is positioned within the <TD> tag of the second table. Therefore, the new table is inside the second table. Figure 8.9 illustrates the output of the HTML we placed into embedTable.html.

Figure 8.9 ■ **New HTML added to embedTable.html.**

LAB 8.2 SELF-REVIEW QUESTIONS

To test your progress, you should be able to answer the following questions.

1) The COLSPAN attribute is used within which of the following tags?
    a) _____ <TABLE>
    b) _____ <TR>
    c) _____ <TD>

2) To add color to table cells, which of the following attributes would you use?
   a) _____ `FONT COLOR`
   b) _____ `HEX`
   c) _____ `COLOR`
   d) _____ `BGCOLOR`

3) `ROWSPAN` allows you to span across as many columns as you need.
   a) _____True
   b) _____False

4) In order to extend more than one row in a table, which of the following attributes would you use?
   a) _____ `ROWSPAN`
   b) _____ `COLSPAN`
   c) _____ `WIDTH`
   d) _____ `HEIGHT`

5) Cell color will not display in Internet Explorer without the use of either the nonbreaking space or the inclusion of cell text.
   a) _____True
   b) _____False

6) To display a table cell without a border, which of the following would you use?
   a) _____ ` `
   b) _____ `BORDER = "0"`
   c) _____ Nothing
   d) _____ Either a or c
   e) _____ Both a and b

7) Which of the following uses the correct table data syntax?
   a) _____ `<TD><B><FONT = "Arial"><SIZE = "+2">Hello</TD></B></FONT></SIZE>`
   b) _____ `<TD><B>Hello<B></TD>`
   c) _____ `<TR><TD><I><FONT = "BLUE">Hello</FONT></I></TD></TR>`
   d) _____ `<TR><TD><B><I><FONT SIZE="+3">Hello</FONT></I></B></TD></TR>`

8) Which of the following are the attributes used to center an image within a table cell?
   a) _____ `CENTER, TOP, BOTTOM`
   b) _____ `HALIGN` and `VALIGN`
   c) _____ `ALIGN, WIDTH, HEIGHT`
   d) _____ `ALIGN` and `VALIGN`

Quiz answers appear in Appendix A, Section 8.2.

C H A P T E R   8

TEST YOUR THINKING

In this Chapter, you learned how to create HTML tables. The different combinations of table attributes, properties, images, font, links, and embedded table HTML are endless. We encourage you to practice the table skills you have learned here. This Chapter will undoubtedly be one of the most useful to you in your HTML page creation process. Each of the following projects is designed to help you become more familiar with HTML table creation. Design each project to include the specified attributes. Additional table enhancements may be added, if you choose to do so. Good luck and have fun!

1)   Create a new HTML file. Name the file `tableProj1.html`. Add two tables to the file. Design the first table with three rows and two columns. This table should occupy 40% of the width of the browser window. The second table should appear next to the first table when displayed in the browser window. Create the second table with one cell containing an image and a short textual description. Place the text below the image.

2)   Create a new HTML file. Name the file `tableProj2.html`. Add one table with two rows. Design the top row with four cells across. The first cell of the top row should represent 45% of the width of the table. What width will you need to use for the other three cells? Design the bottom row as one cell that fills the width of the table. Assign the bottom row a dark hex color. Add your name to the bottom row in white. Center your name horizontally and vertically within the cell.

3)   Create a new HTML file. Name the file `tableProj3.html`. Add a left-aligned table to the file. This table should occupy 30% of the width and 100% of the height of the page. Design this table with three rows, each containing one cell. Pad the cells using both cellpadding and cellspacing. Place a link in each of the three rows. Connect the hyperlinks to `tableProj1.html`, `tableProj2.html`, and `tableProj3.html`.

CHAPTER 9

CASCADING STYLE SHEETS

Each problem that I solved became a rule which served afterwards to solve other problems.

—Rene Descartes

In Chapter 7, "Formatting The Page," you learned how to format the text of your HTML pages using tags. In this Chapter, you will learn how to use a much more advanced method of formatting known as cascading style sheets (known as CSS). The primary purpose of HTML is to define the structure of a document. It is not very good at defining how a document is going to look when viewed in a browser. To a limited extent, you can overcome this by using the various formatting tags (such as <b>,<font>, and so forth), but even these do not allow full control. It is for this reason that so many Web sites use large images instead of text to ensure that the sites look the way the authors want them to. Cascading style sheets are the solution to this problem.

239

L A B   9 . 1

CREATING EMBEDDED AND LINKED STYLE SHEETS

> After this Lab, you will be able to:
>
> • Create an Embedded Style Sheet
> • Add Multiple Style Definitions to an Embedded Style Sheet
> • Create a Linked Style Sheet

Style sheets allow you to separate the formatting from the content of the HTML page and define exactly how the page will look when rendered by the browser. More specifically, style sheets allow you to:

- Control the appearance of all paragraphs, headings, lists, and so forth using a single document.
- Specify font, size, color, and appearance more precisely.
- Improve the cross-browser compatibility of your pages.
- Allow the rapid updating of multiple HTML pages.

With style sheets, you have the kind of control over style that you previously only had with word processing software.

The Whole Truth

Of course, style sheets are not a perfect solution: Like everything on the World Wide Web, they are subject to the differing compliance of different browsers. Internet Explorer 3.0 was the first browser to attempt to implement style sheets. Netscape first supported them in Navigator 4. No current browser supports style sheets completely yet. Despite these problems, style sheets are a vast improvement on formatting HTML using tags.

There are three methods of using style sheets to format Web pages:

- Creating a link within the Web page to an external style sheet.
- Embedding a style sheet in the Web page.
- Adding inline styles to elements within the Web page.

Each has its advantages and disadvantages. As you progress through this Chapter, you will see when and how to use each of these formatting methods. We will begin by using embedded style sheets. An embedded style sheet is a style sheet that is contained within an HTML document. It only affects the appearance of the HTML document within which it appears.

LAB 9.1 EXERCISES

9.1.1 CREATE AN EMBEDDED STYLE SHEET

In this Exercise, we will be setting the font size for different page elements using an embedded style sheet. Font size is just one of numerous attributes that can be set using style sheets. Here are the attributes that we will be using in this chapter's Exercises:

- **font size**—sets the size of the font.
- **font weight**—sets the font to bold.
- **color**—sets the color of the font.
- **background**—sets the background color that appears behind the text.

Appendix C lists many more attributes and how to set them. More complete guides can be found in Appendix D (also at the end of the book).

Create a simple HTML document by entering the following in your text editor:

```
<HTML>
<HEAD>
<TITLE>AN EMBEDDED STYLE SHEET EXAMPLE</TITLE>
</HEAD>
<BODY>
 <H1>This is an H1 Heading</H1>
 <H2>This is an H2 Heading</H2>
<P>This Is A Normal Paragraph
</BODY>
</HTML>
```

Save it as an HTML file and open it in your browser.

a) What does the page look like?

_____

_____

Next, you are going to embed a style sheet into this HTML document. Open the HTML file in the text editor and enter the following code between the `</title>` **tag and the** `</head>` **tag:**

```
<STYLE TYPE="text/css">
<!-
H1 { font-size: 18 }
H2 { font-size: 14 }
P { font-size: 12 }
-->
</STYLE>
```

Save this file as an HTML file and open it again in your browser.

b) Now what does the page look like? What are the differences between the HTML page without the style sheet and the HTML page with the style sheet?

_____

_____

9.1.2 ADD MULTIPLE STYLE DEFINITIONS TO AN EMBEDDED STYLE SHEET

So far, we have only controlled the font size of the text using style sheets. To control additional attributes of the text, we have to add new attribute definitions to our style sheet, separating each definition with a semicolon. This time, we are going to define the color attribute, which controls the color of the text.

Open the HTML file you created in your text editor and edit the style sheet to match the following example:

```
<STYLE TYPE="text/css">
<!—
H1 { font-size: 18; color: blue }
H2 { font-size: 14; color: red }
P { font-size: 12; color: yellow }
-->
</STYLE>
```

After you have entered the text, save the file and open it in your browser.

a) What is the difference between how the HTML page without the style sheet and the HTML page with the style sheet display?

_____

_____

b) How would you edit the style sheet so that H1, H2, and P all use the same font size of 12?

_____

_____

c) BACKGROUND is the attribute that controls the background color of the text enclosed within a tag. How would you edit the style sheet so that all text enclosed within <P> tags had an orange background?

_____

_____

9.1.3 CREATE A LINKED STYLE SHEET

An embedded style sheet is an excellent way to format a single Web page, but suppose you want to give a common format to a collection of Web pages. To do this, you have to use the linked style sheet.

A linked style sheet consists of a series of style definitions that are placed in a separate text file. The file is identified as a style sheet by adding .css as a file extension.

To use this style sheet to format an HTML document, you simply place a special type of link to the style sheet in the head section of the document. This allows you to change the style of every linked document by editing the style sheet file.

Open a new file in your text editor and enter the following text:

```
H1 { font-size: 18; color: blue }
H2 { font-size: 14; color: red }
P { font-size: 12; color: yellow }
```

You do not have to enter any style tags.

Save the file as text and name it `stylesheet.css` (or any name you wish as long as it ends with .css). You have created your first style sheet file. Now, we need to link an HTML document to this external style sheet.

Open the HTML file we created in Exercise 9.1.1 in the text editor, delete the embedded style sheet, and enter the following text into the head section of the document:

```
<LINK REL="stylesheet" TYPE="text/css"
HREF="stylesheet.css">
```

Then change the title so it reads:

```
<TITLE>A LINKED STYLE SHEET EXAMPLE</TITLE>
```

When you are done, the file should look like the following:

```
<HTML>
<HEAD>
<TITLE>A LINKED STYLE SHEET EXAMPLE</TITLE>
```

```
<LINK REL="stylesheet" TYPE="text/css"
HREF="stylesheet.css">
</HEAD>
<BODY>
 <H1>This is a H1 Heading</H1>
 <H2>This is an H2 Heading</H2>
<P>This Is A Normal Paragraph
</BODY>
</HTML>
```

You have created your first HTML document with a linked style sheet. Save the file and open it in your browser.

a) What is the difference between how the HTML page with the embedded style sheet and the HTML page with the link to the external style sheet display?

_____

_____

b) How would you edit the external style sheet so that H1, H2, and P all use the same background color of black?

_____

_____

c) Font weight controls the heaviness of the text enclosed within a tag. How would you edit the external style sheet so that all text enclosed within <P> tags had a font weight of bold?

_____

_____

LAB 9.1 EXERCISE ANSWERS

9.1.1 ANSWERS

a) What does the page look like?

Answer: You should see something like the output shown in Figure 9.1.

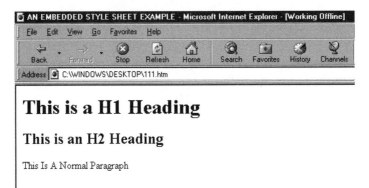

Figure 9.1 ■ **A simple HTML page with three different headings.**

However, because HTML formats the *structure* of a document, not its precise display, you probably will not see exactly what is shown in Figure 9.1. The font size, color, and placement of the text will all vary depending upon which browser you are using and how the user's preferences are set. By inserting a style sheet into the HTML document we have already created, we can control how the text appears.

b) Now what does the page look like? What are the differences between the HTML page without the style sheet and the HTML page with the style sheet?

Answer: In part, this depends upon your browser settings. Generally, however, the text on the HTML page with the style sheet will be smaller in the sections enclosed within the <H1> and <H2> tags and larger in the section enclosed in the <P> tags. As long as your browser supports cascading style sheets, you should see something almost exactly like the output shown in Figure 9.2.

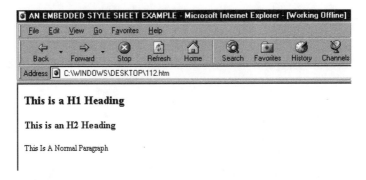

Figure 9.2 ■ **The style sheet you added to the previous example changed the appearance of the text.**

The text you inserted created an embedded style sheet. It is defined as a style sheet by the pair of style tags. These tags tell a browser that supports style sheets that what appears between the tags is a style sheet. The TYPE="text/css" declaration defines the type of style sheet. This declaration, combined with the HTML comment tags (see Chapter 4) that are placed within the style tags, prevents browsers that don't support style sheets from rendering the text that appears within the tags.

The text between the style tags and HTML comment tags contains the actual style definitions. Each definition consists of the name of an HTML tag (in this case the H1, H2, and P tags) followed by a pair of braces (braces are those curly brackets). Within the braces are the actual style attributes that control how the text associated with each type of tag is displayed. The attributes consist of the name of the attribute, followed by a colon, followed by the value to which the attribute is set. In the case of our example, we are setting the font size attribute for the <H1>, <H2> and <P> tags within our document. The values we are setting the attribute to is the size in points.

9.1.2 ANSWERS

a) What is the difference between how the HTML page without the style sheet and the HTML page with the style sheet display?

Answer: In part, this depends upon your browser settings. Generally, however, the text on the HTML page with the style sheet will be smaller in the sections enclosed within the <H1> and <H2> tags and larger in the section enclosed in the <P> tags. As long as your browser supports cascading style sheets, you should see something almost exactly like the output in Figure 9.3.

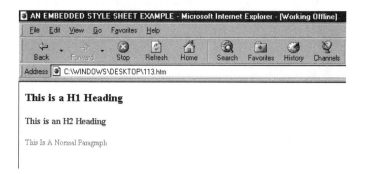

Figure 9.3 ■ **Although you can't see it here, there is now color added to the display.**

b) How would you edit the style sheet so that H1, H2, and P all use the same font size of 12?

Answer: You would change the font size attribute in each of the style definitions, so that the style sheet looked like the following:

```
H1 { font-size: 12; color: blue }
H2 { font-size: 12; color: red }
P { font-size: 12; color: yellow }
```

It is very important that you do not mix up where to use the colons and the semicolons. The colons separate each attribute from its setting. The semicolons separate each attribute definition.

c) BACKGROUND is the attribute that controls the background color of the text enclosed within a tag. How would you edit the style sheet so that all text enclosed within <P> tags had an orange background?

Answer: You would edit the <P> style definition so that it read as follows:

```
P { font-size: 12; color: yellow; background: orange }
```

Make sure that you do not forget the braces (those squiggly brackets) that surround the style settings for each HTML tag. If you leave them off, the style sheet will not be read properly by the browser.

9.1.3 ANSWERS

a) What is the difference between how the HTML page with the embedded style sheet and the HTML page with the link to the external style sheet display?

Answer: There should be no difference in the way the two different pages display. In both cases, you should see something almost exactly like the output shown in Figure 9.4.

Your choice of which method to use to control the page's display would depend upon how you are going to use the page. If you have a group of pages that need to have the same style, you should use linked style sheets. A single sheet, with its own unique formatting, should use an embedded style sheet.

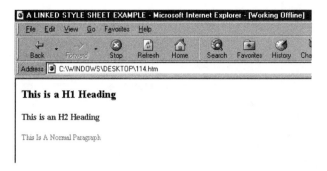

Figure 9.4 ■ Embedded style sheets and cascading style sheets work the same way on a single page.

b) How would you edit the external style sheet so that H1, H2, and P all use the same background color of black?

Answer: You would edit the style sheet so that it read as follows:

```
H1 { font-size: 18; color: blue; background: black }
H2 { font-size: 14; color: red; background: black }
P { font-size: 12; color: yellow; background: black }
```

The way that the background color displays will differ from browser to browser, though. Some browsers display the background color only behind the actual characters (and the spaces between them). Other browsers display the background color over the entire width of the screen for each line occupied by an element for which you have set the background color. These display differences can make the use of the background setting problematic.

c) Font weight controls the heaviness of the text enclosed within a tag. How would you edit the external style sheet so that all text enclosed within <P> tags had a font weight of bold?

Answer: You would edit the <P> style definition so that it read as follows:

```
P { font-size: 12; color: yellow; font-weight: bold }
```

In design terms, setting the font weight of paragraphs to bold lessens the contrast between regular text and the text enclosed in heading tags. Therefore, you probably would not use this setting for many pages. Setting the font weight of the different heading tags to bold, though, is frequently done.

LAB 9.1 SELF-REVIEW QUESTIONS

In order to test your progress, you should be able to answer the following questions.

1) Font weight is the style attribute that accomplishes which of the following?
   a) _____ Sets how big text is.
   b) _____ Sets whether a text is bold or not.
   c) _____ Sets the width of letters.

2) COLOR sets the background color behind text.
   a) _____ True
   b) _____ False

3) Embedded style sheets are which of the following?
   a) _____ Inside an HTML document.
   b) _____ Linked to a separate .css file.
   c) _____ Placed inside the tags surrounding text.

4) Linked style sheets are which of the following?
   a) _____ Inside an HTML document.
   b) _____ Linked to a separate .css file.
   c) _____ Placed inside the tags surrounding text.

5) You can use a style definition for a <P> tag to format text within <H1> tags.
   a) _____ True
   b) _____ False

Quiz answers appear in Appendix A, Section 9.1.

L A B   9 . 2

COMBINING INLINE STYLES AND CLASSES WITH STYLE SHEETS

LAB OBJECTIVES

After this Lab, you will be able to:

- Create Inline Styles
- Combine Inline Styles with Style Sheets
- Combine Styles within Documents
- Use Classes with Style Sheets

In addition to setting style attributes in both embedded and linked style sheets, you can also use them to set style within the tags of a page directly. This method of setting styles is known as inline styles. When you use *inline styles*, the style definition only affects the text that is surrounded by the particular tag that they are modifying. At first, this seems to defeat the whole purpose of using styles. After all, if you have to format tags directly, you might as well use formatting tags. However, inline styles do have a place when you want to make minor alterations to the overall styling that you have applied to a group of pages.

■ *FOR EXAMPLE:*

To set the font size of a particular paragraph to 12, you would type the initial paragraph tag as follows:

```
<P STYLE="font-size: 12">
```

This would set the font size to 12 for all text between the `<P>` tag and the next `</P>` tag. Just as in embedded and linked style sheets, additional attribute settings are separated by semicolons. With inline styles, however, you do not need any braces.

LAB 9.2 EXERCISES

9.2.1 CREATE INLINE STYLES

Open the HTML document we modified in Exercise 9.1.2 and delete the link to the external style sheet. Then, modify the text in the body of the document so that it matches the following code. When you are finished, the document should look like this:

```
<HEAD>
 <TITLE>An Inline Style Example</TITLE>
</HEAD>

<BODY>
<H1 style="font-size: 18; color: blue">
 This is a H1 Heading
</H1>
<H2 style="font-size: 14; color: red">
 This is an H2 Heading</H2>
<P style="font-size: 12; color: yellow">
 This Is A Normal Paragraph
</P>
<H1>This is a H1 Heading</H1>
<H2>This is an H2 Heading</H2>
<P>This Is A Normal Paragraph
</BODY>
```

Save the file and open it in your browser.

a) What is the difference between how the text enclosed within the tags containing inline styles displays and how the text enclosed within the tags that do not contain inline styles displays?

_____

_____

b) How would you edit the inline styles so that all text enclosed within the first set of <H1> tags has a font weight of bold?

9.2.2 COMBINE INLINE STYLES WITH STYLE SHEETS

So far, you have learned different ways of using styles to format Web pages. Suppose, however, that you decide to combine two or more of the styling methods. How does the browser know which style to use? Well, that is why they are officially known as *cascading* style sheets.

According to the CSS specification, the closer the styling is to the text being styled, the more importance is placed upon that styling. Therefore, inline styles should overrule embedded styles, which should overrule linked styles. In practice, though, this does not always work out. As a result, it's best where possible to avoid mixing different types of style sheets. If you must, stick to mixing inline styles with embedded or linked style sheets.

Style sheets also have rules to define which style to use when style definitions at the same level conflict.

■ FOR EXAMPLE:

If you have an embedded style sheet in a document that reads as follows:

```
<BODY> { font-size: 12 }
<P> { font-size: 11}
```

then the <P> style will be the one that is implemented for all <P> tags in the document.

If the conflicting style definitions are equally specific—for example if you have two HI definitions—then the browser will use whichever definition came last. The cascading style sheet specification has many more rules to decide between conflicting styles, but don't worry about them. None of them are implemented in today's browsers.

The Whole Truth

Neither Netscape nor Microsoft has managed to implement cascading correctly in their browsers (at least through version 4). While inline styles reliably overrule both linked and embedded styles, embedded styles do not overrule linked. Most other cascading rules (other than those listed previously) are also not reliably implemented.

In the text editor, open the HTML file you created in the previous Exercise. Type an embedded style sheet by adding the following text below to the head section of the document. When you are done, the file should read as follows:

```
<HTML>
<HEAD>

<STYLE TYPE="text/css">
 <!–
  H1 { font-size: 18; color: blue }
  H2 { font-size: 14; color: red }
  P { font-size: 12; color: yellow }
 -->
</STYLE>

</HEAD>

<BODY>
 <H1 style="font-size: 18; color: blue">
  This is an H1 Heading
 </H1>

 <H2 style="font-size: 14; color: red">
  This is an H2 Heading
 </H2>
<P style="font-size: 12; color: yellow">
 This Is A Normal Paragraph
</P>

<H1>This is an H1 Heading</H1>
<H2>This is an H2 Heading</H2>

<P>This Is A Normal Paragraph

</BODY>

</HTML>
```

Save the file and open it in your browser.

> **a)** What is the difference between how the text within the tags for-matted by the embedded style sheet displays and how the text within the tags formatted by the inline styles displays?

_____

_____

Create a style sheet file that contains the following code:

```
H1 { font-size: 18; color: blue }
H2 { font-size: 14; color: red }
P { font-size: 12; color: yellow }
```

Open the HTML file we created previously in your text editor. Delete the em-bedded style and replace it with a link to an external style sheet that contains the same style definitions as the embedded style sheet did.

> **b)** What changed about how the page displayed?

_____

_____

9.2.3 COMBINE STYLES WITHIN DOCUMENTS

Open the HTML file you created in the previous Exercise. Delete the link to the external style sheet. Edit the `<Body>` tag of the document so that it reads as follows:

```
<BODY STYLE="color:green; font-size: 24">
```

Save the file and open it in your browser.

> **a)** Which text was displayed in green with a 24-point font?

_____

_____

b) If you added a link to an external style sheet that defined a style for the body to have black text, would it change the way the page displayed?

_____

_____

9.2.4 USE CLASSES WITH STYLE SHEETS

A common formatting problem is the need to modify a small percentage of paragraphs in a collection of HTML documents. For example, suppose you have a group of documents where you want 90% of the paragraphs to use black text and the remaining 10% to use red text.

a) How would you solve this formatting problem using inline styles?

_____

_____

Using inline styles is a good solution. Inline styles, however, are not the only way to modify how text that is formatted by a style sheet is displayed. A more convenient way is to use class definitions in your style sheet.

A class is a style definition within a style sheet that modifies or replaces a previous style definition for the same type of tag.

Open your text editor and create a style sheet file that reads as follows:

```
H1 { font-size: 18; color: black }
H2 { font-size: 14; color: black }
P { font-size: 12; color: black }
P.red { font-size: 12; color: red }
```

Save this file as `stylesheet.css`. Then, create an HTML document that reads as follows:

```
<HTML>
<HEAD>
<TITLE>A LINKED STYLE SHEET EXAMPLE</TITLE>
<LINK REL="stylesheet" TYPE="text/css"
HREF="stylesheet.css">
</HEAD>
<BODY>
 <H1>This is an H1 Heading</H1>
 <H2>This is an H2 Heading</H2>
```

```
<P>This Is A Normal Paragraph
<P class="red">This Is A Class Red Paragraph</P>
</BODY>
</HTML>
```

Save this file and open it in your browser.

b) How does the text within the `<P class="red">` tag display?

The advantage of classes over inline styles is that if you decide that you want the 10% of paragraphs to be in 14-point type instead of 12, you only have to modify the single class definition in the style sheet instead of modifying every inline style.

You can also create a generic class definition that can modify any type of tag. To do this, edit `stylesheet.css` so that it reads as follows:

```
H1 { font-size: 18; color: black }
H2 { font-size: 14; color: black }
P { font-size: 12; color: black }
.red { font-size: 12; color: red }
```

Then edit the HTML document so that it reads as follows:

```
<HTML>

<HEAD>
<TITLE>A LINKED STYLE SHEET EXAMPLE</TITLE>
<LINK REL="stylesheet" TYPE="text/css"
 HREF="stylesheet.css">
</HEAD>

<BODY>
<H1>This is an H1 Heading</H1>
<H1 class="red">This is a class red H1 Heading</H1>

<H2>This is an H2 Heading</H2>
<H2 class="red">This is a class red H2 Heading</H2>

<P>This Is A Normal Paragraph

<P class="red">This Is A Class Red Paragraph</P>

</BODY>
```

```
</HTML>
```

Save the file and open it in your browser.

c) How does the text within the tags containing `class="red"` display?

_____

_____

d) How would you create a class that sets the font weight of H1 elements to bold? How would you create a class that could be used to set the font weight of any text to bold?

_____

_____

LAB 9.2 EXERCISE ANSWERS

9.2.1 ANSWERS

a) What is the difference between how the text enclosed within the tags containing inline styles displays and how the text enclosed within the tags that do not contain inline styles displays?

Answer: The text formatted by the inline styles is colored and the size is controlled by the style definitions. When you open the file in your browser, it will look like Figure 9.5.

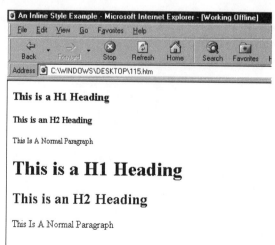

Figure 9.5 ■ It's obvious which headings were formatted with the inline styles.

b) How would you edit the inline styles so that all text enclosed within the first set of <H1> tags has a font weight of bold?

Answer: You would edit the style definition within the first <H1> tag so that it read as follows:

```
<H1 style="font-size: 18; color: blue">
```

9.2.2 ANSWERS

a) What is the difference between how the text within the tags formatted by the embedded style sheet displays and how the text within the tags formatted by the inline styles displays?

Answer: As long as the style definitions in the inline styles match those in the embedded style sheet, there should be no difference in how the text formatted by inline styles displays, and how the text formatted by the embedded style sheet displays. When you open the page in your browser, it will look like Figure 9.6.

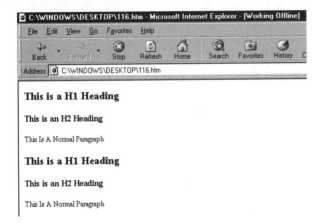

Figure 9.6 ■ There is no difference in formatting between inline styles and embedded styles, provided the definitions are the same.

b) What changed about how the page displayed?

Answer: As long as the style definitions in the embedded and linked style sheets were the same, nothing should have changed in the way the page displayed. When you opened the file in your browser, it should have looked like the screenshot in Figure 9.7.

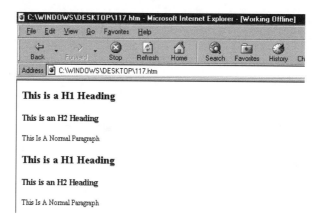

Figure 9.7 ■ **Again, provided the definitions are the same, there is no difference in formatting between embedded and linked style sheets.**

9.2.3 ANSWERS

a) Which text was displayed in green with a 24-point font?

Answer: All text that was not formatted using an inline style is displayed in green. When you opened the file in your browser, it should have looked like the screenshot in Figure 9.8.

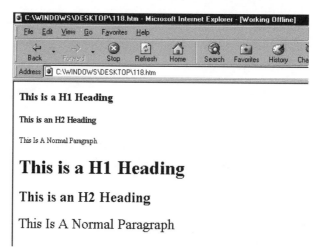

Figure 9.8 ■ **You can combine several styles into one HTML document, but inline styles will rule.**

b) If you added a link to an external style sheet that defined a style for the body to have black text, would it change the way the page displayed?

Answer: No, because the inline style in the body would have overruled the body style in the external style sheet.

9.2.4 ANSWERS

a)   How would you solve this formatting problem using inline styles?

**LAB
9.2**

Answer: In each 10% of the paragraphs that you want to display with red text, you would modify the <P> tags to read as follows:

```
<P Style="color: red">
```

It would be better to use classes for this formatting, though, because if you later decided to change the red to green, you would only have to change a single class definition instead of all those inline style declarations.

b)   How does the text within the `<P class="red">` tag display?

Answer: It looks identical to the other paragraph, except that the text color is red.

c)   How does the text within the tags containing `class="red"` display?

Answer: It looks identical to the text enclosed in the same type of tag, except that the text color is red. When you opened the file in your browser, it should have looked like the screenshot in Figure 9.9.

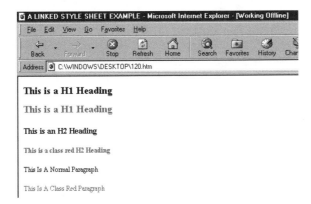

Figure 9.9 ■ You can use the class attribute to modify any type of tag.

d)   How would you create a class that sets the font weight of H1 elements to bold? How would you create a class that could be used to set the font weight of any text to bold?

Answer: To create a bold class that only modifies H1 elements, enter the following class definition in your style sheet:

```
H1.bold { font-weight: bold }
```

To create a class that can modify any text, the class definition in your style sheet should read as follows:

```
.bold { font-weight: bold }
```

LAB 9.2 SELF-REVIEW QUESTIONS

In order to test your progress, you should be able to answer the following questions.

1) Style sheets are called cascading style sheets for which of the following reasons?
   a) _____ Text can be formatted by more than one style definition according to defined rules.
   b) _____ Style sheets were first used at Cascade University.
   c) _____ You can mix them up any way you want in a cascade of styles.

2) According to the CSS specification, which of the following is true of style definitions in embedded style sheets?
   a) _____ They override inline style definitions.
   b) _____ They override linked style definitions.
   c) _____ They override neither.

3) Inline styles are which of the following?
   a) _____ Inside an HTML document.
   b) _____ Linked to a separate CSS file.
   c) _____ Placed inside the tags surrounding the text.

4) In Internet Explorer 4 and Netscape Navigator 4, which of the following is true of style definitions in embedded style sheets?
   a) _____ They override inline style definitions.
   b) _____ They override linked style definitions.
   c) _____ They override neither.

5) The background property sets which of the following?
   a) _____ The background image that appears.
   b) _____ The background color that appears.
   c) _____ Both of the above.

6) Class definitions are used to create which of the following?
   a) _____ Different styles for the same type of tags.
   b) _____ Inline styles.
   c) _____ New kinds of tags.

   Quiz answers appear in Appendix A, Section 9.2.

CHAPTER 9

TEST YOUR THINKING

In this Chapter, you learned how to format HTML documents using cascading style sheets. You learned about the three different ways of using styles and what they are best suited for. Finally, you learned how to combine the different types of style sheets and how they interact with each other.

1) Create a set of Web pages (perhaps the beginnings of a small site) that are all linked to a single style sheet. Use the style sheet to control the font size, font weight, and color of the text used in the pages.

2) Modify the Web pages by using inline styles to control the text align and background properties of the headings in the pages. Try doing the same thing using embedded style sheets. Which works better and why?

3) Create two style classes for paragraphs (the <P> tag) that have different colors for their text, but the same font size and font weight. In some of your pages, alternate the two classes.

UNDERSTANDING FRAMES

The attempt and not the deed confounds us.

—William Shakespeare (Macbeth)

Frames are one of the most-used features in HTML. If you have gone to a Web site that has a navigation bar on one part of the page and content that changes on another part of the page, then you have been to a site that uses frames. Frames allow you to display more than one HTML document at a time, and that allows you to make more interesting Web sites.

You will begin by learning to create the documents that set up the frames.

L A B   1 0 . 1

CREATING FRAMES

LAB OBJECTIVES

After this Lab, you will be able to:

- Create a Frameset Document
- Use the Noframes Tag

The frameset document is the document that contains the HTML code that creates the frames. It tells the browser whether to divide the page horizontally or vertically (or sometimes both) and how much space to assign to each frame. Figure 10.1 shows the page created by a simple frameset document that divides the page vertically and assigns 40% of the page to the left frame and 60% of the page to the right frame.

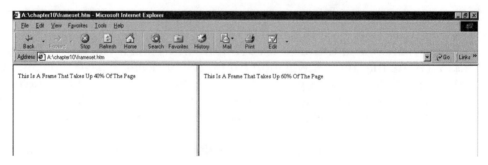

Figure 10.1 ■ A simple frameset document displayed in a browser.

The frameset document also tells the browser which HTML documents to display in each frame. A frameset document contains no content of its own. It can only display complete HTML documents. For example, the frameset document shown in Figure 10.1 displays two simple HTML pages, each containing a single line of text.

LAB 10.1 EXERCISES

10.1.1 CREATE A FRAMESET DOCUMENT

Before you can create the frameset document, however, you need to create some HTML documents to fill the frames. So create two HTML documents. The first document should display the text "This is frame one," when displayed in the browser. The other document should display the text "This is frame two," when displayed in the browser. By this time, you shouldn't need any help to create these files, but we'll give an example below, just in case.

```
<HTML>
<HEAD>
<TITLE>Frame One</TITLE>
</HEAD>
<BODY>
 <P>This Is Frame One</P>
</BODY>
</HTML>
```

Save the first file as `frame1.htm` and the other file as `frame2.htm`. Now that you have created the content, you can create the frameset document.

Make sure that you save all of the files for this Chapter in the same directory on your hard drive. If you do not do so, none of the examples in this Chapter will work!

In Chapter 2, "Introduction to HTML," you learned that every HTML document has a `<BODY>` section. The one exception to this rule is the frameset document. It contains a `<FRAMESET>` section instead of a `<BODY>` section. An empty frameset document looks like this:

```
<HTML>
<HEAD>
</HEAD>
 <FRAMESET COLS="50%,50%">
  <FRAME>
  <FRAME>
 </FRAMESET>
</HTML>
```

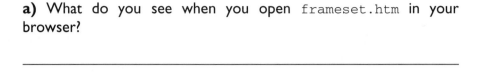

Save it as an HTML file called `frameset.htm`, and open it in your browser.

> **a)** What do you see when you open `frameset.htm` in your browser?
>
> _____
>
> _____

Open `frameset.htm` in your text editor and edit it so that it reads as follows:

```
<HTML>
<HEAD>
</HEAD>
 <FRAMESET COLS="50,25%,*">
  <FRAME>
  <FRAME>
  <FRAME>
 </FRAMESET>
</HTML>
```

Save it as an HTML file and open it in your browser.

> **b)** What changed about the way the page displayed?
>
> _____
>
> _____

> **c)** What do you think would change about the way the page displayed if you replaced the word COLS with the word ROWS in the `<FRAMESET>` tag?
>
> _____
>
> _____

Now, you are going to put some content inside the frames. Reopen `frameset.htm` and edit it so that it reads as follows:

```
<HTML>
<HEAD>
</HEAD>
 <FRAMESET COLS="50%,50%">
```

```
<FRAME SRC="frame1.htm">
<FRAME SRC="frame2.htm">
</FRAMESET>
</HTML>
```

Save `frameset.htm` and open it in your browser.

d) How does the file display in your browser now?

_____

_____

Just like other tags, you can nest `<FRAMESET>` tags. Before we do that, however, we will need another HTML file called `frame3.htm`. Create `frame3.htm` in your text editor. It should be exactly like `frame1.htm` and `frame2.htm`, except that it should display the text "This Is Frame 3" when opened in a browser. Then, open `frameset.htm` in your text editor and edit it so that it reads as follows:

```
<HTML>
<HEAD>
</HEAD>
 <FRAMESET ROWS="50%,50%">
   <FRAMESET COLS="50%,50%">
    <FRAME SRC="frame1.htm">
    <FRAME SRC="frame2.htm">
   </FRAMESET>
  <FRAME SRC="frame3.htm">
 </FRAMESET>
</HTML>
```

Save the text as an HTML file and open it in your browser.

e) How does the page display in your browser now that you have nested frames?

_____

_____

10.1.2 USE THE NOFRAMES TAG

So far in this Chapter, you have learned to create pages with frames. However, there are some browsers that cannot display frames. Therefore, you have to take these browsers into account when you create a page using frames. Open the HTML file you created earlier in your text editor and edit it to match the following example:

```
<HTML>
<HEAD>
</HEAD>

 <FRAMESET COLS="50%,50%">
  <FRAME SRC="frame1.htm">
  <FRAME SRC="frame2.htm">
 </FRAMESET>

 <NOFRAMES>
  <P>
    You Must Have A Browser That Can Display
    Frames To See This Web Page
  </P>
 </NOFRAMES>
</HTML>
```

Save it as an HTML file and open it in your browser.

a) How does the file display in your browser now that you have inserted the <NOFRAMES> tag?

_____

_____

Of course, telling the person attempting to view a Web page to get a better browser is not a great solution if you want to encourage more people to see your Web page.

b) What would be a better message to include within the <NOFRAMES> tag?

_____

_____

LAB 10.1 EXERCISE ANSWERS

10.1.1 ANSWERS

a) What do you see when you open `frameset.htm` in your browser?

Answer: When you view the file in a Web browser, it should look like the page shown in Figure 10.2.

Figure 10.2 ■ An empty frameset document.

The page is divided in half because you used the COLS attribute of the <FRAMESET> tag to set the width of each frame to 50% of the Web page. You could also have set the width in pixels by leaving off the percentage. For example, to set the columns to be 100 and 400 pixels wide, you would use the following code:

```
<FRAMESET COLS="100,400">
```

In this case, however, you would have a problem if the browser was displaying a screen more than 500 pixels wide. You can deal with this problem by rewriting the code as follows:

```
<FRAMESET COLS="100,*">
```

The asterisk (*) directs the browser to make the second column as wide as the screen that remains after the 100-pixel-wide column is made. You can replace any one value of the COLS attribute with a *, but no more than one.

You should know that if you select View Source in a browser displaying a frameset page, you will only see the HTML code of the frameset page. You will not see the HTML code that is in the frames. To see the HTML code of a page enclosed in a frame, right-click on the page, and then select View Source *on the pop-up menu. Similarly, the title displayed by a browser displaying a frameset page is the title of the frameset page itself. Titles included in frameset pages are never displayed! So, remember to include a title in your frameset page!*

You edited Frameset.htm to have three column values.

b) What changed about the way the page displayed?

Answer: It should look like the page shown in Figure 10.3.

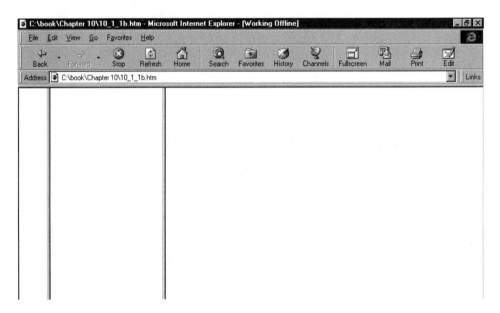

Figure 10.3 ■ A frameset document with three columns.

If you see a gray area instead of a third empty page, then you probably forgot to insert one of the <FRAME> tags. You can have as many columns as you want, but you must have a frame tag for each one, because you use the <FRAME> tags to define the content that appears in each frame.

c) What do you think would change about the way the page displayed if you replaced the word COLS with the word ROWS in the <FRAMESET> tag?

Answer: After you replace the word COLS with the word ROWS, your frameset tag should read as follows:

```
<FRAMESET ROWS="50,25%,*">
```

When you view the file in a Web browser, it should look like the page shown in Figure 10.4.

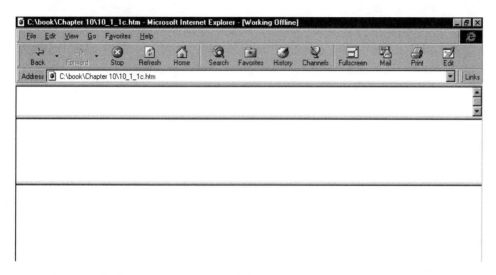

Figure 10.4 ■ A frameset page with three rows.

You have replaced the COLS attribute of the frameset tag with the ROWS attribute. The ROWS attribute takes the same values as the COLS attribute. You may be wondering whether you can use both the ROWS and COLS attributes in a frameset tag? The answer is yes, but it gets confusing trying to remember which frame is which. Therefore, we recommend that you never do this! You will learn later in the Chapter how best to combine columns and rows in frames.

You edited `frameset.htm` *to add some content in the frames.*

d) How does the file display in your browser now?

Answer: It should look the like the page shown in Figure 10.5.

You edited the <FRAME> tags so that they read as follows:

```
<FRAME SRC="frame1.htm">
<FRAME SRC="frame2.htm">
```

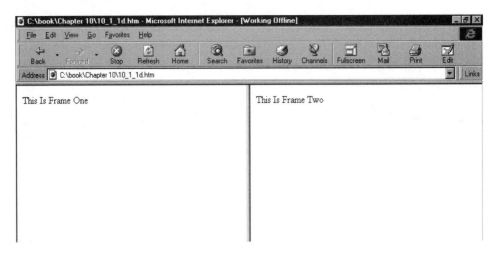

Figure 10.5 ■ A frameset page with content added.

By using the SRC (or *Source*) attribute of the frame tag, you tell the browser which HTML file to display in the frame. Each frame tag requires a SRC attribute or else it will be blank as the frames were in the earlier Exercises. You can use any valid HTML document as the source for a frame—even other people's Web pages. For instance, to make Microsoft.com the source of a frame's content, you would edit the SRC attribute to read as follows:

```
SRC="http://www.microsoft.com"
```

Then, when you displayed your frameset document in the browser, you would see Microsoft.com displayed in one frame.

You should note that it is generally not considered ethical to place other people's pages within frames on your own Web site. Moreover, many Web sites have methods (using scripting or server-side code that we don't cover in this book) that automatically prevent you from doing so. If you really want to include other people's content in your site, provide a link that opens in a full browser window (we show you how to do that later in this Chapter) and give them proper credit.

You edited frameset.htm to include nested frameset tags.

e)   How does the page display in your browser now that you have nested frames?

Answer: It should look the like the page shown in Figure 10.6.

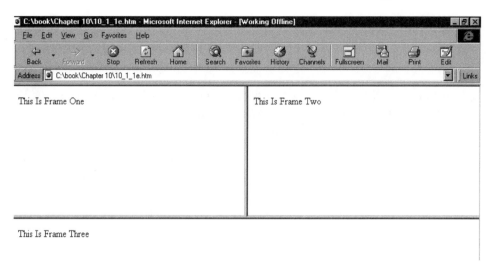

Figure 10.6 ■ A frameset page with nested frameset tags.

Earlier, we told you that we would show you the proper way to combine rows and columns using the frameset tags. The proper way is to use nested frameset tags, as you just did. You can replace any frame tag, within a set of frameset tags, with another set of frameset tags.

Please, do not get carried away in your use of frames. You should not use more than three frames in any Web page, and you are better off limiting yourself to two. Viewers of Web pages find multiframe pages highly confusing. And it is not too easy for the Web page designer to keep everything straight either!

10.1.2 ANSWERS

You inserted <NOFRAME> tags in frameset.htm.

a) How does the file display in your browser now that you have inserted the <NOFRAMES> tag?

Answer: When you view the file in a Web browser, it should look exactly like the page shown in Figure 10.1.

You will not see any of the text placed within the noframes tag, because your browser can display frames. Only viewers of the Web page who use a browser that cannot display frames will see the text. Of course, by now, there are very few people using a browser that cannot display frames. You still, however, have to allow for this small group of Web users.

b) What would be a better message to include within the <NOFRAMES> tag?

Answer: The best message to include is a link to a version of your Web site that does not use frames.

You may think that it is a lot of work to create both a version of you Web site with frames and a version without frames, but actually, it is pretty easy. Generally, all you have to do is to create a new introductory page with links to the content. After all, your content is already in separate HTML pages. Alternatively, you could include the frameless version of the page within the <NOFRAMES> tag. For example, if your frames version of the site has a list of links in a left-hand frame that displays in the right-hand frame, then you would simply place the entire list of links from the left-hand frame document between the <NOFRAMES> tags.

LAB 10.1 SELF-REVIEW QUESTIONS

In order to test your progress, you should be able to answer the following questions.

1) All HTML documents must include <BODY> tags.
   a) _____ True
   b) _____ False

2) Which of the following is not an attribute of the <FRAMESET> tag?
   a) _____ COLS
   b) _____ SRC
   c) _____ ROWS

3) Which of the following is correct HTML?
   a) _____ <FRAMES>
   b) _____ <NOFRAME SRC="stuff.htm">
   c) _____ <FRAME ROWS="30%,*">
   d) _____ <FRAMESET ROWS="30%,*">

4) Which of the following is not a unit in which you can set the COLS attribute?
   a) _____ Pixels
   b) _____ Inches
   c) _____ Percent of the page

5) Why should you not use more than three frames on a Web page?
   a) _____ Because it is confusing to the reader of the page.
   b) _____ Because the COLS attribute cannot have a value higher than three.
   c) _____ Because it is confusing to the author of the page.
   d) _____ Both a) and d)

Quiz answers appear in Appendix A, Section 10.1.

L A B   1 0 . 2

FORMATTING FRAMES

LAB OBJECTIVES

After this Lab, you will be able to:

- Set Margins and Borders on Frames
- Set Resizing and Scrolling on Frames

In the previous Lab, you learned to create basic frames. In this Lab, you will learn how to format the frames displayed by the frameset document. This will allow you to have greater control over the "look and feel" of the Web pages that you create.

LAB 10.2 EXERCISES

10.2.1 SET MARGINS AND BORDERS ON FRAMES

Open `frameset.htm` in your text editor and edit it so that it reads as follows:

```
<HTML>

<HEAD>
 <TITLE>A Frameset Document With Margins</TITLE>
</HEAD>

<FRAMESET COLS="50%,50%">
 <FRAME SRC="frame1.htm" MARGINHEIGHT="100">
 <FRAME SRC="frame2.htm" MARGINWIDTH="100">
</FRAMESET>

<NOFRAMES>
 <P>
  You Must Have A Browser That Can Display
  Frames To See This Web Page
```

```
    </P>
</NOFRAMES>

</HTML>
```

Save it as an HTML file and open it in your browser.

a) How does the document display in your browser now that you have added margins to the frames?

_____

_____

b) How would you edit the HTML document so that both frames displayed their content with 100 pixel vertical and horizontal margins?

_____

_____

Now that you have set the margins, you are going to add borders to the frames. You do this just as you set the margins through the use of attributes of the <FRAME> tag. Open `frameset.htm` in your text editor and edit it so that it reads as follows:

```
<HTML>

<HEAD>
 <TITLE>A Frameset Document With Borders</TITLE>
</HEAD>

<FRAMESET COLS="50%,50%">
 <FRAME SRC="frame1.htm"FRAMEBORDER="No">
 <FRAME SRC="frame2.htm" FRAMEBORDER="No">
</FRAMESET>

<NOFRAMES>
 <P>
  You Must Have A Browser That Can Display
  Frames To See This Web Page
</NOFRAMES>

</HTML>
```

Save it as an HTML file and open it in your browser.

c) How does the document display in your browser now that you have set the FRAMEBORDER attribute for the frames?

_____

_____

You can also set the color of the border. Edit `frameset.htm` in you text editor so that it reads as follows:

```
<HTML>

<HEAD>
 <TITLE>
  A Frameset Document With
  Colored Borders
 </TITLE>
</HEAD>

<FRAMESET COLS="50%,50%">
 <FRAME SRC="frame1.htm" BORDERCOLOR="Black">
 <FRAME SRC="frame2.htm" BORDERCOLOR="Black">
</FRAMESET>

<NOFRAMES>
 <P>
  You Must Have A Browser That Can Display
  Frames To See This Web Page</P>
</NOFRAMES>

</HTML>
```

Save it as an HTML file and open it in your browser.

d) How does the document display in your browser now that you have set the BORDERCOLOR attribute for the frames?

_____

_____

10.2.2 SET RESIZING AND SCROLLING ON FRAMES

So far in this Lab, you have controlled the borders and margins of the frames when they display in the browser. A lot of decisions remain regarding the way the frames display on the user's browser. For example, the user of the browser can still change the size of the frames that you set in your frameset document.

To see how this works, open `frameset.htm` in your browser, position the mouse pointer over the frame border so that it changes to a `<->` symbol, and then hold down the left mouse button and drag the mouse to the left.

a) What happens when you drag the mouse to the left?

_____

_____

Now, suppose you want to prevent the viewers of your Web page from making the frames different sizes. Open `frameset.htm` and edit it so that it reads as follows:

```
<HTML>

<HEAD>
 <TITLE>
  A Frameset Document You Can't Resize
 </TITLE>
</HEAD>

<FRAMESET COLS="50%,50%">
 <FRAME SRC="frame1.htm" NORESIZE>
 <FRAME SRC="frame2.htm" NORESIZE>
</FRAMESET>

<NOFRAMES>
 <P>
  You Must Have A Browser That Can Display
  Frames To See This Web Page</P>
</NOFRAMES>

</HTML>
```

Save the file, open it in your browser, and try to change the size of the frames.

b) Can you change the size of the frames now that you have added the NORESIZE attribute?

_____

_____

The user of the browser can also make scrollbars appear within your frames. To see how this works, edit frameset.htm so that it reads as follows:

```
<HTML>

<HEAD>
 <TITLE>
  A Frameset Document With Set Frame Widths
 </TITLE>
</HEAD>

<FRAMESET COLS="300,300">
 <FRAME SRC="frame1.htm" MARGINWIDTH="150" NORESIZE>
 <FRAME SRC="frame2.htm" MARGINWIDTH="150" NORESIZE>
</FRAMESET>

<NOFRAMES>
 <P>
  You Must Have A Browser That Can Display
  Frames To See This Web Page</P>
</NOFRAMES>

</HTML>
```

Save the file, open it in your browser, and reduce the size of the browser until the width of the browser window is less than 600 pixels.

c) What happens when you reduce the width of the browser window to less than 600 pixels?

_____

_____

Now, reopen frameset.htm and edit it so that it reads as follows:

```
<HTML>

<HEAD>
```

```
<TITLE>
A Frameset Document With No Scrolling
</TITLE>
</HEAD>

<FRAMESET COLS="300,300">
 <FRAME SRC="frame1.htm" MARGINWIDTH="150"
  SCROLLING="No">
 <FRAME SRC="frame2.htm" MARGINWIDTH="150"
  SCROLLING="No">
</FRAMESET>

<NOFRAMES>
 <P>
  You Must Have A Browser That Can Display
  Frames To See This Web Page</P>
</NOFRAMES>

</HTML>
```

Save the file, open it in your browser, and reduce the size of the browser until the width of the browser window is less than 600 pixels.

d) What happens, now that you have set the SCROLLING attribute, when you reduce the width of the browser window to less than 600 pixels?

_____

_____

LAB 10.2 EXERCISE ANSWERS

10.2.1 ANSWERS

a) How does the document display in your browser now that you have added margins to the frames?

Answer: The page should now look like the one shown in Figure 10.7.

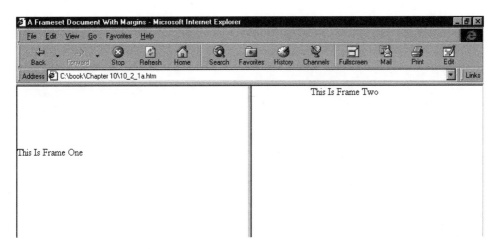

Figure 10.7 ■ The Web page after the frame margins have been set.

The margin of a frame is the distance between the edge of the frame and the edge of the text contained in the frame. When you set the MARGIN-HEIGHT and MARGINWIDTH attributes, you set the width of the margin in pixels. The MARGINHEIGHT attribute sets the top and bottom margins of the frame. The MARGINWIDTH attribute sets the left and right margins of the frame. If you do not set the margins of the frame, the browser will set them itself. Depending upon which browser you are using, this default margin can vary from 8 to 14 pixels.

 If you only set either the MARGINHEIGHT *or* MARGINWIDTH *attribute in a frame, then the browser will set the value of the one you didn't specify to 0 pixels. So, unless you want your text right up against the edge of a frame, make sure you set both the* MARGINHEIGHT *and* MARGINWIDTH *attributes.*

b) How would you edit the HTML document so that both frames displayed their content with 100-pixel vertical and horizontal margins?

Answer: You would edit frameset.htm *so that the* <FRAME> *tags read as follows:*

```
<FRAME SRC="frame1.htm" MARGINHEIGHT="100"
  MARGINWIDTH="100">
<FRAME SRC="frame2.htm" MARGINHEIGHT="100"
  MARGINWIDTH="100">
```

When you displayed the file in your browser, it would look like the Web page shown in Figure 10.8.

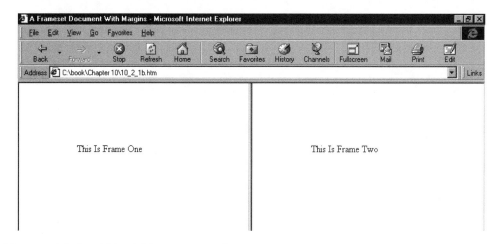

Figure 10.8 ■ The Web page after the frame margins have been set to 100 pixels.

c) How does the document display in your browser now that you have set the FRAMEBORDER attribute for the frames?

Answer: How the document displays depends upon which browser you are viewing it in. If you view the document in Internet Explorer, you will see a page that looks like the one shown in Figure 10.9.

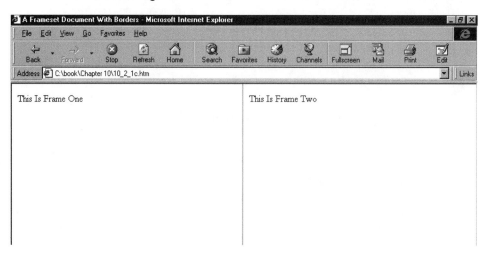

Figure 10.9 ■ The Web page with frame borders in Internet Explorer.

If you view the document in Netscape Navigator, you will see a page that looks like the one shown in Figure 10.10.

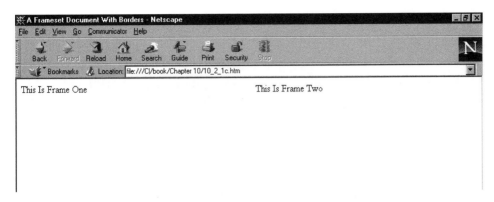

Figure 10.10 ■ The Web page with frame borders in Netscape Navigator.

In Internet Explorer, you cannot truly set the FRAMEBORDER attribute to *No.* The viewer of the page will always see, at least, a very thin border. In Netscape Navigator, though, you can really set the attribute to *No.* The viewer of the page, in Navigator, sees no visible border between the frames at all. There is one thing to be careful of, though. Make sure that when you set the FRAMEBORDER attribute to *No,* that you do it for all of the frames within the same set of <FRAMESET> tags. Otherwise, you may still get borders displayed, depending upon which browser is being used to view the page. Alternatively, you can set the FRAMEBORDER attribute within the <FRAMESET> tag and not within the <FRAME> tags. This will apply the same FRAMEBORDER attribute value to all of the frames within the <FRAMESET> tags. The best rule is to leave nothing about the way your pages display to be determined by the browser!

d) How does the document display in your browser now that you have set the BORDERCOLOR attribute for the frames?

Answer: The page displayed in your browser should look like the one shown in Figure 10.11.

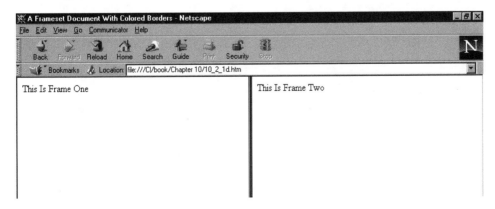

Figure 10.11 ■ The Web page with the *BORDERCOLOR* attribute set.

You can set the color of the BORDERCOLOR attribute in any of the 140 named colors accepted by either Internet Explorer or Netscape Navigator, or you can use a hex color value. You should take the same approach when setting the BORDERCOLOR attribute that we recommend for setting the FRAMEBORDER attribute. Avoid setting the borders of adjacent frames to different colors or setting one frame and not the other. Again, you could get inconsistent results, depending upon which browser the viewer of your page is using.

10.2.2 ANSWERS

a) What happens when you drag the mouse to the left?

Answer: The width of the left-hand frame decreases, and the width of the right-hand frame increases, so that the page now looks like the one displayed in Figure 10.12.

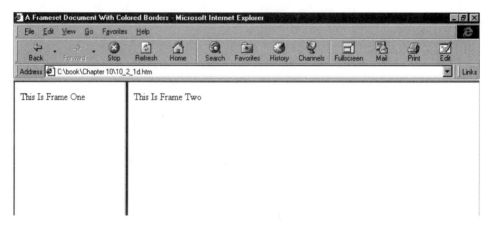

Figure 10.12 ■ The Web page after the frames have been resized.

b) Can you change the size of the frames now that you have added the NORESIZE attribute?

Answer: No, you cannot. Now, when you position your mouse pointer over the border between the frames, it does not change to the resize pointer (the resize pointer is the one that looks like <->). The screen in Figure 10.13 shows an example of this.

There are very few situations in which you do not want to allow the viewer of a page to resize the frame. The most common one is where you are running an advertisement in a separate frame, and you want to make sure that the viewer of the page has to see the whole ad. Generally, though, it is best to leave the size of the frames up to the viewer of the page. After all, if the reader wants to resize the page, it probably means that he or she are trying to see the page better, which is something that you, the Web page author, want as well.

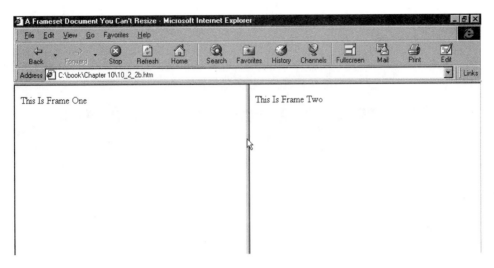

Figure 10.13 ■ The Web page with the frames set to NORESIZE.

c) What happens when you reduce the width of the browser window to less than 600 pixels?

Answer: Horizontal scrollbars will appear along the bottom of the frames so that the page appears similar to the one shown in Figure 10.14.

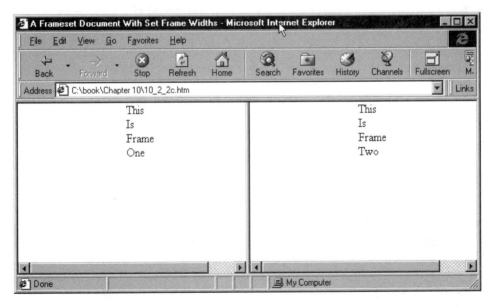

Figure 10.14 ■ The Web page after the width of the browser window has been reduced.

If you reduced the height of the browser window in a similar fashion, then vertical scrollbars will appear on the right side of each frame.

**LAB
10.2**

d) What happens, now that you have set the SCROLLING attribute, when you reduce the width of the browser window to less than 600 pixels?

Answer: No scrollbars appear, regardless of how much you reduce the width of the browser window, so that the page appears similar to the one shown in Figure 10.15.

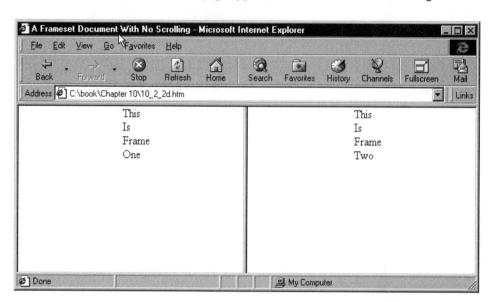

Figure 10.15 ■ The Web page after the width of the browser window has been reduced and the SCROLLING attribute set to *No*.

The SCROLLING attribute of the frame tag can take the following values:

- **Yes**—Horizontal and vertical scrollbars are always displayed.
- **No**—No scrollbars are ever displayed, however small the frame gets.
- **Auto**—Scrollbars are displayed whenever any of the frame content is hidden.

If you do not set the SCROLLING attribute, then the browser acts as if you had set the attribute to *Auto*. The only reason to set the SCROLLING attribute of a frame to *No* are aesthetic ones. In other words, you don't like the way the frame looks with scrollbars. The price you pay for this visual appeal is that the viewer of a page may not be able to see all the content of the frame. You have to decide which is more important: conveying information or making your page look nice. Generally, it is better to place a priority on conveying information to the viewer of the page and leave the default setting of *Auto*. After all, are you more likely to come back to a page that is unattractive, but useable, or one that looks nice, but is hard to use? (Of course, hopefully, you can make your pages both attractive and useful!)

LAB 10.2 SELF-REVIEW QUESTIONS

In order to test your progress, you should be able to answer the following questions.

1) Which of the following is correct HTML?
   a) _____ `<FRAME MARGIN="25">`
   b) _____ `<FRAME MARGINHEIGHT="25">`
   c) _____ `<FRAME BORDER="30">`
   d) _____ `<FRAME FRAMEBORDER="Auto">`

2) Which of the following tags has a FRAMEBORDER attribute?
   a) _____ `<FRAME>`
   b) _____ `<FRAMESET>`
   c) _____ Neither a) nor b)
   d) _____ Both a) and b)

3) You cannot include both COLS and ROWS attributes in the same `<FRAME SET>` tag.
   a) _____ True
   b) _____ False

4) Which of the following is not an attribute of the `<FRAME>` tag?
   a) _____ Marginheight
   b) _____ Frameborder
   c) _____ Border
   d) _____ Noresize

5) Which of the following is the default setting for the SCROLLING attribute?
   a) _____ *No*
   b) _____ *True*
   c) _____ *Auto*
   d) _____ *Yes*

Quiz answers appear in Appendix A, Section 10.2.

L A B   1 0 . 3

USING LINKS
WITH FRAMES

LAB OBJECTIVES

After this Lab, you will be able to:

- Create Links Between Frames
- Use Reserved Names with Links

The most common use of frames in HTML is to create a Web page with two frames—a menu bar in one frame and content displayed in another frame. When you click on an item in the menu frame, the page displayed in the other frame changes. In this Lab, you will learn to create a page with links between frames.

LAB 10.3 EXERCISES

10.3.1 CREATE LINKS BETWEEN FRAMES

Open `frameset.htm` and edit it so that it reads as follows:

```
<HTML>

<HEAD>
 <TITLE>
  A Frameset Document With Links
 </TITLE>
</HEAD>

<FRAMESET COLS="50%,50%">
 <FRAME SRC="frame1.htm" NAME="menuframe">
```

```
<FRAME SRC="frame2.htm" NAME="targetframe">
</FRAMESET>

<NOFRAMES>
 <P>
  You Must Have A Browser That Can Display
  Frames To See This Web Page</P>
</NOFRAMES>

</HTML>
```

Save `frameset.htm` as an HTML file. Now, open `frame1.htm` in your text editor and edit it so that it reads as follows:

```
<HTML>

<HEAD>
 <TITLE>Frame One</TITLE>
</HEAD>

<BODY>
<P>
 <A HREF="frame3.htm" TARGET="targetframe">
  Click Here To Display Frame3.htm
 </A>

<P>
 <A HREF="frame2.htm" TARGET="targetframe">
  Click Here To Display Frame2.htm
 </A>
</BODY>


</HTML>
```

Save `frame1.htm` as an HTML file. Now, open `frameset.htm` in your browser.

a) What happens when you click on the link `Click Here To Display Frame3.htm`? What happens when you next click on the link `Click Here To Display Frame2.htm`?

_____

_____

Open `frame1.htm` in your text editor and edit it so that it reads as follows:

```
<HTML>

<HEAD>
 <TITLE>Frame One</TITLE>
</HEAD>

<BODY>
<P>
 <A HREF="frame3.htm" TARGET="noframe">
  Click Here To Display Frame3.htm
 </A>

<P>
 <A HREF="frame2.htm" TARGET="noframe">
  Click Here To Display Frame2.htm
 </A>
</BODY>

</HTML>
```

Save the file as an HTML file and open it in your browser.

> **b)** What happens when you click on the link Click Here To Display Frame2.htm, now that you set the TARGET attribute equal to a NAME attribute of a frame that doesn't exist?

_____

_____

Now, reopen frame1.htm in your text editor and edit it so that it reads as follows:

```
<HTML>

<HEAD>
 <TITLE>Frame One</TITLE>
</HEAD>

<BODY>
<P>
 <A HREF="frame3.htm" TARGET="menuframe">
  Click Here To Display Frame3.htm
 </A>

<P>
 <A HREF="frame2.htm" TARGET="menuframe">
  Click Here To Display Frame2.htm
```

```
  </A>
</BODY>

</HTML>
```

Save the `frame1.htm` as an HTML file and open `frameset.htm` in your browser.

> **c)** What happens when you click on the link `Click Here To Display Frame3.htm`, now that you have set the `TARGET` attribute equal to *menuframe*? Would the same thing happen if you had not set the `TARGET` attribute at all?

10.3.2 USE RESERVED NAMES WITH LINKS

In the previous Exercise, we told you that you have to set `TARGET` attributes equal to existing `NAME` attributes. This is not quite true. You don't always have to set the `TARGETS` of links only to the `NAMES` of different frames, because there are also several reserved names that you can use. A reserved name is a name that has a set meaning specified by the HTML standard. It is called *reserved* because you cannot use it as a name for anything other than its standard purpose. In this Exercise, you are going to use several of these reserved names in links.

Open `frame2.htm` in your text editor and edit it so that it reads as follows:

```
<HTML>

<HEAD>
 <TITLE>Frame Two</TITLE>
</HEAD>

<BODY>
<P>
<P>
 <A HREF="frame1.htm" TARGET="_parent">
  Click Here To Display Frame1.htm
  with _parent as the target.
 </A>
</BODY>

</HTML>
```

Save `frame2.htm` as an HTML file. Open `frame1.htm` in your text editor and edit it so that it reads as follows:

```
<HTML>

<HEAD>
 <TITLE>Frame One</TITLE>
</HEAD>

<BODY>
<P>
 <A HREF="frame3.htm" TARGET="_top">
  Click Here To Display Frame3.htm
  with _top as the target
 </A>

<P>
 <A HREF="frame2.htm" TARGET="_blank">
  Click Here To Display Frame2.htm
  with _blank as the target.
 </A>

<P>
 <A HREF="frame2.htm" TARGET="_self">
  Click Here To Display Frame3.htm
  with _self as the target.
 </A>

</BODY>

</HTML>
```

Save `frame1.htm` as an HTML file and open `frameset.htm` in your browser.

a) What happens when you click on the link `Click Here To Display Frame2.htm` with `_blank` as the `target`?

_____

_____

Close one of the browser windows and make sure that `frameset.htm` is open in the remaining browser window.

b) What happens when you click on the link `Click Here To Display Frame1.htm` with _parent as the target?

_____

_____

Click on the `back` button of the browser. Make sure that `frameset.htm` is displayed in the browser.

c) What happens when you click on the link `Click Here to Display Frame3.htm` with _top as the target?

_____

_____

Click on the `refresh` button of the browser to reload `frameset.htm`.

d) What happens when you click on the link `Click Here To Display Frame3.htm` with _self as the target?

_____

_____

LAB 10.3 EXERCISE ANSWERS

10.3.1 ANSWERS

a)   What happens when you click on the link `Click Here To Display Frame3.htm`? What happens when you next click on the link `Click Here To Display Frame2.htm`?

Answer: When you click on the link `Click Here To Display Frame3.htm`, *the file displayed in the right-hand frame should change to* `frame3.htm`. *The browser window should now look like the one shown in Figure 10.16.*

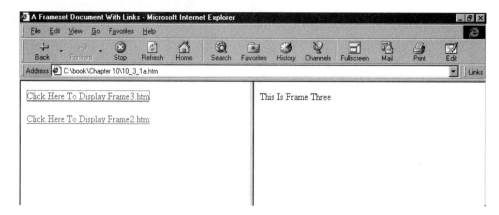

**LAB
10.3**

Figure 10.16 ■ The view of the browser window after the user clicks on the first targeted link.

When you next click on the link Click Here To Display Frame2.htm, the file displayed in the right-hand frame should change to frame2.htm. The browser window should now look like the one shown in Figure 10.17.

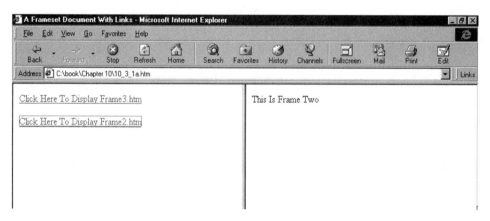

Figure 10.17 ■ The view of the browser window after the user clicks on the second targeted link.

The NAME attribute of the <FRAME> tag tells the browser that the frame has a name that can be used in HTML to refer to the frame. The TARGET attribute of the <A> tag then tells the browser the name of the frame in which the linked HTML document should be opened. By using a combination of NAME attributes and TARGET attributes, you can control where the linked document is displayed in the browser.

b) What happens when you click on the link `Click Here To Display Frame2.htm`, now that you set the `TARGET` attribute equal to a `NAME` attribute of a frame that doesn't exist?

Answer: `Frame2.htm` is displayed in a new browser window instead of being displayed in any part of the first browser window. Your screen should now contain two browser windows, like those shown in Figure 10.18.

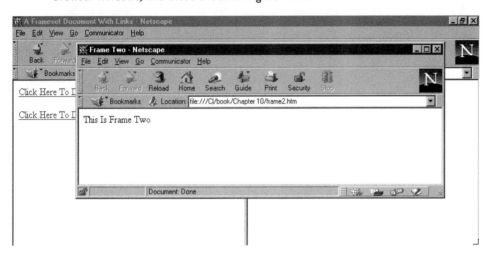

Figure 10.18 ■ The screen with two browser windows open.

You should never use the `TARGET` attribute without assigning it to existing `NAME` attributes of your frames because, as you saw above, the browser will become confused as to where you are telling it to open the linked document. It will become similarly confused if you misspell the name when you set the target. Generally, if you set a `TARGET` attribute of a link to a `NAME` attribute that doesn't exist, the browser will respond by opening the linked document in a new browser window. However, there is no guarantee that this will always be the browser's response.

You especially have to be careful of how you assign names when working with Internet Explorer. Internet Explorer will only recognize `NAME` attributes, which have identical capitalization. For example, if you set the `NAME` attribute of a frame to Myframe, and the `TARGET` attribute of a link to myframe, Internet Explorer will treat them as different words and open the link in a new browser window instead of in the named frame.

c) What happens when you click on the link `Click Here To Display Frame3.htm`, now that you have set the `TARGET` attribute equal to *menuframe*? Would the same thing happen if you had not set the `TARGET` attribute at all?

Answer: When you click on the link `Click Here To Display Frame3.htm`, now that you have set the `TARGET` attribute equal to menuframe, *the page displayed should* look like the one shown in Figure 10.19. The same thing would happen if you had not set the TARGET attribute at all.

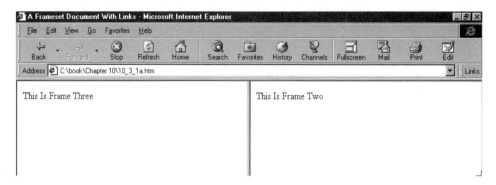

Figure 10.19 ■ The browser after clicking on the link targeted to menuframe.

The reason that setting the TARGET attribute to the name of the frame in which the link is contained is the same as not setting the TARGET attribute at all, because by default a link opens in the same frame or window that the link is in.

10.3.2 ANSWERS

a) What happens when you click on the link Click Here To Display Frame2.htm with _blank as the target?

Answer: When you click on the link Click Here To Display Frame2.htm *with* _blank *as the target, the linked document is opened in a new browser window. Your screen should now look like the one shown in Figure 10.20.*

The names that you are setting the TARGET attributes equal to in this Exercise are known as reserved names, because the browser sets their meanings. This means that you cannot set the NAME attributes of any frame created by you to these values. In fact, you cannot even use a name that begins with the same sequence of characters as any of the reserved names, because the browser treats any name that starts with the same characters as the reserved name. For example, the name _toplevelname is considered by the browser to be exactly the same as the reserved name _top. There are four reserved names, all of which begin with an underscore (_) character.

The reserved name _blank always opens a linked document in a new browser window. This is an excellent target to use with links to other people's Web pages. Remember, we said earlier that it was not good practice to open other people's Web pages inside a frame. If you set the target of the link to _blank, then the other person's Web page will open in its own window, but your Web page will still be open as well.

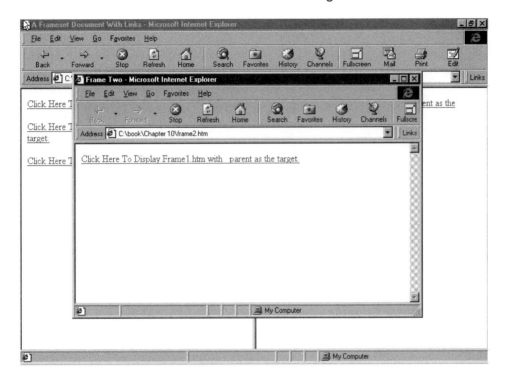

Figure 10.20 ■ **The screen after clicking on the link** `targeted at _blank.`

b) What happens when you click on the link `Click Here To Display Frame1.htm with _parent as the target`?

Answer: When you click on the link `Click Here To Display Frame1.htm with _parent as the target, your browser should look like the one shown in Figure 10.21.`

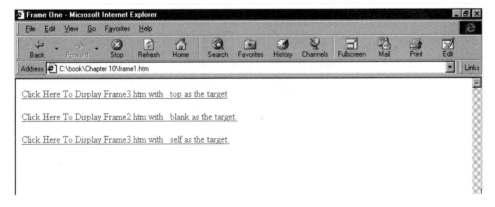

Figure 10.21 ■ **The screen after clicking on the link** `targeted at _parent.`

Clicking on a link, with a TARGET attribute set to _parent, opens the linked document in the previous window. If you are not using nested frames, this is usually the window displaying the frameset document. If there is no previous window, then _parent is treated just like _self.

c) What happens when you click on the link Click Here to Display Frame3.htm with _top as the target?

Answer: When you click on the link Click Here to Display Frame3.htm *with* _top *as the* target, *your browser should look like the one shown in Figure 10.22.*

Figure 10.22 ■ The screen after clicking on the link targeted at _top.

Clicking on a link, with a TARGET attribute set to _top, opens the linked document in the main browser window. It does not matter how many frames-deep the link is placed: The linked document still opens in the main window.

There are two common uses for links with _top target. The first use is to link to external sites without placing them inside your frames. Many Web page viewers prefer loading the next site within the same browser window, because they do not want multiple browsers open on their computer. As a Web page author, though, this method has the disadvantage of closing your Web site. Once the reader leaves your Web site, they may never come back. The second use is to display pages that do not fit within a frame. If the linked page contains a lot of information, then it is usually easier to read when it is displayed in a complete browser window than when it is in a frame. Remember, the whole point of a Web page is to get someone to read your content. Don't let your design get in the way!

d) What happens when you click on the link Click Here To Display Frame3.htm with _self as the target?

Answer: When you click on the link Click Here To Display Frame3.htm *with* _self *as the* target, *your browser should look like the one shown in Figure 10.23.*

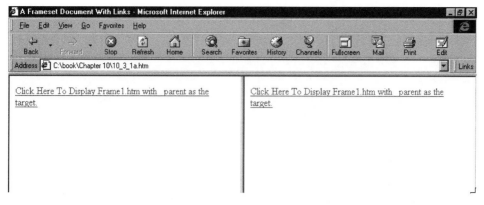

LAB 10.3

Figure 10.23 ■ **The screen after clicking on the link `targeted at _self`.**

Clicking on a link with a TARGET attribute set to _self opens the linked document in the same frame in which the link itself is contained. It does not matter how many frames-deep the link is placed: The linked document still opens in that frame. Setting the TARGET attribute to _self is the same as not setting the target at all, because _self is the default setting for the TARGET attribute.

In actual practice, there is no real use for setting the target equal to _self, other than to make your HTML completely clear to anyone reading it. It is standard practice in computer science, however, to allow programmers to set default values explicitly, and the creators of HTML followed this standard.

LAB 10.3 SELF-REVIEW QUESTIONS

In order to test your progress, you should be able to answer the following questions.

1) Which of the following is correct HTML?
   a) _____ `<FRAMESET NAME="Main">`
   b) _____ `<FRAME NAME="Main>`
   c) _____ `<A HREF="frame1.htm" NAME="Main">`
   d) _____ `<A HREF="frame1.htm TARGET="Main">`

2) Which of the following is not a reserved name?
   a) _____ `_top`
   b) _____ `_own`
   c) _____ `_new`
   d) _____ `_self`

3) Clicking on a link targeted at _parent opens the linked document in which of the following?

a) _____The previous window.

b) _____The main browser window.

c) _____The current window, if there is no previous window.

d) _____Both a) and c)

e) _____Both a) and b)

4) You can set the NAME attribute of a frame to _top.

a) _____ True

b) _____ False

5) Setting the TARGET attribute of a link to the name of the frame in which it is displayed is the same as.

a) _____Setting it to _self

b) _____Setting it to _top

c) _____Not setting it at all

d) _____Both a) and c)

d) _____None of the above

Quiz answers appear in Appendix A, Section 10.3.

C H A P T E R   1 0

TEST YOUR THINKING

1) Visit several Web sites that use frames. View the sources of the various frame documents. How are the frames linked to each other? Are the Web sites using frames for purposes which increase the usefulness of the site, or are they just an unnecessary complication? Try to think of ways in which you could make the same site work without using frames.

2) Take a menu from a restaurant that divides its meals into several sections or categories (menus from Chinese restaurants are usually good for this). Create a Web site which has a list of the categories on the left in one frame. When you click upon a category, the list of meals in that category should display in another frame. Then, place these two frames below a third frame containing the name, address, and phone number of the restaurant.

APPENDIX A

ANSWERS TO SELF-REVIEW QUESTIONS

CHAPTER 1
Lab 1.1 ■ Self-Review Answers

Question	Answer	Comments
1)	d	The Netscape browser is called Netscape Navigator. The complete Netscape package, which also contains features like Smart Browsing, Instant Messaging, and a scalable address book, is known as Netscape Communicator.
2)	a	True. Executables are self-contained programs. An executable may be the file that is downloaded to your machine. An executable may also be the program that runs to install the browser on your PC.
3)	c	An Internet Service Provider is a company that provides you and your PC with a connection to the World Wide Web. Some of the most well-known ISPs are AOL, MSN, Erol's, and ATT, to name a few.
4)	a	Pressing CTRL + A simultaneously selects all of the files within a folder.
5)	b	HTML is not case-sensitive.
6)	b	False. However, there are browser cache settings available in both Internet Explorer and Netscape Navigator that enable you to set how often the cache is emptied.
7)	c	Memory Cache is the name of the location where cached files are kept.
8)	b	False. It is perfectly safe to delete a cookie.
9)	b	False. Choosing and clicking on the Refresh option from within the browser menu options will load a newer version (if available) of a Web page.

Lab 1.2 ■ Self-Review Answers

Question	Answer	Comments
1)	b	A server responds to a client's request.
2)	d	Most often, the name of the server is the main word in the URL. For example, the name of the server for `http://www.microsoft.com` is Microsoft.
3)	b	False. The benefit of a cached file allows your PC to load a Web page you have previously visited within your browser without having to do complete the task of requesting the file across the network once again.
4)	a	True. It is possible to open a Web page that has been cached onto your PC without the Web server. Also, it is not necessary to be connected to the Internet while viewing the cached HTML.
5)	b	False. Numerous servers are not necessary for each client. Yet, it is possible.
6)	c	The Internet functions as a series of requests and responses. You may think of this process as a series of questions and answers, as well.
7)	b	HTTP is the acronym for Hypertext Transfer Protocol.
8)	c	The exchange between browsers and servers is known as HTTP.

CHAPTER 2
Lab 2.1 ■ Self-Review Answers

Question	Answer	Comments
1)	b	False. HTML tags that do not format text do not come in pairs.
2)	b	Don't put angular brackets around it. It is proper to place text that you want displayed in the body section, but you don't have to.
3)	a	Always. The browser doesn't care whether the text is in the head section. It will display it anyway.
4)	b	`</BODY>`
5)	b	No, but it is good practice. Browsers will assume that the document they are displaying is HTML.

Lab 2.2 ■ Self-Review Answers

Question	Answer	Comments
1)	d	Both b) and c). The text enclosed within the `<TITLE>` tags is displayed in the browser's title bar and is used in the bookmark list when the page is bookmarked.
2)	a	True. `<META>` tags can be used to convey information about the HTML document to the Web browser.
3)	b	False. You cannot make up your own `HTTP-EQUIV` attributes.
4)	b	`<META HTTP-EQUIV="Keywords" CONTENT="Peanuts">` is correct.

Lab 2.3 ■ Self-Review Answers

Question	Answer	Comments
1)	d	Both a) and c). HTML comments can be placed in both the <HEAD> and <BODY> sections.
2)	b	False. Everything in the <BODY> section is not displayed by the browser.
3)	d	All of the above. While we suggest that you place the date an HTML document was last modified at the end of the document, it could be placed anywhere.
4)	a	The information on how to contact the author of an HTML document typically appears at the end of the document.
5)	b	It is important to include the date a document was last modified so the reader knows how current the information on the page is.

CHAPTER 3
Lab 3.1 ■ Self-Review Answers

Question	Answer	Comments
1)	b	There are six levels of headings in HTML.
2)	b	Heading tags do not have a SIZE attribute.
3)	b	Left is the default alignment for horizontal rules in Netscape Navigator and Internet Explorer.
4)	a	True. A blank line always follows headings in HTML.
5)	c	You can use either pixels or the percent of the page as the unit to set the width of a horizontal rule.

Lab 3.2 ■ Self-Review Answers

Question	Answer	Comments
1)	c	Text formatted with <BLOCKQUOTE> is indented from both side margins of the page.
2)	b	The tag does not have an ALIGN attribute.
3)	a	True. Many Web designers find text formatted with the block quote tag visually unappealing.
4)	b	<P ALIGN="Center"> is the correct HTML.
5)	c	Left is the default alignment for paragraph tags.

CHAPTER 4
Lab 4.1 ■ Self-Review Answers

Question	Answer	Comments
1)	b	To create an ordered list, you would use the <OL> tag.
2)	b	False. There is no such thing as the NUMBER attribute. The VALUE attribute sets which number an <LI> tag displays.

3)	a	The START attribute is used with the <OL> tag.
4)	a	True. You can include more than one paragraph in a list item.
5)	b	1, 2, 3 is the default TYPE setting for an Ordered list.

Lab 4.2 ■ Self-Review Answers

Question	Answer	Comments
1)	b	To create an unordered list, you would use the <UL> tag.
2)	b	False. There is no such thing as the SHAPE attribute. The TYPE attribute sets which shape an <LI> tag displays.
3)	c	The TYPE attribute can be used with both the <UL> and <LI> tags.
4)	b	False. The Type="Square" attribute setting displays differently in some Macintosh browsers.
5)	c	The black circle (or *bullet*) is the default TYPE setting for an unordered list.

Lab 4.3 ■ Self-Review Answers

Question	Answer	Comments
1)	d	You often need to combine lists when you make a page containing a recipe.
2)	b	False. You can put an unordered list within an ordered list.
3)	b	False. You can combine more than two lists at a time.
4)	a	True, in Internet Explorer and Netscape Navigator. In these two browsers, an unordered list enclosed in an ordered list defaults to this bullet type.

CHAPTER 5
Lab 5.1 ■ Self-Review Answers

Question	Answer	Comments
1)	a	True. Images are stored as a series of dots known as *pixels*.
2)	b	False. Compressed images are the same physical size as their non-compressed counterparts. The higher the compression, the less storage space the file consumes on your hard drive. Visibly, the (compressed) image appears the same size.
3)	c	The properties of an image downloaded from an external Web site can be checked by opening the folder in which the image resides on your PC, right-clicking the image, and then choosing Properties. Answer choice a) is a valid answer, as well. However, you must open your image editor to check the properties. Therefore, choice c) is the easiest.
4)	c	An image may consist of as many as 16,555,216 colors. Wow!
5)	e	All of the choices are correct. Remember, HTML is not case-sensitive. Either of the Joint Photographics Experts Group image extensions are valid and recognizable.

6)	b	The `.gif` file format may use up to 256 colors.
7)	b	The `.gif` file format is used in association with animated images.

Lab 5.2 ■ Self-Review Answers

Question	Answer	Comments
1)	b	The `SRC` attribute of the `<IMG>` tag informs the HTML of the source of the image file.
2)	a	True. In order to ensure that the HTML is able to interpret the file location of the image, you must enclose the entire path in double quotes.
3)	b	False. Unlike many of the HTML tags, the `<IMG>` tag does not require an ending `</IMG>` tag.
4)	b	False. The `HEIGHT` and `WIDTH` properties enable you to resize the image within your HTML page.
5)	c	Using percentage values for the `HEIGHT` and `WIDTH` properties resizes the image in relation to the size of the browser window.
6)	b	When specifying a border for an image, the default border color is black.
7)	c	The `ALT` attribute displays a tool tip when you hover the mouse over the image. Also, if the intended image does not display (for whatever reason), the `ALT` attribute displays the text to inform the user which image was supposed to display.

Chapter 6
Lab 6.1 ■ Self-Review Answers

Question	Answer	Comments
1)	c	*Links* is the abbreviated name for *hyperlinks*.
2)	d	URL is the acronym for Uniform Resource Locator. Generally speaking, it is the global address or site that houses the Web server files, or directory.
3)	b	A URL is the address at which the Web files live.
4)	a	The hand icon is most often displayed while hovering your mouse over a link.
5)	e	The status bar is located at the bottom of the Web browser window. The status bar often contains the words "Document Done" when a file has completed loaded itself onto your PC.
6)	b	An HTML page may contain as many internal and external links as you wish.
7)	c	The anchor tag, `<A>`, must contain the `HREF` attribute.
8)	b	The anchor tag does require a closing anchor tag.
9)	b	Internal links do not require the full URL.
10)	a	As of this writing, Internet Explorer recognizes the `TITLE` attribute. Netscape does not recognize this attribute.

Lab 6.2 ■ Self-Review Answers

Question	Answer	Comments
1)	d	The MAILTO must not contain a space after the MAILTO keyword.
2)	a	True.
3)	a	True. A guestbook is a type of form. Therefore, it must be created within the confines of the <FORM> tags.
4)	a	True. Browsers with version numbers lower than 3 do not recognize the guestbook form.
5)	b	False. The INPUT TYPE informs the browser what type of field to create within the form.
6)	b	The NAME attribute helps you identify what text the Web surfer entered into the given field.
7)	b	False. Option buttons are used to allow the user only one choice within a given group.
8)	d	This is the correct syntax for implementing a TEXTAREA text box.
9)	b	The MAILTO ACTION is POST.

CHAPTER 7
Lab 7.1 ■ Self-Review Answers

Question	Answer	Comments
1)	a	The three primary computer colors are red, green, and blue.
2)	d	The two color attributes for the <BODY> tag are BGCOLOR and TEXT.
3)	c	BGCOLOR is used to specify the background color of an HTML document.
4)	c	The correct color usage of the body text attribute is <BODY TEXT = "#76BB00">.
5)	g	To display color for links, you may use the LINK, ALINK, and VLINK attributes.
6)	b	False. Older browsers are able to understand hex colors only.
7)	b	False. Hex color codes can use any 6-digit combination of 16 possible hexadecimal digit choices.
8)	a	The absence of color in computing is the color white.

Lab 7.2 ■ Self-Review Answers

Question	Answer	Comments
1)	d	The available attributes for the <FONT> tag are FACE, COLOR, and SIZE.
2)	b	False. Using multiple font styles for a single line of text is good HTML design practice.
3)	c	The range of available font sizes range from –1 to –6 and +6 to +1.
4)	b	False. The largest available font size in HTML is +6.
5)	b	False. HTML headings have the ability to separate themselves from other HTML without the use of additional formatting tags.

6)	a	The font attributes work no matter the order in which they are used.
7)	b	The correct syntax to complete a Heading 4 tag is as follows: <H4></H4>.
8)	d	There are six heading tag sizes available in HTML.
9)	a	True. Any font must exist on the user's PC in order to display as intended.
10)	a	True. When using font tags, they should be placed within the heading tags.

Lab 7.3 ■ Self-Review Answers

Question	Answer	Comments
1)	b	False. Proper use of the <B> tag requires an ending tag.
2)	d	Embedding tags properly helps to ensure your HTML displays as you intend.
3)	b	False. You may use as many or as few formatting tags as you desire.
4)	b	False. A <P> or tag is not needed to separate text when using the <PRE> tag.
5)	c	A registered trademark may be displayed in HTML by using ®.
6)	c	The <PRE> tag enables you to display text exactly the way it is typed within your HTML document.
7)	b	False. Links are able to use formatting tags.
8)	c	All "funky" tags begin with an ampersand and end with a semicolon.

CHAPTER 8
Lab 8.1 ■ Self-Review Answers

Question	Answer	Comments
1)	a	The <TR> and the <TD> tags are the defining row and column tags used to create HTML tables.
2)	a	The intersection of a row and column is known as a *cell*.
3)	c	Table data is represented in HTML with the use of the <TD> tag.
4)	c	The BORDER attribute defines the outline of a table.
5)	a	Cellpadding is the space between the cell border and the table border. Cellpadding is also the space between the borders of each cell.
6)	b	False. Using percentage values for the WIDTH attribute will size the table as it relates to the users' screen and window settings.
7)	a	Internet Explorer does not understand the Middle property of the ALIGN attribute when used in association with the alignment of an HTML table. However, Internet Explorer does recognize the Middle property of the ALIGN attribute when used in association with cell alignment.
8)	b	False. An HTML is still a table with or without the physical representation of a border.

Lab 8.2 ■ Self-Review Answers

Question	Answer	Comments
1)	c	The COLSPAN attribute is used within the <TD> tag.
2)	d	The BGCOLOR attribute is used to add background color to an HTML table cell.
3)	b	False. ROWSPAN is used within table columns to span as many rows as needed.
4)	a	Using ROWSPAN allows you to extend your HTML columns to as many rows as needed.
5)	b	False. Internet Explorer will display cell color with or without the use of or text. However, Netscape does not recognize the use of BGCOLOR within a table cell unless you include some cell text or the nonbreaking space.
6)	d	Utilizing proper HTML conventions, the BORDER="0" attribute will display a table without a border. In turn, using no attribute within the <TABLE> tag will result in the display of a table without a border.
7)	d	This choice uses proper HTML embedding of tags as well as utilizing the correct attribute for the <FONT> tag to ensure the browser understands that we are setting the font size to +3.
8)	d	ALIGN and VALIGN are the attributes used to align an image or any other item within a table cell. You may use the properties of Center, Top, and Bottom to set the alignment to the desired position.

CHAPTER 9
Lab 9.1 ■ Self-Review Answers

Question	Answer	Comments
1)	b	Font weight is the style attribute that sets whether text is bold or not.
2)	b	False. The COLOR property sets the color of the text.
3)	a	Embedded style sheets are inside an HTML document.
4)	b	Linked to a separate .css file.
5)	b	False. You cannot use a style definition for a <P> tag to format text within <H1> tags.

Lab 9.2 ■ Self-Review Answers

Question	Answer	Comments
1)	a	Style sheets are know as cascading style sheets, because text can be formatted by more than one style definition according to defined rules.
2)	b	According to the CSS specification, style definitions in embedded styles sheets override definitions in linked style sheets.
3)	c	Inline styles are placed inside the tags surrounding text.

4)	c	In Internet Explorer 4 and Netscape Navigator 4, style definitions in embedded style sheets do not override either linked or inline style definitions.
5)	b	The background property sets the background color that appears.
6)	d	Class definitions are used to create different styles for the same type of tags.

CHAPTER 10
Lab 10.1 ■ Self-Review Answers

Question	Answer	Comments
1)	b	Frameset documents do not have to include body tags.
2)	b	SRC is not an attribute of the <FRAMESET> tag.
3)	d	<FRAMESET ROWS="30%,*"> is correct HTML.
4)	b	You cannot set the COLS attribute in inches.
5)	d	You should not use more than three frames on a Web page, because it is confusing to both the reader and the author of the page.

Lab 10.2 ■ Self-Review Answers

Question	Answer	Comments
1)	b	<FRAME MARGINHEIGHT="25"> is the correct HTML.
2)	d	Both the <FRAME> and <FRAMESET> tags have FRAMEBORDER attributes.
3)	b	You can include both COLS and ROWS attributes in the same <FRAMESET> tag, we just don't recommend it.
4)	c	BORDER is not an attribute of the <FRAME> tag.
5)	c	*Auto* is the default setting for the SCROLLING attribute.

Lab 10.3 ■ Self-Review Answers

Question	Answer	Comments
1)	d	<A HREF="frame1.htm" TARGET="Main"> is the correct HTML.
2)	b	_own is not a reserved name.
3)	d	Clicking on a link targeted at _parent opens the linked document in the previous window, or the current window if there is no previous window.
4)	b	_top is a reserved name. Therefore, you cannot set a NAME attribute to it.
5)	d	Setting the TARGET attribute of a link to the name of the frame in which the link is displayed is the same as setting it equal to _self or not setting it at all.

APPENDIX B

HTML TAGS

`<A>`   **anchor**

Attributes: HREF, TITLE, NAME

The anchor tag is used in HTML to specify a hyperlink. The `<A>` tag does require a closing `</A>` tag. HREF stands for Hypertext Reference and points to any URL, whether it is an internal or external link.

Example:

```
<A HREF = "http://www.phptr.com/phptrinteractive/"> HTML
Assistance </A>
```

`<B>`   **bold**

Attributes: NONE

The bold tag is used to format text as bold. The `bold` tag requires an ending tag.

Example:

```
<B> Use me to create bold text. </B>
```

`<BODY>`   **body**

Attributes: BACKGROUND, BGCOLOR, LINK, ALINK, VLINK, TEXT

The starting and ending body tags enclose the bulk of your HTML page design. Each and every HTML page should begin with opening `<HTML><BODY>` tags and end with closing `</BODY></HTML>` tags.

Example:

```
<HTML>
<BODY BGCOLOR="#0AC4C2">
<H1>All HTML design is enclosed within the body of the
page.</H1>
<A HREF = "http://www.zdnet.com/pcmag"> PC Week </A>
</BODY>
</HTML>
```

`<BR>` break

Attributes: NONE

The `<BR>` tag forces a line break within your HTML document. Any text placed after a `<BR>` tag is forced to a new line. This tag does not require an ending tag.

Example:

```
<B>This is one line of text.</B>
<BR>
<I>This is another line of text.</I>
```

The example appears within an HTML page as follows:

This is one line of text.
This is another line of text.

`<CENTER>` center

Attributes: NONE

Text within the starting `<CENTER>` and ending `</CENTER>` tag appears centered within the page.

Example:

```
<CENTER> Once upon a time there was an HTML designer who
created amazing and fabulous Web sites.</CENTER>
```

The example appears within an HTML page as follows:

```
Once upon a time there was an HTML designer who created
amazing and fabulous Web sites.
```

`<FONT>` font

Attributes: SIZE, COLOR, FACE

The font tag combined with one or more of the attributes allows you to format HTML text. An ending `</FONT>` tag is required.

The SIZE attribute changes the size of the font. You may use font sizes from 0 to 7.

The COLOR attribute changes the color of HTML text. You may use named or hexadecimal colors. Refer to Chapter 7, "Formatting the Page," for a partial HTML color chart.

The FACE attribute enables you to change the font of HTML text. You may use one or more font attributes for any given group of text.

Example:

```
<FONT FACE = "Arial, Helvetica" SIZE = "3" COLOR =
"#4040FF"> This is a formatting tag. </FONT>
```

`<FORM>` form

Attributes: ACTION, METHOD

The form tag is used within HTML to create guestbooks. The form tag does require an ending tag.

The ACTION and the METHOD attributes work together to complete the assigned task. Refer to Chapter 6, "Creating Hyperlinks," for a more in-depth discussion.

Example:

```
<FORM METHOD="POST" ACTION="[Enter URL here]">

</FORM>
```

`<H1>`-`<H6>` headings

Attributes: ALIGN

There are six headings, H1, H2, H3, H4, H5, and H6. H6 is the smallest and H1 is the largest. All heading tags require ending tags. For more information on heading tags, refer to Chapter 7, "Formatting the Page."

Example:

```
<H3>Text placed within this tag has a certain font size, ap-
pears bold, and forces a paragraph break before and after
the heading. </H3>
```

`<HEAD>` **head**

Attributes: NONE

Each and every HTML page should contain a `<HEAD>` tag. The `<HEAD>` tag does require an ending tag. The title is the only thing that should be placed within the head tags.

Example:

```
<HEAD>
<TITLE>This text will appear in the title bar of the browser
window.</TITLE>
</HEAD>
```

`<HR>` **horizontal rule**

Attributes: ALIGN, WIDTH, SIZE, COLOR

Note: At the time of this writing, Internet Explorer 5 recognizes the COLOR attribute, Netscape Navigator 4.61 does not.

Horizontal rules may be used to separate an HTML document into sections. The `<HR>` tag does not require a closing tag.

Example:

```
<HR>This line appears on a new line without the need of a
BREAK tag.
```

`<HTML>` **html**

Attributes: NONE

The HTML opening and closing tags define a file as an HTML document.

Example:

```
<HTML>
<HEAD>This is the title.</HEAD>
<BODY>This is where the meat of the page is written.</BODY>
 </HTML>
```

`<I>`   italic

Attributes: NONE

Text typed within the opening and closing italic tags appear italic.

Example:

```
<I>You may use this tag to emphasize certain text within
your HTML document.</I>
```

This example appears as follows in an HTML page:

```
You may use this tag to emphasize certain text within your
HTML document.
```

`<IMG>`   image

Attributes: SRC, ALT, ALIGN, BORDER HEIGHT, WIDTH

To place images within an HTML document, use the image tag. It does not require an ending tag.

The SRC attribute is required. It defines the location of the image. For more information on placing images in an HTML document, see Chapter 5, "Adding Images to your Web Pages." The other attributes may or may not be used to enhance the location or the appearance of the image on the Web page.

Example:

```
<IMG SRC = "C:/Images/flower.gif">
```

`<INPUT>`   input

Attributes: TYPE, NAME, SIZE, VALUE, CHECKED, DISABLED

The input type identifies an entry field within an HTML form.

The `TYPE` attribute may identify the input field as a textbox, option button, or a check box, to name a few. A more detailed description of the `TYPE` attribute and other `INPUT` attributes may be found in Chapter 6, "Creating Hyperlinks".

Example:

```
<INPUT TYPE = "text" NAME = "UserName" SIZE = "20">
```

`<LH>`   **list heading**

Attributes: NONE

The list heading tag identifies an item as the heading of an HTML list. It does utilize an ending tag.

Example:

```
<OL>
<LH>People in my family</LH>
<LI>Fred</LI>
<LI>Wilma</LI>
<LI>Pebbles</LI>
</OL>
```

`<LI>`   **list item**

Attributes: `VALUE`, `TYPE`

List item identifies an item in an ordered or unordered list. For more information on using lists, refer to Chapter 4, "Using Lists".

The `VALUE` attribute allows you to set a starting value (or number) for your lists.

Example:

```
<UL>
<LI>Gateway</LI>
<LI>Dell</LI>
<LI>Compaq</LI>
<UL>
```

<OL>   ordered list

Attributes: TYPE

The <OL> tag informs the Web browser to interpret the enclosed items within an ordered list.

The TYPE attribute allows you to define the list item. For further information related to ordered lists and the TYPE attribute, refer to Chapter 4, "Using Lists".

Example:

```
<OL TYPE = "A">
<LI>Buckle your seat belt.</LI>
<LI>Place the key in the ignition.</LI>
<LI>Start the engine.</LI>
</OL>
```

<P>   paragraph

Attributes: ALIGN

The <P> tag forces a paragraph break within your HTML document.

Example:

```
<CENTER>We, the people, in order to form a more perfect union
</CENTER>
<P>
<CENTER>swear to write HTML according to the W3C.</CENTER>
```

<PRE>   preformatted

Attributes: NONE

Any text typed within the opening and closing <PRE> tags appear exactly as you type it.

Example:

```
<PRE>T hi    s     is    kin    d a     coo      l.</PRE>
```

<TABLE>   **table**

Attributes: BORDER, HEIGHT, WIDTH, CELLPADDING, CELLSPACING, ALIGN

The table tag is crucial to format an HTML document as you wish it to appear within a Web browser. An HTML table consists of rows and columns. The <TABLE> tag does require a closing tag. For more information on tables, refer to Chapter 8, "Designing and Formatting Tables."

Example:

```
<TABLE BORDER = "1">
<TR>
<TD>Spanish</TD>
<TD>English</TD>
<TD>French</TD>
</TR>
</TABLE>
```

<TD>   **table data**

Attributes: WIDTH, HEIGHT, ROWSPAN, COLSPAN, VALIGN, BGCOLOR

The <TD> tag defines a cell within a table row. The table data tag must always be embedded in the <TR> tags. The <TD> tag does require an ending tag.

For a complete description of the <TD> attributes, refer to Chapter 8, "Designing and Formatting Tables."

Example:

```
<TABLE>
<TR>
<TD BGCOLOR = "BLUE"><FONT COLOR = "WHITE">Hello out there
in Cyberland.</FONT></TD>
</TR>
</TABLE>
```

<TEXTAREA>   **text area**

Attributes: NAME, ROWS, COLS, WRAP

The <TEXTAREA> tag defines a large input text box within an HTML form. An ending tag is required.

Example:

```
<TEXTAREA NAME = "FirstName" ROWS = 3 COLS = 30></TEXTAREA>
```

`<TITLE>`　　　　　　**title**

Attributes: NONE

The title tag is used to define the Web page. The title appears in the title bar of the Web browser. A closing tag is required.

Example:

```
<TITLE>Tour de France 1999</TITLE>
```

`<TR>`　　　　　**table row**

Attributes: ALIGN, VALIGN

The `<TR>` tag allows you to set the number of rows displayed within an HTML table.

Example:

```
<TABLE>
<TR VALIGN = "BOTTOM">
<TD><FONT SIZE = "+2">Welcome</FONT></TD>
</TR>
</TABLE>
```

`<UL>`　　　　　**unordered list**

Attributes: TYPE

Unlike ordered list, unorderd lists are not numbered. Unordered lists have bulleted list items. The `<UL>` tag does require an ending tag.

The TYPE attribute of the unordered list may be a disc, circle, or a square. For a detailed description of the `<UL>` tag and its TYPE attribute, refer to Chapter 4, "Using Lists".

Example:

```
<UL TYPE = "SQUARE">
```

```
<LH>Ingredients</LH>
<LI>Sugar</LI>
<LI>Flour</LI>
<LI>Butter</LI>
<UL>
```

`<!--`   **comment**

Attributes: NONE

The `<!--` tag designates an HTML comment. Any text placed within an opening `<!--` tag and a closing `-->` tag is recognized as a comment.

Example:

```
<!-- What you see here will not appear on the Web page. -->
```

A P P E N D I X   C

CSS ATTRIBUTES

BACKGROUNDCOLOR

Acceptable Values: any valid color name, rgb value, or hex value

The BACKGROUND COLOR attribute is used to set the background color for an element. The default value is transparent. You can set it using an acceptable color name for browsers by specifying the red, green, and blue values (0 to 255 for each value) or by using a valid hex value for a color.

Examples:

```
<P> { background-color: red }
<H2> { background-color: #FFFFFF }
<H1> { background-color: rgb(255,132,0) }
<H1 Style="background-color: red">Red Background-Color
Example</H1>
```

Red Background-Color Example

Light Blue Background-Color Example

BACKGROUND IMAGE

Acceptable Values: url (image name)

The BACKGROUND IMAGE attribute sets the background image for an element. The image name must be preceded by "url(," and followed by ")." If you set both a background image and a background color, then the image will display. The default value is no image.

Examples:

```
<H2> { background-image: url(background.jpg)}
<H2 Style="background-image: url(./background.jpg)">
Background-Image Example
</H2>
```

Background-Image Example

BACKGROUND REPEAT

Acceptable Values: repeat, no-repeat, repeat-x, repeat-y

The BACKGROUND REPEAT attribute sets whether a background image should repeat. The default value is *repeat*. The *repeat-x* value makes it only repeat across the page. The *repeat-y* value makes it only repeat vertically on the page.

Examples:

```
<H1> { background-image: url(background.jpg); background-
repeat: repeat-y }
<H2 Style="background-image: url(./background.jpg);
background-repeat: repeat-x">Background-Repeat Example</H2>
```

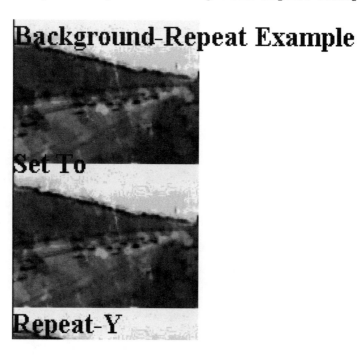

COLOR

Acceptable Values: any valid color name, rgb value, or hex value

The color attribute sets the text color for an element. The default value is black. You may set the value using any of the acceptable named colors for browsers, or you can use the red, green, blue value, or hex value of a color.

Examples:

```
<P> { color: blue }
<H2> { color: rgb(0,0,255) }
<H6 Style="color: #ABFFFF">Text Color Example</H6>
```

Text Color Set To Red Example

Text Color Set To Orange Example

Text Color Set To Yellow Example

FONT SIZE

Acceptable Values: xx-small, x-small, small, medium, large, x-large, xx-large—size in points (pt) or in ems (em)

The font-size attribute sets the size of the font used in an element. You can set it in the relative values listed above, but the sizes will differ from browser to browser. You can also set the value in points or ems by specifying a number followed by the unit.

Examples:

```
<P> { font-size: 12pt }
<H2> { font-size: xx-small }
<P Style="font-size: 44em">Font Size Example</P>
```

Font Size Set To 12 Pixels Example

Font Siz Set To 12 Points Example

12 Ems

FONT FAMILY

Acceptable Values: font names or generic font names separated by commas

The FONT FAMILY attribute sets the font used to display text in an element. You can specify more than one font, separating the names with commas, and the browser will use the first named font that exists on the system. Font names that contain a space must be contained in quotes. You should always end your list of font names with a generic font name such as serif, sans-serif, or monospace, since all of these families are available on the standard browsers.

Examples:

```
<P> { font-family: arial, helvetica, "comic sans",sans-serif }
<H1 Style="font-family: arial">Font Family Example</H1>
```

Font Family Set to Serif Example

Font Family Set to Sans-Serif Example

```
Font Family Set To Monospace Example
```

FONT STYLE

Acceptable Values: normal, italic, oblique

The FONT STYLE attribute sets the style of font used to render an element. You should recognize that if an appropriate font is not available on the user's system, the quality of the rendering will not be good. The default value is normal.

Examples:

```
<P> { font-style: italic }
<P Style="font-style: italic">Font Style Example</P>
```

Font Style Set To Italic Example

Font Style Set To Oblique Example

Font Style Set To Italic Example

FONT VARIANT

Acceptable Values: normal, small caps

The FONT-VARIANT attribute sets the way in which the text in an element is displayed. The default value is *normal*. The small caps value causes text to be displayed all in capitals regardless of how it was typed. This attribute is not available in Netscape Navigator.

Examples:

```
<H3> { font-variant: small-caps }
<H3 Style="font-variant: normal">Font Variant Example</H3>
```

Font Variant Set To Normal Example

<small>FONT VARIANT SET TO SMALLCAPS EXAMPLE</small>

FONT WEIGHT

Acceptable Values: bold, bolder, lighter, normal, 100, 200, 300, 400, 500, 600, 700, 800, 900

The FONT WEIGHT attribute sets the heaviness with which a font is rendered in an element. The default value is *normal.* You can use the named values or the numeric values. The numeric value of 400 is equivalent to normal.

Examples:

```
<H3> { font-weight: bolder }
<P> { font-weight: 800 }
<P Style="font-weight: 200">Font Weight Example</P>
```

Font Weight Set To 100 Example

Font Weight Set To 300 Example

Font Weight Set To 500 Example

Font Weight Set To 700 Example

Font Weight Set To 900 Example

LETTER SPACING

Acceptable Values: normal, length in pixels (px), length in inches (in), length in ems (em), length in centimeters (cm)

The LETTER SPACING attribute sets the distance between letters in the element. The default value is *normal.*

Examples:

```
<P> { letter-spacing: 10px }
<H1> { letter-spacing: 12cm }
<P Style="letter-spacing: 1em">Letter Spacing Example</P>
```

L e t t e r   S p a c i n g   S e t   T o   1   E m   E x a m p l e

Letter Spacing Set To 1 Pixel Example

Letter Spacing Set To 1 Point Example

LINE HEIGHT

Acceptable Values: normal, height in pixels (px), height in inches (in), height in ems (em), height in centimeters (cm), height in number of lines, height in percent

The LINE HEIGHT attribute sets the height of the line in an element. The default setting for line height is determined by which font is used. Setting the height in number of lines is equivalent to using spacing. For example the value 2 would be equivalent to double spacing. Setting the height in percent produces similar results. For example, the value 200% would also be roughly equivalent to double spacing. It is possible to set the line height to a smaller value than the height of the letter used. Doing so can cause display problems.

Examples:

```
<P> { line-height: 12pt }
<H2> { line-height: 200% }
<H6 Style="line-height: 3">Line Height Example</H6>
```

Line Height Set

To 2 Example

Line Height Set

To 20 Points Example

Line Height Set

To 200 Percent Example

LIST STYLE TYPE

Acceptable Values: For unordered lists: disk, square, circle, none. For ordered lists: lower-roman, upper-roman, lower-alpha, upper-alpha, decimal.

The LIST STYLE TYPE attribute sets the shape of the bullet that is used to precede each list item. The default value for unordered lists is disk. The default value for ordered lists is decimal.

Examples:

```
<OL> { list-style-type: upper-roman }
<UL> { list-style-type: disk }
<UL Style="list-style-type: disk><LI>List Style Type
Example</UL>
```

- List Style Type Disk Example
- List Style Type Square Example
- I.   List Style Type Upper Roman Example
- i.   List Style Lower Roman Example

LIST STYLE IMAGE

Acceptable Values: none, url(image name)

The LIST STYLE IMAGE attribute replaces the bullet used for an unordered list with an image. The image must be preceded by "url(," . and followed by ")." The default value is none.

Examples:

```
<UL> { list-style-image: none }
<UL> { list-style-image: url(bullet.gif) }
<UL style="list-style-image: url(smiley.gif)"><LI>List Style
Image Example</UL>
```

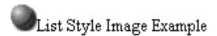
List Style Image Example

LIST STYLE POSITION

Acceptable Values: inside, outside

The LIST STYLE POSITION attribute sets the alignment of the text for any line following the first line which is displayed as a list item. If the value is set to *inside,* then the text is aligned with the bullet, and the bullet is indented with the text. If the value is set to *outside,* then the text is aligned with the beginning of the text on the first line, and the bullet is "outdented" from the text. The default value is *outside.*

Examples:

```
<UL> { list-style-position: inside }
<UL Style="list-style-position: inside"><LI>List Style
Position Example</UL>
```

- List Style Position
  Set To Inside Example

- List Style Position
  Set To Outside Example

TEXT ALIGN

Acceptable Values: center, left, right

The TEXT ALIGN attribute sets the alignment of the element. The default value is left.

Examples:

```
<P> { text-align: center }
<P Style="text-align: center">Text Align Example</P>
```

Text Align Set To Left Example

Text Align Set To Center Example

Text Align Set To Right Example

TEXT DECORATION

Acceptable Values: blink, line-through, overline, underline, none.

The TEXT DECORATION attribute sets the way the text is displayed in an element. The default value is *none*. Internet Explorer does not recognize *blink* as a value, and Netscape Navigator does not recognize *overline*.

Examples:

```
<H1> { text-decoration: blink }
<H1 Style="text-decoration: underline">Text Decoration
Example</H1>
```

<u>Text Decoration Set To Underline Example</u>

Text Decoration Set To Overline Example

~~Text Decoration Set To Line Through Example~~

TEXT INDENT

Acceptable Values: length in pixels (px), length in inches (in), length in ems (em) length in percent (%), length in centimeters (cm)

The TEXT INDENT attribute sets the indentation of the first line of an element. The default value is 0, and negative values are allowed. Some negative values, though, may take the beginning of the line off the left side of the browser screen (see example below).

Examples:

```
<H2> { text-indent: 10px }
<P> { text-indent: 23em }
<H1 Style="text-indent: -10%">Text Indent Example</H1>
```

Text Indent Set To 10 Ems Example

Text Indent Set To 10 Pixels Example

dent Set To -10 Percent Example

TEXT TRANSFORM

Acceptable Values: capitalize, lowercase, uppercase, none

The TEXT TRANSFORM attribute sets the case of text in an element, overriding the way the text was typed. The default value is *none*. Setting TEXT TRANSFORM equal to capitalize will capitalize the first letter of every word. Setting it to uppercase or lowercase will cause every letter to be displayed as uppercase or lowercase, respectively.

Examples:

```
<P> { text-transform: uppercase }
<P Style="text-transform: capitalize">Text Transform
Example</P>
```

Text Transform Set To Capitalize Example

TEXT TRANSFORM SET TO UPPERCASE EXAMPLE

text transform set to lowercase example

A P P E N D I X   D

HTML WEB SITE REFERENCES

HTML AND WEB DESIGN HELP

http://www.phptr.com/phptrinteractive/

Prentice Hall, Professional Technical Reference

Access the Prentice Hall Book Series. Use this URL as your number-one reference point for answers, questions, errata, or discussions with us and/or with other students.

http://www.w3.org/

World Wide Web Consortium

The W3C was founded in October 1994. It serves to set the standards for the World Wide Web in order to promote common protocols for Internet operation around the globe. Refer to this Web site to read up-to-date technical and reference materials. The W3C is an excellent source for news and updates on new Internet technology.

http://developer.netscape.com/

Netscape's DevEdge Online Magazine

This developer site is run by Netscape, the makers of the Netscape Navigator browser. Lots of useful information for the Web page designer, although it is obviously slanted toward Netscape's products.

`http://msdn.microsoft.com/default.asp`

Microsoft's MSDN Online

MSDN stands for Microsoft Developer's Network. This site has lots of information useful to Web designers, although it is all slanted toward Microsoft products.

`http://www.cnet.com`

CNET: The source for computers and technology.

CNET is a multipurpose Web site. Refer to CNET for new freeware and shareware software downloads. CNET is a great source for technology news and happenings. CNET Shopper offers great computer hardware/software comparison price and quality advice.

`http://www.bensplanet.com`

Ben's Planet: Complete HTML Reference Guide

This site is filled with useful news and HTML help.

`http://www.hotwired.com/webmonkey/`

Webmonkey: A How-to Guide for Web Developers

Everything you ever wanted to know about the Web can be found here.

`http://www.zdnet.com/devhead/filters/html/`

ZDNet's DevHead—HTML

Refer to ZDNet to read up on HTML Devheadlines, Reviews, News, Downloads, and Resources. This site promises to be a trip well worth the visit. Check it out!

`http://www.htmlgoodies.com`

HTML Goodies

Joe Burns, Ph.D, offers endless tips and advice.

http://www.webpagesthatsuck.com

Vincent Flanders' Web Pages That Suck

Learn good HTML design by viewing some not-so-good HTML design.

http://www.devx.com

The Development Exchange

Want to advance your Web development knowledge and skills? If so, this site is for you.

http://www.builder.com

CNET's Builder.com

The CNET site specifically devoted to Web designers. Has lots of useful tutorials and articles on Web design, HTML, and lots of other Web subjects.

http://www.newmedia.com

NewMedia online magazine

An online magazine devoted to covering the World Wide Web. If you want to know what is going on in the Internet industry, this site will help.

http://www.projectcool.com/

The Project Cool Network

In their words, "A network of websites sharing the common belief that anyone can make a great Web site if given knowledge, guidance and inspiration. There's something for everyone within, from the first time Webmaker to the designer with years of experience."

http://www.webstandards.org

The Web Standards Project

A professional group for Web page creators that is dedicated to ensuring that all browsers support the standards created by the World Wide Web Consortium. Join this group, and help make every Web designer's life easier. This site has lots of useful information about making HTML work in all browsers.

`http://www.webreference.com`

Internet.com's Web reference page

Another handy site with lots of tutorials, design examples, and articles on Web design.

`http://www.highfive.com`

High Five Online Magazine

A site devoted to excellence in Web page design. Lots of interesting design examples and reviews of Web sites. Really, it's the cutting edge in Web design.

`http://www.webreview.com`

Web Review Online Magazine

Another site devoted to HTML, Web design, and reviews of tools for developers.

`http://www.designer.com`

Corel's Designer.com

A site for Web designers from the makers of Corel Draw and the Word Perfect Office suite. Has lots of free graphics, tutorials, and other articles of interest to Web designers.

`http://www.htmlhelp.com`

The Web Design Group

In their words, "The Web Design Group was founded to promote the creation of *non-browser specific, non-resolution specific, creative* and *informative* sites that are accessible to **all** users worldwide. To this end, the WDG offers material on a wide range of HTML related topics."

`http://www.webtools.com`

CMP's Web Tools

A great site with lots of tips, information, and articles devoted to solving the problems encountered in Web design.

`http://www.mozilla.org`

The Mozilla Project

The site devoted to the development of the next generation of Netscape's browser. Check out this site if you want to know what is going on with Netscape's browser development.

`http://www.ibm.com/developer/`

IBM DeveloperWorks site

IBM's developer site. This site has some HTML information, but it is mixed in with information about every other IBM product that has anything to do with the Web.

HTML COLOR

`http://st-ives.net/dlv/html/colorsamples.html`

140 HTML Colors Acceptable to Browsers

Use this Web site as a reference for HTML named colors.

`http://msdn.microsoft.com/workshop/design/color/`
`colorpick.asp`

MSDN Web Workshop: The Safety Palette Color Picker

This serves as a nice, quick reference for Web-friendly colors.

`http://www.habanero.com/hex/`

Habanero Computing Solutions: Hex Colors

This page shows a brief yet useful listing of hex colors.

`http://www.correlationsystems.com/colors/`

Correlation Systems: Hex Colors

This page lists 4096 different hex colors organized according to their first hex number.

HTML IMAGES/GRAPHICS

`http://www.gifworks.com/`

GIFWorks: Free Online GIF eTools

This Web site offers some free animated GIFs, borders, icons, and lines, to name a few.

`http://www.freegraphics.com/`

Free Graphics

Free Graphics offers links to Web sites supplying Web designers with free downloadable images.

`http://www.animfactory.com/gif_graphics/af_misc.html`

Animation Factory

Animation Factory is a great resource for quality animated GIFs. Search this Web site for GIFs listed alphabetically A through Z.

`http://www.eyewire.com/`

Adobe's Eyewire

A graphics site created by the makers of Adobe Photoshop. A great source for graphics collections to use on your Web sites.

HTML EDITING TOOLS

The following Web sites provide trial-version HTML Editors.

`http://www.allaire.com/products/homesite/index.cfm`

Allaire Software: HomeSite

Download this easy-to-use HTML editing tool that is highly rated by ZDNet.

`http://commerce.allaire.com/download/`

Allaire Software: Cold Fusion

Cold Fusion is a Web development tool you may use to create simple HTML pages or full-blown Web applications. Allaire requires you to register prior to the download.

`http://www.htmlworks.com`

HTMLWorks: Free Online HTML eTools

HTMLWorks come to you via the same folks that provide GIFWorks. Utilize this free tool to analyze and validate your HTML.

`http://www.netobjects.com/`

NetObjects, Inc.—Fusion 4.0

Download a demo version of NetFusion to design and create your Web site.

INDEX

343